# *Twenty Three Years*

# Twenty Three Years:

## A Study of the Prophetic Career of Mohammad

by

'ALI DASHTI

*Translated from the Persian*

by

F. R. C. Bagley

**MAZDA PUBLISHERS**
Costa Mesa, California
1994

**CIP Data is available from The Library of Congress**

Copyright © 1985,1994 by F. R. C. Bagley
First published in hardcover edition by George Allen & Unwin (Publishers) Ltd, London.
All rights reserved under International and Pan-American Copyright Conventions. No part of this publication may be used or reproduced in any manner whatsoever without written permission except in the case of brief quotations embodied in critical articles and reviews. For information write to: Mazda Publishers, P.O. Box 2603, Costa Mesa, California 92626 U.S.A.

ISBN: 1-56859-029-6

# Contents

# Note on the Author

## by F. R. C. Bagley

The religion of Islam, founded by Mohammad in his prophetic career which began in 610 and ended with his death in 632, has helped to shape the cultures and lifestyles of many nations.

In the last hundred years, numerous scholarly books have been written about Mohammad, the Qor'ān, and Islamic theology, laws, sects, and mystic movements. Foreign scholars have accomplished essential tasks of gathering and analysing data. Indigenous scholars have for the most part written expositions and apologia, and with exceptions such as the Egyptian Tāhā Hosayn, who lived from 1889 to 1973 and was blind, have not paid much attention to difficulties.

The book *Bist o Seh Sāl* (Twenty Three Years) by the Iranian scholar 'Ali Dashti (1896–1981–2) is valuable because it discusses both values and problems which Islam presents to modern Moslems.

Born in 1896 in a village in Dashtestān, a district adjoining the port of Bushehr on the Persian Gulf, 'Ali Dashti was the son of Shaykh 'Abd ol-Hosayn Dashtestāni. At a young age he was taken by his father to Karbalā in Iraq, which then belonged to the Ottoman empire. Karbalā, where the Prophet Mohammad's grandson Hosayn was martyred in 680, and Najaf (about 70 km. or 43 m. to the south), where the Prophet's cousin and son-in-law 'Ali was martyred in 661, are visited by Shi'ite Moslem pilgrims and have colleges (*madrasa*s) where Shi'ite clergy (*'olamā*) are trained and theological studies are pursued. Despite the unsettled conditions in the First World War, 'Ali Dashti received a full training in these *madrasa*s and acquired a thorough knowledge of Islamic theology and history, logic, rhetoric, and Arabic and Persian grammar and classical literature.

After his return from Iraq to Iran in 1918, however, he decided against a clerical career. Having strong patriotic feelings and an awareness of world developments, he preferred to devote his fluent pen to journalism. Eventually he succeeded in establishing his own newspaper at Tehrān, *Shafaq-e Sorkh* (Red Dawn), which lasted from 1 March 1922 until 18 March 1935. He was its editor until 1 March 1931, when Mā'el Tuyserkāni took over. In 1919 'Ali Dashti was imprisoned for a time after he had written articles criticizing the proposed Anglo-Iranian treaty of that year (which was later dropped), and in 1921 and subsequently he spent some more short spells in prison. He described his experiences and thoughts in articles which were collected in a book, *Ayyām-e Mahbas* (Prison Days). With its radical and modernizing tone, shrewd observations, pleasant humor, and fluent style, this book won immediate popularity and was several times reprinted in amplified editions. *Shafaq-e Sorkh* became noted for the high quality of its articles on social and literary subjects written by 'Ali Dashti and his then young collaborators, among whom were distinguished men such as the poet and literary historian Rashid Yāsemi and the scholarly researchers Sa'id Nafisi, 'Abbas Eqbāl, and Mohammad Mohit Tabātabā'i.

During those years, 'Ali Dashti taught himself French and began to read widely in modern French literature and in English and Russian literature in French translations. He also read material in French on current affairs, music and painting (in which he was interested), and Islamic subjects. He was one of the few Iranians who took an interest in modern Arabic, particularly Egyptian, literature. At a time when most writers of Persian prose were still addicted to elaborate metaphors and complex sentences, he developed a fluent but elegant style which was widely admired and copied, the only adverse criticism being that he used too many borrowed French words. Not only his original writings gained popularity, but also his translations of Edmond Demolins's *A quoi tient la supériorité des Anglo-Saxons* and of an Arabic version of Samuel Smiles's *Self-Help*.

In 1927 'Ali Dashti was invited to visit Russia for the tenth anniversary of the Bolshevik revolution, and he took the opportunity to extend his journey and see France and other Western European countries. He was elected to the Majles (Parliament) as deputy for Bushehr in 1928 and again in the next two parliaments, and won a reputation for forceful speaking. After the expiry of the Ninth Majles in 1935, however, he was again detained and kept under house arrest for fourteen months. In 1939 he was re-elected to the Majles as deputy for Damāvand (near Tehrān), and after the Anglo-Russian occupation of Iran he won the same seat in the elections of 1941 and 1943. He was the leading figure in the 'Adālat (Justice) party, a group favoring moderate and practicable social reforms. As a patriot he expressed alarm at the risks taken in 1946 by the then prime minister, Qavām os-Saltana, in admitting members of the Soviet-backed Tuda party into the cabinet and in negotiating on the Soviet demand for an oil concession. His outspokenness landed him in prison in April 1946. After his release six months later, he went to France and stayed there until the end of 1948, when he was appointed ambassador to Egypt and the Lebanon. He was briefly minister of foreign affairs in the cabinet of Hosayn 'Alā, which held office for a fortnight before Mohammad Mosaddeq's rise to the premiership on 2 April 1951. In 1954 he was appointed a senator (half of the members of the Senate being elected and half appointed by the Shah). He remained in the Senate until the Islamic revolution of 11 February 1979 and won further esteem for his contributions to its debates, which often carried more weight than those of the Majles.

In the literary world, 'Ali Dashti was best known during the early post-war years as an essayist and novelist. In *Sāya* (1946), a collection of reprinted articles and sketches, his tone remains modernizing, but is less radical than in his previous writings. During and after Rezā Shah's reign, the social problem which was most discussed in Iran, or at least in upper and middle class circles, was the status of women. Iranian women had been compulsorily unveiled on 7 January 1936, but after the war women of the lower classes resumed the veil and women of the upper and middle classes came under strong pressure to do likewise. 'Ali Dashti sympathized with the desire of educated Iranian women for freedom to use their brains and express their personalities; but he does not present a very favorable picture of them in his collections of novelettes *Fetna* (1943 and 1949), *Jādu* (1951), and *Hendu* (1955). His heroines engage in flirtations and intrigues with no apparent motive except cold calculation. Nevertheless these stories are very readable, and they provide a vivid, and no doubt partly accurate, record of the social life of the upper classes and the psychological problems of the educated women in Tehrān at the time.

'Ali Dashti's literary reputation, however, rests on his work as a scholar and critic of the Persian classics. The Iranians take legitimate pride in their heritage but have shown reluctance to discuss the difficulties which the classics present to their own younger generation, let alone to foreigners. One difficulty is the archaic language of the classics, another is their medieval atmosphere, and another is their bulk. Sā'eb, the leading poet of the Safavid period, wrote 300,000 verses, most of which were probably not intended to be more than ephemeral. In any case, nobody can read all the classics. Modern Iranian scholars have generally taken a classical author's greatness for granted and have concentrated their research on matters such as the influence of the author's training and career, and his forerunners and patrons, on the form and content of his work, and his own influence on successors. 'Ali Dashti, while not neglecting such points, tried to pick out and explain the elements in the works of certain classical poets which have continuing artistic and moral value for the modern reader. He also makes candid criticisms, mentioning for instance that Sa'di gives some very immoral pieces of advice in addition to ever popular maxims of common sense, good manners, and good humor. Although there is necessarily a measure of subjectivity in 'Ali Dashti's appraisals, his new approach met a widely felt need and helped to revive popular interest in the classics. His books in this field, which were several times reprinted, are as follows:

*Naqshi az Hāfez* (1936), on the poet Hāfez (ca. 1319–1390).

*Sayri dar Divān-e Shams*, on the lyric verse of the poet Mawlavi Jalāl od-Din Rumi (1207–1273).

*Da qalamraw-e Sa'di*, on the poet and prose-writer Sa'di (1208?–1292).

*Shā'eri dir-āshnā* (1961), on Khāqāni (1121?–1199), a particularly difficult but interesting poet.

*Dami bā Khayyām* (1965), on the quatrain-writer and mathematician 'Omar Khayyām (1048?–1131); translated by Laurence P. Elwell Sutton, *In Search of Omar Khayyam*, London 1971.

*Negāhi be-Sā'eb* (1974), on the poet Sā'eb (1601–1677).

*Kākh-e ebdā', andishahā-ye gunāgun-e Hāfez*, on various ideas expressed by Hāfez.

In his later years 'Ali Dashti returned to the study of Islam, for which he was well qualified by his *madrasa* training and his wide reading of modern Egyptian and European works. His approach was the same as in his literary studies, namely to emphasize elements of lasting value and to discuss problems frankly. His writings in this field are as follows:

*Parda-ye pendār* (1974 and twice reprinted), on Sufism (Islamic mysticism).

*Jabr yā ekhtiyār* (anonymous and undated, contents first published in the periodical *Vahid* in 1971), dialogues with a Sufi about predestination and free will.

*Takht-e Pulād* (anonymous and undated, contents first published in the periodical *Khāterāt* in 1971–72), dialogues in the historic Takht-e Pulād cemetery of Esfahān with a learned *'ālem* who sticks to the letter of the Qor'ān and the Hadith.

*'Oqalā bar khelāf-e 'aql* (1975 and twice reprinted, revised versions of articles first published in the periodicals *Yaghmā* in 1972 and 1973, *Vahid* in 1973, and *Rāhnomā-ye Ketāb* in 1973, with two additional articles), on logical contradictions in arguments used by theologians, particularly Mohammad ol-Ghazzāli (1058–1111).

*Dar diyār-e Sufiyān* (1975), on Sufism, a continuation of *Parda-ye pendār*.

*Bist o Seh Sāl* (anonymous and without indication of place and date of publication, but evidently not later than 1974 and according to 'Ali Dashti's statement printed at Beirut), a study of the prophetic career of Mohammad.

The government of Mohammad Rezā Shāh Pahlavi and his prime minister from 1965 to 1977, Amir 'Abbās Hovaydā, maintained a censorship which offended many Iranian intellectuals, though it seemed to foreigners to be less oppressive than the contemporary censorships in most other Middle Eastern countries. The Iranian censorship was tightened after the start of terrorist attacks in 1971 and directed mainly against Marxist and Islamic revolutionary writings; but it was also used to prevent the printing of any sort of potentially trouble-causing matter. Publication of criticism of orthodox or popular religion was not allowed in Iran between 1971 and 1977. 'Ali Dashti was therefore obliged to have *Bist o Seh Sāl*, his major work in this field, printed abroad (at Beirut) and to issue it anonymously.

Only oral and scanty information about 'Ali Dashti's experiences after the Islamic revolution is available. He was arrested, and during an interrogation he received a beating and fell and broke his thigh. To what extent he recovered is not clear. After release he was not allowed to return to his home, a pleasant, small house with a garden at Zarganda, a northern suburb of Tehrān. It is unlikely that he saw his books and papers again. A notice in the Iranian periodical *Āyanda* reported his death in the month of Dey of the Iranian year 1360, i.e. between 22 December 1981 and 20 January 1982.

# Note on the Translation

## by F. R. C. Bagley

A mutual friend introduced me to 'Ali Dashti when I was staying in Tehrān in the spring of 1975. I well remember his upright bearing and fine physique at a ripe age and the perspicacity and wit of his conversation. It seemed likely that he would have several more years of vigorous and useful life ahead.

He presented a copy of *Bist o Seh Sāl* to me and requested me to translate it but not to talk about it and not to publish the translation until after his death. He repeated these requests when I met him again at Tehrān in September 1977, and when he telephoned and wrote to me from London during a short journey to Paris and London which he made in June 1978. I lost touch with him after the revolution, but remained bound by my promises to fulfill his requests.

I have tried to produce a readable translation while remaining faithful to 'Ali Dashti's text. In some places I have abbreviated slightly, and in others I have inserted explanations. In chapter V,I have changed the positions of paragraphs obviously printed in wrong order in the Persian original. I found a small number of misprinted or erroneous dates and names, and have checked and corrected them. I have incorporated 'Ali Dashti's few footnotes into the text and added notes of my own to provide identifications and explanations which may be helpful to non-specialist readers.

'Ali Dashti quotes passages from the Qor'ān in the original Arabic, which would be understood by many of his readers, and then gives Persian renderings which are more often explanatory paraphrases than literal translations. I have translated the Qor'ānic passages as literally as possible into modern English after consideration of 'Ali Dashti's renderings and English, French, and German versions. I preferred not to quote from the widely used English versions of Arthur J. Arberry and Marmaduke Pickthall because their strict literalism and archaic English often make comprehension difficult. Systems of Qor'ānic verse-numbering differ, and I have not followed 'Ali Dashti in this respect, but have used the system of Gustav Flügel.

Although this is a translation of a Persian book, the subject-matter requires a transliteration system reproducing Arabic rather than Persian pronunciations of names and words. The chosen system dispenses with diacritical points, which have to be used for identification of Arabic consonants, but distinguishes between long and short vowels as follows: long *ā* (as in *father*), short *a* (like the vowel of *cut* rather than *cat*), long *u* (as in *peruse*), short *o* (like the vowel of *put* rather than *pot*), long *i* (as in *prestige*), short *e* (like the vowel of *sit* rather than *set*). The diphthongs are spelt *ay* and *aw* (though sometimes the former is pronounced as in *my* rather than *may* and the latter as in *now* or *know* rather than *gnaw*). The guttural is transcribed as ' and the glottal stop as '; elision is indicated by '. Unless separated by a hyphen (e.g. *s-h* in Es-hāq), *th* represents the initial consonant of *thing*, *kh* the final consonant of *loch*, *dh* the initial consonant of *this*, *sh* the consonant of *shoe*, and *gh* a consonant similar to the French *r grasseyé*. In constructs with the Arabic article, the Arabic nominative case is used (e.g. *'Abdollāh*, not *'Abdallāh*). The article when preceding the so-called "sun letters" is transliterated as it is pronounced (e.g. *'Abd or-Rahmān*, not *'Abd ol-Rahmān* as it is spelt).

Apologies are offered to Arabists and others accustomed to spellings such as *Ibn 'Abbās* instead of *Ebn 'Abbās*. Conventional English spellings, such as Islam, Iraq, are retained. Arabic names which have the definite article (e.g. *ol-Madina, ot-Tā'ef, ol-Basra, ol-Hasan, ol-Hosayn*) are, for convenience, given without it (e.g. Madina, Hosayn). The abbreviation b. stands for the Arabic *ebn* or *ben* (son of) and *bent* (daughter of). *Banu* (sons of) means tribe or clan.

Dates are given with the *hejri* lunar year preceding the Gregorian solar year (e.g. 10/632).

Below are some explanations of technical terms in the text:

*Sura*: Chapter of the Qor'ān. The chapters are divided into verses which are called *āya*. Both words occur in the Qor'ān, where *sura* appears to mean scripture (e.g. in *sura* 2, verse 21) and *āya* means sign (of God's existence, power, or bounty).

Companions (*sahāba*): early converts and other close associates of the Prophet Mohammad.

*hejra*: the emigration of the Prophet Mohammad and a number of Meccan converts to Madina in September 622. The Islamic era is called the *hejri* era, but its starting point is 16 July 622.

*Mohājerun* (emigrants): the Meccan converts who accompanied or followed the Prophet Mohammad to Madina.

*Ansār* (supporters): the members of the Madinan Khazraj and Aws tribes whose leaders invited Mohammad to Madina and who supported him there.

*Hadith* (news): reports of the Prophet Mohammad's sayings and actions attributed to his companions, his wives, men who knew or saw him, and men who knew his companions. The Shi'ite Islamic *Hadith*, also called *Akhbār* (reports), includes sayings and examples of the *Emāms*. The Hadith supplemented the Qor'ān as a source of Islamic law and theology, and was written down in the 9th and following centuries in massive compilations which are thought by modern scholars to include material absorbed from many Eastern sources.

*Sonna* (custom): the custom of the Prophet Mohammad, as recorded in the Hadith, and of Moslems generally in the early centuries of Islam.

Sonnites: Moslems who believe that, after the Qor'ān, the *sonna* and the consensus of the community are authoritative in religious and legal matters.

Caliph (*Khalifa*): Successor of Mohammad in his role as head of the Islamic state.

*Emām* (Leader): head of the Islamic religious community.

Shi'ites: Moslems who believe that the Prophet Mohammad designated 'Ali to be the next Emām and head of the state, and that only Emāms descended from 'Ali, and each likewise designated by his predecessor, can give authoritative guidance. Shi'ite sects differed over the line of succession of the Emāms and over matters of doctrine. The Twelver Shi'ites, who are the majority in Iran and numerous in Iraq, believe that the Twelfth Emām disappeared in 939 and that since then authoritative guidance is given by the most learned and pious *'olamā* acting as the Emām's representatives.

*'olamā* (plural), *'ālem* (singular): scholars of the Islamic religion who fulfill the function of clergy and used also to act as lawyers.

Readers wishing to pursue the study of subjects treated in this book can find bibliographical guidance in the *Encyclopaedia of Islam*, 2nd ed., Leiden, 1960– (up to Ma in 1984); the *Encyclopaedia Iranica*, New York, 1982– (up to Al in 1984); D. Grimwood-Jones, D. Hopwood, and J. D. Pearson, ed., *Arabic-*

*Islamic Bibliography*, Hassocks, Sussex/Atlantic Highland, New Jersey, 1977; L. P. Elwell Sutton, ed., *Bibliographical Guide to Iran*, Hassocks, Sussex/Totowa, New Jersey, 1983; J. D. Pearson, ed., *Index Islamicus* (articles in periodicals etc. since 1906), Cambridge, 1958.

# CHAPTER I

# *Mohammad*

## HIS BIRTH

I search for the way, but not the way to the Ka'ba and the temple.
For I see in the former a troop of idolaters and in the latter a band of
self-worshippers.

Mawlavi Jalāl od-Din Rumi

At Mecca in 570 Āmena b. Wahb gave birth to a child named
Mohammad. His father 'Abdollāh had died before he opened his
eyes, and he lost his mother when he was five years old. A little
later his influential and generous grandfather 'Abd ol-Mottaleb b.
Hāshem, who had been his sole protector and sustainer, also
passed away. Thereafter this child, who had several quite wealthy
paternal uncles, was brought up by the poorest but bravest of
them, Abu Tāleb. Ahead lay an astonishing career, perhaps
unique in the world's record of self-made men who have created
history.

Thousands of books have been written about this extraordinary
man's life, about the events of the twenty three years of his
mission, about everything that he did and said. Scholars and
researchers actually have at their disposal more information about
him than about any of the great men of history before him. Yet we
still lack an objective and rationally acceptable book presenting a
portrait of him unclouded by preconceptions, suppositions, and
fanaticisms; or if such a book has been written, I have not seen it.

Moslems, as well as others, have disregarded the historical facts.
They have continually striven to turn this man into an imaginary
superhuman being, a sort of God in human clothes, and have
generally ignored the ample evidence of his humanity. They have
been ready to set aside the law of cause and effect, which governs
real life, and to present their fantasies as miracles.

About Mohammad's life up to 610, when he reached the age of forty, nothing of any importance is recorded. In the accounts of the period, and even in the biographies of the Prophet, there are no reports of anything remarkable or out of the ordinary. Yet by the end of the 3rd/9th century the great historian and Qor'ān-commentator Tabari,[1] in his exegesis of verse 21 of *sura 2* (*ol-Baqara*), could insert an unsubstantiated statement about the Prophet's birth which shows how prone the people were in those days to create and repeat impossible myths, and how even a historian could not stick to history. The verse says, "If you are in doubt over what We have sent down to Our servant, bring a *sura* like it, and call your witnesses, other than God, if you are truthful!" The statement which Tabari adds to his explanation of the verse is as follows: "Before the Prophet's appointment, a rumor had spread in Mecca that a messenger from God with the name Mohammad would appear and that the east and the west of the world would fall under his sway. At that time forty women in Mecca were with child, and every one of them, after giving birth, named her son Mohammad in case he might be the expected messenger."

The fatuity of this statement is too obvious for comment. Nobody in Mecca could have heard such a rumor or foreseen the appearance of a prophet named Mohammad. Mohammad's protector and guardian Abu Tāleb, who died without embracing Islam, must certainly have heard nothing and seen nothing. Mohammad himself did not know before his appointment that he was going to be a prophet, as verse 17 of *sura 10* (*Yunos*) eloquently attests: "Had God so willed, I should not have recited it to you, and He would not have made it known to you. I dwelt among you for a lifetime before it." There were no registration statistics at Mecca to show that in the year 570 only forty women gave birth and that all without exception named their sons Mohammad. Did Mohammad in his childhood have forty playmates of the same age and name?

The historian Wāqedi[2] tells a different sort of story about the Prophet's birth: "As soon as he came out of his mother's womb, he said 'God is great'. At one month he crawled, at two months he stood, at three months he walked, at four months he ran, and at nine months he shot arrows." It is noteworthy that Mirzā Jāni Kāshāni (d. 1268/1852) makes a similar statement about Sayyed 'Ali Mohammad Shirāzi, the founder of Bābism, in his book *Noqtat ol-Kāf*,[3] which the Bahā'is tried to suppress. According to this, as soon as Sayyed 'Ali was born he uttered the words "Sovereignty belongs to God."

If such extraordinary things as Wāqedi relates had occurred, surely they would have become known to all the people of Mecca, and surely those people, who worshipped stone idols, would have bowed down to Mohammad instead.

This story is an example of myth-making and history-fabrication by Moslems. Conversely certain Western Christian writers were moved by religious bias to describe Mohammad as a liar, impostor, adventurer, power-seeker, and lecher. Neither group was capable of objective study of the facts.

The reason for this is that ideologies, whether political, religious, or sectarian, prevent men and women from using their brains and thinking clearly. Subjects thus become veiled by preconceived notions of good and evil. Inculcated love or hatred and fanaticism or prejudice envelop the person who is being discussed in a fog of unreal imagination.

Without question the Prophet Mohammad is an outstanding figure. Among the qualities which distinguished him from his fellow men were sharpness of mind, profundity of thought, and impatience with the illusions and superstitions prevalent in his time. Most important of all were the extraordinary will-power and energy which carried him into single combat with evil. In fervent words he warned the people against dishonesty and immorality, reprehended wickedness, untruthfulness, and selfishness, stood up for the deprived and needy lower class, rebuked his compatriots for worshipping stone idols instead of the one great God, and ridiculed the uselessness of the idols. Naturally those who enjoyed prestige and held positions of strength in the Meccan community took no notice of his words. Acceptance would have required abandonment of customs and beliefs which had been rooted for centuries and, like all inherited ideologies, were supposed to have absolute and incontestable validity.

What most offended the Meccan chiefs was the fact that this call for overthrow of the traditional social structure came from a man of lower status than themselves. Although he was of the same tribe, the Qoraysh, he was not of the same rank, being an orphan whom an uncle had compassionately housed and reared. After a childhood spent in tending the camels of his uncle and his neighbors, he had at a quite young age entered the service of a wealthy woman, Khadija, and begun to gain some esteem. Such a man,

3

seen hitherto as an ordinary Qorayshite tribesman lacking any kind of distinction, suddenly claimed authority to teach and lead on the ground that God had appointed him to be a prophet.

The attitude and mentality of the chiefs is illustrated by a reported remark of Walid b. ol-Moghira, who was head of the Makhzum clan of the Qoraysh tribe in the early years of Mohammad's mission and died some time before 615: "When the Qoraysh have a chief like me and the Banu Tamim one like 'Orwa b. Mas'ud, how can Mohammad claim to be a prophet?" There is a reference to this crude notion in verses 30 and 31 of *sura* 43 (*oz-Zokhrof*): "And they said, 'If only this Qor'ān had been sent down to some great man of the two towns (i.e. Mecca and Tā'ef)!' Is it they who apportion your Lord's mercy? It is We who have apportioned their sustenance among them in the life of the lower world."

The Makhzum clan had been gaining ground in Meccan affairs. The powerful 'Abd Manāf clan of the Qoraysh had split into smaller clans called after 'Abd Manāf's sons; among these were the clan of Hāshem, into which Mohammad was born, and the wealthy clan of 'Abd Shams and the latter's son Omayya. The clan mentality is expressed in the reported words of Abu Jahl,[4] the next head of the clan of Makhzum, to Akhnas b. Shariq, a head of another clan: "We were rivals with the Banu 'Abd Manāf for the ascendancy, and we have caught up with them. So one of them has come out with a claim to be a prophet. This is how the Banu 'Abd Manāf hope to regain the upper hand over us."

These and other reports enable us to understand the thinking of the Qoraysh chiefs and their reaction to Mohammad's preaching. They took a negative view because they did not believe either in the existence of one God or in the divine appointment of a man from their own people to teach and guide them. Their objection, several times quoted in the Qor'ān (e.g. in *suras* 6, verse 8; 11, verse 15; 25, verse 8) was that if a god had wished to guide them, he would not have appointed a man of their own people to do so, but would have sent an angel to them. The reply, also given in the Qor'ān (*sura* 17, verse 97), is that if the angels lived on earth, a prophet from among their people would likewise be sent to them. Significantly the Meccan chiefs paid no attention to the basic issue. They never listened to Mohammad's teaching with any willingness to ascertain its truth and assess its compatibility with reason and the good of the community.

4

In any community, however wicked or immoral, there are a few clear-thinking and well-meaning persons ready to accept words of truth, no matter from whose mouth they may come. Among the men of influence in Meccan society, Abu Bakr must be counted the first to have acknowledged Mohammad's teachings as true. Following his example some other Qorayshite notables, such as 'Abd or-Rahmān b. 'Awf, 'Othman b. 'Affān, Zobayr b. ol-'Awwām, Talha b. 'Obaydollāh, and Sa'd b. Abi Waqqās, embraced Islam.

In any community there is also a group which has not shared in the good fortune of the wealthy group and naturally forms the poor and discontented class. At Mecca members of both groups rallied to Mohammad and joined in praise of him and his ideas. Conflict between the two groups was bound to arise in the Meccan situation. The wealthy, who enjoyed the support of the majority of the people, were proud of their wealth and their money. The minority supporting Mohammad were convinced of the rightness of their cause, and in order to propagate it, they ascribed special faculties and merits to their leader. The tendency to do this was kept within reasonable bounds during his lifetime but continually gathered strength after his death. Popular imagination soon dehumanized him and endowed him with the qualities of a son of God, cause of creation, controller of the universe.

To show how most of these fantasies came into being and proliferated, an important example will be discussed. The evidence in this case is clear and uncontrovertible. For Moslems the Qor'ān is the conclusive proof. Verse 1 of *sura* 17 (*ol-Esrā*), which is one of the Meccan *suras*, was the source of the belief that the Prophet made a night journey to heaven. The words of the verse, however, are simple and rationally explicable: "Exalted is He who carried His servant by night from the Mosque of the Sanctuary to the Furthest Mosque, whose precincts We have blessed, so that We might show him some of Our signs. He is (all-)hearing, (all-)seeing." The words may certainly be taken to mean a spiritual journey. Other instances of spiritual journeys by visionary thinkers are known.

In Moslem minds, however, this simple verse is overlaid with wondrous and rationally unacceptable myths. Here it will suffice to quote the relatively temperate account given in the *Tafsir ol-Jalālayn*, which is one of the trustworthiest Qor'ān-commentaries because the learned Egyptians Jalāl od-Din ol-Mahalli, who began it, and Jalāl od-Din os-Soyuti (848/1445–910/1505), who finished it, were virtually free from sectarian prejudice, their only concern being to explain the meanings of the verses and in some cases the occasions of the revelations. Even so, in their exegesis of verse 1 of *sura* 17, they put unsubstantiated words into the Prophet Mohammad's mouth. Was their purpose to explain the meaning and the occasion of the revelation of the verse, or to summarize the stories about it circulating among Moslems? In any case, they cite no evidence that the Prophet ever said such things. The authors of the Hadith compilations took great pains to check the transmission of sayings ascribed to the Prophet, though this does not necessarily prove the reliability of the trans-mitters. The authors of the *Tafsir ol-Jalālayn* do not mention any source at all. This suggests that perhaps they did not believe the story which they were telling. According to it, the Prophet said:

"That night Gabriel came, bringing a quadruped bigger than a donkey and smaller than a mule, with outward-facing hoofs on its feet. I mounted it and rode to the House of the Sanctuary. I tied Borāq's (the animal's) bridle on the ring on which prophets usually tied it. In the Furthest Mosque I lowered my head to the ground three times in prayer. When I came out, Gabriel brought two vessels to me, one filled with milk and one filled with wine. I chose the one filled with milk, and Gabriel approved my choice. Then we flew to the first heaven. At the gate of the first heaven a guard asked, 'Who is it?' Gabriel answered, 'It is Gabriel.' The guard asked, 'Who is with you?' Gabriel answered, 'Mohammad.' The guard asked, 'Has he been summoned?' Gabriel said, 'Yes.' Then the guard opened the gate of the heaven. Adam came to meet me and said, 'You are welcome.' [In like manner Mohammad traverses the seven heavens and in each of them is greeted by a prophet]. In the seventh heaven I saw Abraham reclining in the populous abode into which seventy thousand angels go every day and out of which none ever come. Next Gabriel took me to the last lote tree,[5] whose leaves were as big as elephant's ears and whose fruits were like . . . . . . Then a revelation came ordering me to pray fifty times every day and night. On my way back, the Prophet Moses said to me, 'Fifty prayers are too many. Ask the Lord to reduce them!' So I went back to God and asked for a reduction. The Lord granted a reduction to forty prayers. This time Moses said, 'I have tested the matter in my own community. The people cannot pray forty times every day and night.' I went back to God again . . . . . . . . . ."

[In short, the Prophet went on haggling until God reduced the number of the daily prayers to five.]

This statement about the Prophet's night journey in the *Tafsir ol Jalālayn* is pale beside the extravaganzas of Tabari's *Tafsir* (Qor'ān-commentary) and the writings of Abu Bakr 'Atiq Nishā-puri. Islamic portrayals of the night journey turn it into fables like the adventures of the folklore hero Amir Arslān. Even the Prophet's modern and generally rational biographer, Mohammad Hosayn Haykal,[6] while denying that the night journey was a bodily ascension, presents the mythical account in a modified form taken from a book by Emile Dermenghem.[7]

To anyone acquainted with the Qor'ān, which reflects the events and experiences of Mohammad's prophetic career, it is obvious that the Prophet did not say such things and that these childish fables are figments of the imaginations of simple-minded people who conceived of the divine order as a replica of the court of their own king or ruler. For in the same *sura* 17, whose first verse gave rise to the myth, the Prophet is told in verse 95 how to answer those who demanded a miracle from him: "Say 'Glory to my Lord! Am I other than a human, a messenger?'" Verse 50 of *sura* 42 (*osh-Shawrā*) states clearly that "it would not be (vouchsafed) to a human that God should speak to him, except through revelation."

When revelations were being sent down to the Prophet, there was no need that he should go up to the heavens. Even on the assumption of such a need, why should a winged or air-borne quadruped have been provided? Was the Furthest Mosque on the route to the heavens? Does God, who is omnipotent, have any need for prayers from His worshippers? Why had not the guards of the heavens been forewarned of the Prophet's journey?

Credulous minds relate cause to effect without reference to reality. The Prophet needs a mount because he is going on a long journey; therefore the mount, while resembling a mule, has to possess some sort of wings to enable it to fly like a pigeon. God wants to dazzle Mohammad with His Majesty and therefore commands Gabriel to show Mohammad the wonders of the heavens. Like a mighty king who orders his officials to collect higher taxes to meet the state's expenses, and whose finance minister warns against impoverishment of the subjects through overtaxation, the Lord demands prayers from the worshippers and His Prophet pleads that fifty prayers are too many.

Mohammad's greatness is unquestionable. He was one of the

most outstanding men of genius who have appeared in human history. If the social and political circumstances of his time are taken into account, he has no equal among the initiators of major historical change. Men such as Alexander, Caesar, Napoleon, Hitler, Cyrus, Chengiz Khān, or Timur do not bear comparison with him. They all had the support of the armed forces and public opinion of their peoples, whereas Mohammad made his way into history with empty hands and in a hostile society.

Perhaps Lenin can be rated the most potent man of the present century and compared with Mohammad. For nearly twenty years (1904–1924), with tireless energy and resourcefulness and with stubborn fidelity to his principles, he thought, wrote, kept remote control over revolutionary activities, and never relaxed until he established the first communist state in the physically and socially unfavorable environment of Russia. He certainly overcame huge internal and external obstacles. On the other hand, a revolutionary movement had been developing in Russia for half a century before him, and hundreds of thousands of revolutionaries and malcontents were ready to support him. Another striking difference is that he always lived in poverty or self-chosen austerity.

It is natural and normal that legends about great men should arise after their deaths. After a time their weak points are forgotten and only their strong points are remembered and passed on. The lives of many thinkers and artists were by no means morally irreproachable, but their works survive and are admired. We do not know how Nasir od-Din Tusi[8] managed to become a minister to the Mongol conqueror Hulāgu Khān;[9] but even if his expedients were immoral, his scientific writings have made him an honored son of Iran.

No wonder, then, that after the death of a great spiritual leader imaginations should get to work and endow him with a profusion of virtues and merits. The trouble is that this process does not stay within reasonable limits but becomes vulgarized, commercialized, and absurd.

The Prophet Mohammad's birth took place in the normal way and with no immediate consequences, just like the births of millions of other infants; but the craze for miracles made people invent and believe fables about it, for instance that as soon as he was born the arch at Ctesiphon[10] cracked and the fires in the fire-temples of Fārs went out. Even if such events occurred at that time, how could they be effects of the Prophet's birth and how could they be warnings from God?

Reason, observation, and mathematics require effects to have causes. All the world's phenomena, whether physical, social, or political, have causes. Sometimes these seem obvious; sunshine gives warmth and light, fire burns if not obstructed, water flows downward unless it can be pumped upward. Sometimes they are not obvious and have only been discovered through long effort, such as the causes of thunder and lightning or diseases and cures.

Between the birth of a child at Mecca and the extinction of temple-fires in Iran, no relation of cause and effect is possible. If a crack appeared in the arch at Ctesiphon, it must have been due to subsidence. The miracle-mongers of a later age described these events as divine warnings, meaning that God wished to tell the inhabitants of Ctesiphon, and in particular the king of Iran, about an impending cataclysm, and to let the guardians of the fire-temples of Fārs know about the advent of a man who would overthrow fire-veneration. Yet how could the Iranian king or the Zoroastrian priests have recognised the cracking of the arch and extinction of the fires as indications of the birth of a child who was only to begin his religious mission forty years later? Why should God, who is wise and understanding, have wanted the Iranians to take heed of Islam forty years before Mohammad was appointed to preach it? All that is known about the situation in pre-Islamic Arabia confirms the Qor'ānic statement that Mohammad himself had no premonition of his future prophethood. If God had wished to signalize the extraordinary importance of Mohammad's birth, why did He give no sign to the Meccans? In His omnipotence He could have caused the Ka'ba's roof to fall and its idols to topple, which would have been a stronger warning to the Qorayshites than the extinction of fires in faraway temples. In any case, why was not the Prophet's appointment accompanied by a miracle which would have convinced all the Qorayshites and spared God's chosen messenger from thirteen years of enmity and persecution? Why was not a light kindled in the heart of King Khosraw Parviz[11] to guide him to the true faith and dissuade him from tearing up the Prophet's letter? The Iranians would then have been guided by their king's example, and they would have become Moslems without having to suffer defeat at the battles of Qādesiya and Nehāvand.

Many years ago, I read the *Vie de Jésus* of the great French writer

Ernest Renan (1823–92), who has painted a realistic and vivid portrait of the Messiah with masterly skill. Sometime later, I came across another book, entitled *Son of Man*, whose painstaking German author, Emil Ludwig, claimed that it is as factual as any book on the subject can be when reliable historical documentation is so scarce.

In the present short work, I do not attempt to give a full account of twenty three of the sixty three years of the Prophet Mohammad's life. Without false modesty, I do not see myself as possessing Ernest Renan's talent and sensitivity or Emil Ludwig's patience and capacity for research, all of which qualities would be needed in plenty for adequate portrayal of a man whose spiritual and moral strength changed the course of human history.

My purpose in this short work is to sketch an outline and to dispel a phantom. The shape of the book evolved in my mind from study of the Qor'ān and reflection on the genesis of Islam.

To be more precise and candid, I admit that part of the impulse to write it came to me from a psychological theory or rather observation. This is that belief can blunt human reason and common sense. As we all know, ideas which have been inculcated into a person's mind in childhood remain in the background of his or her thinking. Consequently he or she will want to make facts conform with inculcated ideas which have no rational validity. Even learned scholars, with rare exceptions, are burdened with this handicap and inhibited from using their common sense; or if they use it, they only do so when it corroborates their inculcated ideas. Mankind is gifted with faculties of perception and ratiocination which make solution of scientific problems possible, but in matters of religious and political belief is ready to trample on the evidence of reason and even of the senses.

# HIS CHILDHOOD

Information about the Prophet Mohammad's childhood is scarce. He was a fatherless and motherless orphan living in the house of his paternal uncle, Abu Tāleb, a man who had a kind heart but little material wealth. In order that he might be occupied and help to pay for his keep, he was given the task of taking camels owned by Abu Tāleb and others into the plain to graze. He thus spent his days in the grim desert outside Mecca all alone.

For a sensitive and intelligent child, the experience of several years in this occupation must, in the Persian phrase, have been "as bitter as chewing terebinth twigs". He would naturally ask himself why he had come into the world as a fatherless orphan and had so soon lost the young mother to whom alone he could turn for love and caresses. He would wonder too why blind fate had taken away his strong and generous grandfather and sent him for refuge to his uncle's house. His uncle was a good and kind man, but had a large family and could not afford to give him the care which his cousins and other children of the same rank received. His other uncles, such as ʿAbbās and Abu Lahab, lived comfortably and ignored him. Thoughts such as these must have rankled in his mind during long years of sorrow and hardship.

In the monotonous solitude of the arid plain, where the camels strained their necks in search of a thorn or a blade of grass among the stones, what else was there to do but grieve and muse? Misfortune embitters a person and makes him conscious of suffering, especially when he is left to himself with nothing to distract him. It may safely be conjectured that in the course of time this child's thoughts turned to the social system and found in it some of the sources of his unhappiness. The reason why the other boys of his rank and age led pleasant lives was that their fathers had charge of the Kaʿba. They supplied water, bread, and other requisites to the pilgrims who came to Mecca for the annual ceremonies at the Kaʿba, and they made big profits by selling goods which they imported from Syria dearly and buying produce from pilgrims cheaply. These businesses were the source of their children's well-being.

Why did so many tribes sustain the wealth and power of the Qoraysh by coming to the Kaʿba? The reason was that the Kaʿba housed famous idols and contained a black stone which the Arabs held sacred. They thought that walking around the Kaʿba would bring happiness and salvation and that running between the nearby hills of Safā and Marwa, on the tops of which two more idols had been placed, was necessary to make prayers effective. Each group of pilgrims had to shout its entreaties to its idol while circumambulating the Kaʿba and running from Safā to Marwa.

Mohammad's keen eye and intelligence must have prompted him, at the age of eleven or twelve, to start wondering whether any force lay concealed in the black stone and any action could proceed from the lifeless statues. His doubts may well have arisen from a personal experience. It is by no means improbable that in his sorrow and spiritual anguish he had hopefully addressed fervent pleas to the idols and obtained no result. This hypothesis is supported by verses in two *suras* which poured from his mouth thirty years later: "Have no more to do with the filth!" (i.e. the idols; *sura 74, al-Moddather,* verse 5), and "Did not He find you astray and guide you?" (*sura* 93, *od-Dohā,* verse 7).

The Qorayshite leaders themselves could scarcely be unaware of the facts. They lived beside the temple and could see that the stone objects did not move or emit grace or grant mercy. The silence of the Qorayshites and their worship of Lāt, Manāt, and 'Ozzā could only be due to self-interest. There is a Persian saying that the holiness of a saint depends on the guardian of his tomb. If the Qorayshite leaders lost the guardianship of the Ka'ba, their income from it would cease and their flourishing trade with Syria would decline because no more Beduin pilgrims, to whom they could sell dearly and from whom they could buy cheaply, would come to Mecca.

The stirrings in Mohammad's visionary soul must have arisen during the long days which he spent in frightening solitude watching the camels search for their meagre fare in the sun-scorched desert. The approach of sunset, when he would round up the camels and take them to the town, must have brought him back to reality. He had to call them, hustle them, and stop them from straying, in order to return them safe and sound to their owners for the night.

In the darkness of the night the stirrings would give way to visions, and in the morning sunshine they would recommence when he was back in the monotonous desert. Little by little they took shape in the depths of his inner mind.

An introvert personality, prone to musing and dreaming, undistracted by clatter and deprived of normal pleasures, would become more introverted with the passage of every year spent alone in the desert. Then, suddenly, a ghost might appear or a splashing of waves on an unknown sea might be heard.

After several years in the same routine, a new experience made a deep mark on Mohammad's mind. At the age of eleven he accompanied his uncle Abu Tāleb on a journey to Syria. There he saw a different and brighter world with no signs of the ignorance, superstition, and rudeness prevalent among the Meccans. The people whom he met were politer, the social atmosphere was happier, and the accepted customs were of a higher order. These observations must have added to the turmoil in his inner soul. It was probably there that he first perceived how primitive and rough and superstitious his own people were; perhaps there also that he began to wish that they might have a better ordered, less superstitious, and more humane society. It is not known for certain whether he first came into contact with followers of monotheistic religions on this journey, and it would seem that he was then too young to learn anything from such contacts; but the experience must have made an impression on his perceptive and uneasy mind, and perhaps moved him to make another journey. Some of the transmitted reports state that on the second journey he was no longer too young and that he eagerly listened to religious informants.

It is not difficult to understand why so little is known about the Prophet Mohammad's childhood and youth. There was nothing important in the life of an orphan brought up under the guardianship of an uncle. Nobody took enough notice to have any recollection of him as he was at that time. Most of what has been written here is only conjecture based on the theory that the solitude and monotony of daily camel-tending in a desert would make a child introspective, imaginative, and visionary.

It is possible that many of the Qor'ānic verses which at a later time were to flow from his anguished lips echo his youthful musings and impressions of nature and its creation. For instance: "Do they never consider the camels, how they were created? And the sky, how it was raised? And the mountains, how they were erected? And the earth, how it was spread out?" (*sura* 88, *ol-Ghāshiya*, verses 17–20).

Study of the Meccan *suras* gives glimpses into the vision-filled soul of a person remote from life's material blessings and given to communion with himself and with nature. These *suras* also express indignation at the boasting of vain men such as Abu Lahab[12] and Abu'l-Ashadd.[13]

In later times, when the success of Mohammad's preaching had exalted his prestige, believers turned to the fertile fields of their imaginations and invented fables such as those which are found in Tabari's and Wāqedi's works and were cited in the previous chapter.

Another point which needs consideration, though it will not be discussed in detail here, is that the Moslem writers depict conditions in the Hejāz, and particularly at Mecca before the Prophet Mohammad's mission, as darker than they really were. According to most accounts, the Arabs of that time lived in an utter darkness of barbarity and idolatry, and no glimmer of higher thinking and religious belief had appeared. This exaggeration was probably motivated by desire to emphasize the change wrought by the Prophet's rise and teaching. A number of modern scholars in the Arab countries, however, such as 'Ali Jawād, 'Abdollāh Sammān, Tāhā Hosayn,[14] Mohammad Hosayn Haykal, Mohammad 'Ezzat Darwaza, and Professor Haddād, have concluded that the Hejāz in the sixth century possessed a measure of civilization and incipient theism by no means so negligible as is commonly supposed. From the researches of these scholars and from various indications and reports in the early sources, it may be taken for certain that a reaction against idolatry had begun in the Hejāz in the second half of the sixth century.

To some extent this reaction was due to the presence of Jewish tribes, particularly at Yathreb, and of Christians from Syria who made journeys to the Hejāz, and to some extent it was the work of thinking men known by the name *hanif*. The following statement is taken from the biography of the Prophet by Ebn Heshām:[15] "One day the Qorayshites assembled in a palm grove near Tā'ef to celebrate the festival of 'Ozzā, the chief goddess of the Banu Thaqif. Four of them withdrew and said to each other, 'These people are on the wrong track. They have lost the religion of our ancestor Abraham.' Then they cried out to the people, 'Choose a different religion from this! Why do you walk around a stone which neither sees nor hears and can neither help you nor harm you?' These four men were Waraqa b. Nawfal, 'Obaydollāh b. Jahsh, 'Othman b. ol-Howayreth, and Zayd b. 'Amr. From then onward they called themselves *hanif* and came out in favor of the religion of Abraham. The last-named of the four uttered these words in prayer: 'Here I am, in truth, in truth, in worship and humility. I take refuge where Abraham took refuge. I was aloof from You. I deserve whatever may befall me.' Then he knelt and lowered his head to the ground."

While there can be no doubt that ignorance and superstition prevailed in most of Arabia and idolatry was practiced by the great majority, monotheism was not a novelty and was well understood in the Hejāz, particularly at Madina and in the north where Jewish and Christian tribes resided. Before Mohammad, prophets had appeared in various parts of Arabia and warned against idolatry in their preachings; some of them are mentioned in the Qor'ān, namely Hud among the people of 'Ād, Sāleh among the people of Thamud, and Sho'ayb in Medyan. In the Arabic sources there are mentions of preachers named Hanzala b. Safwān, Khāled b. Senān, 'Āmer b. Zareb ol-'Adwāni, and 'Abdollāh ol-Qodā'i. Also mentioned is an eloquent poet and orator, Qass b. Sā'eda ol-Iyādi, who in the annual poetry recitations at the fair at 'Okāz near Mecca, and even at the Ka'ba, appealed to the people in fervent verses and sermons to renounce idolatry. Omayya b. Abi's-Salt, a contemporary of Mohammad and a member of the Thaqif tribe at Tā'ef, was a particularly renowned *hanif* and advocate of monotheism. He made frequent journeys to Syria, where he spent much time in conversation with Christian monks and Jewish men of learning. It was there that he heard news of Mohammad's emergence. Although the two are said to have had a meeting, he did not become a Moslem. After his return to Tā'ef, he is reported to have told one of his friends, "I know more about the books and traditions of the other religions than Mohammad does. I also know the Aramaic and Hebrew languages. So I would have a better right to prophethood." According to Bokhāri,[16] Mohammad said that "Omayya b. Abi's-Salt came near to becoming a Moslem."

Poetry, especially the poetry of a nation in its youth, gives vivid pictures of feelings and customs. In the Arabic poetry of the pre-Islamic period, there are verses which might have been composed by a Moslem, such as these by Zohayr:[17]

> Do not hide what is in your souls from God,
> for however carefully it may be hidden and concealed,
>   God will know it!
> Either it will be adjourned, put into a book, and stored
> for a day of reckoning, or it will come up soon and be
>   requited.

Or these by 'Abdollāh b. ol-Abras:

> It is He whom the people long to worship,
> for seekers of God will not be disappointed.
> Through God all blessings are within reach;
> to mention only a few of them is to urge to victory.
> God has no partners,
> and He knows what hearts conceal.

The Prophet Mohammad is reported to have once quoted a verse by Labid:[18]

> Except through God, all is vain,
> all prosperity is bound to cease.

It is noteworthy that these and some other pre-Islamic poets use the word *Allāh* for God, and that several pagan Qorayshites, including Mohammad's father, were named 'Abdollāh which means slave of God. This indicates that the word *Allāh* was familiar to them, even though the idols were thought to be means of approach to God – a concept which is mentioned in the Qor'ān (*sura* 10, verse 19).

Another pre-Islamic poet, 'Amr b. Fadl, flatly rejected the famous idols of the Arabs:

> I have forsaken Lāt and 'Ozzā altogether.
> Any man who is stalwart and constant will do likewise.
> No longer shall I visit 'Ozzā and her two daughters
> or the two idols of the Banu Ghanm.
> Nor shall I visit Hubal when, as often happens,
> fortune is adverse; for my patience is slight.

The call to reject idolatry and worship the one great God was thus not without precedent. What was new was urgent insistence. Mohammad's miracle was that he unflinchingly faced all insults, harassments, and repulses, and never shrank from any step until he had imposed Islam on Arabia and brought the different Arab tribes under one flag.

The mentality of these tribes was in general still primitive, concerned only with visible and tangible things and unfamiliar with metaphysical ideas. Their only goal was immediate gain. They had no scruples about seizing the property of others and would stop at nothing in the pursuit of power. A good example of their way of thinking is the already quoted remark of Abu Jahl to Akhnas b. Shariq to the effect that Mohammad's prophethood was a ruse of the Banu 'Abd Manāf to regain the ascendancy. The same view reappears in the wish of the Omayyad caliph Yazid b. Mo'āwiya (60/680–64/683) that the men whom Mohammad had defeated at the battle of Badr (in 2/624) might have seen how the Omayyad troops had defeated the Banu Hāshem and killed

Hosayn b. 'Ali at the battle of Karbalā (in 61/680). Yazid is reported to have said, in verse:

> The Hāshemites gambled for power, but
> no word came, no revelation was sent down.

It would be wrong to end this chapter without mentioning that the modern Arab scholars disagree about the pre-Islamic poetry. Some of them doubt whether it is all genuinely pre-Islamic. In any case, there is ample evidence that signs of disillusionment with paganism and movement toward monotheism had appeared in the Hejāz during the sixth century.

## THE PROBLEM OF PROPHETHOOD

In recent times numerous scholars have made detailed studies of the rise and spread of Islam, the meaning and arrangement of the Qor'ān and the occasions of the revelation of its verses, and the origins and development of the Hadith. Valuable work has been accomplished by great Western scholars such as Theodor Nöldeke, Ignaz Goldziher, Alfred von Kremer, Adam Mez, Régis Blachère, and others. They have examined the problems with microscopic precision and from a purely scientific viewpoint. Their writings show no trace of fanaticism or desire to disparage Islam. In their research they have used authentic and reliable Islamic sources.

There are also European writers who have let religious fanaticism dim their vision. They have described Mohammad as an adventurer and impostor and the Qor'ān as his tool for winning power. If they had similarly criticized Moses and Jesus, their views might deserve consideration (though that would be beyond the scope of this book); but they presuppose that Moses and Jesus were appointed by God and that Mohammad was not. Their statements are not supported by any kind of rationally acceptable evidence.

In reply to holders of such views, it is best to begin by discussing the question of principle. They must in logic accept the principle of prophethood because their appraisals imply acceptance in one case and rejection in another.

Some profound thinkers such as Mohammad b. Zakariyā

ol-Rāzi[19] and Abu'l-'Alā ol-Ma'arri[20] rejected the principle of prophethood. They found the theological arguments for the general necessity of prophethood to be illogical and unconvincing. While the theologians said that God in His grace appoints a person to warn His people against sin and wrongdoing, the rationalists argued that if God had been concerned about the virtue and harmony of His people, He would have created all of them sinless and good, in which case there would have been no need to send a prophet. The usual reply is that good and evil were not created by God, who is pure good, and that propensities for good and evil are inherent in human nature. We are then bound to ask who gives an individual his or her particular nature with its good and evil potentialities.

Human beings start life with natures determined by their parents at the moment of conception. Every new-born child comes into the world with certain physical characteristics and consequently with psychological and mental characteristics which depend on his or her physical constitution. Nobody can voluntarily determine his own brain power, nervous energy, and instincts any more than he can choose his eye color, nose shape, heart pressure, stature, or bodily strengths such as eyesight. Some individuals are temperamentally calm and moderate, others are turbulent, stubborn, and prone to excess. Those with well-balanced personalities do not disturb the freedom and infringe the rights of others. Those with aggressive personalities often commit violence.

If it is said that prophets are sent to change people's natures, the question arises whether an ill-balanced personality can be transformed into a well-balanced one any more than a black skin into a white one. If this is possible, why has the history of the human race since its adoption of religion been so stained with violence, cruelty, and crime? We are bound to conclude that God's dispatch of prophets to mankind has not succeeded in making all men and women good and happy. An objective observer might remark that a safer way for God to achieve this aim would have been for Him to create all men and women good in the first place.

The theologians have a ready answer to this criticism. They say that life in the present world is a test, that good and evil must be authoritatively defined, and that the dispatch of a prophet is a sort of ultimatum notifying good-doers, who obey his commands, of future reward in heaven and wrong-doers, who disobey them, of future condign punishment.

The deniers of prophethood say that the notion of life as a test is crude and untenable. Why should God want to test His servants when He knows their secret thoughts better than they do themselves? Why should He want them to become aware of their wrong-doing? They do not think of themselves as wicked and do not see their actions as sins, because otherwise they would not commit them. They act in ways which conform with their natures and temperaments. If all individuals had identical natures, the fact that some obey and others disobey prophets would be inexplicable. In other words, all individuals would necessarily either obey or disobey if the good and evil propensities in their natures were uniformly distributed.

Aside from these general considerations, Moslem theologians ought not to forget the numerous Qor'ānic verses which make human error and rectitude dependent on God's will. For example, "You do not guide those whom you like, but God guides those whom He wills" (*sura* 28, verse 56); "Those whom God leads astray have no guide" (*sura* 39, verse 24); "And if We had so willed, We would have given every soul its guidance" (*sura* 32, verse 13). The number of verses which state that guidance and error are from God alone is so large that it would be impossible to quote them all here.

These verses, and the inability of the prophets to change mankind radically, make nonsense of the efforts of the theologians to prove the general necessity of prophethood.

The basic fallacy in the reasoning of the theologians of Islam and the other religions lies in their concept of the creation. Their belief in the existence of prophets sent by the Cr tor and Sustainer of the universe depends on their belief in the Creator, and their belief in the Creator requires assumption that the universe is contingent and was created *ex nihilo*, in other words that the universe did not exist until the Creator brought it into existence. This assumption is not verifiable. How can we know that there was a time when no universe, no trace of being, existed? The hypothesis that the earth and solar system and the stars and nebulae did not always exist is tenable, but the assumption that their component elements once did not exist and then came into existence seems hardly reasonable. It seems more reasonable to suppose the contrary, namely the pre-existence of the atoms from whose fusion the sun emerged, though we do not know for certain what factors caused the fusion and emergence. This hypothesis is supported by observations which show a continual process of stars emerging and becoming extinguished. Coming into being is accordingly not genesis of substance but change of form. In that case argument for the existence of a Creator becomes difficult.

Another problem which arises if we assume that the universe did not exist until it was created by Almighty God is the purpose of its creation. However much we exert and exalt our minds, we cannot find answers to the two questions: why did not the universe exist before, and why did God choose to create it? Pure reason is as powerless to solve these problems as it is to prove or disprove the existence of the Creator.

In this confusion, one thing seems certain to our earth-bound minds. We humans are not, or do not wish to be, in the same category as other terrestrial animals. Humans can think, and since the earliest remembered times they have supposed that there must be a person who started and controls the system and exerts favorable and unfavorable influences. This idea, whether prompted by reasoning or by pride in distinction from other animals, impelled humans to construct religions.

In all societies, from the most primitive to the most advanced, religious beliefs have arisen and remain strong. Among primitive peoples they are stained with superstition and illusion. Among advanced peoples they have acquired moral and social aspects under the influence of great thinkers, whose teachings eventually led those peoples to adopt more civilized and equitable ways of life. These great men came forth in the roles of legislators, reformers, or philosophers, such as Hammurabi, Confucius, Buddha, Socrates, and Plato. Among the Semitic peoples they always came forth as prophets, that is to say as self-proclaimed spokesmen for God.

Moses walked up Mount Sinai, brought down tablets, and enacted laws to reform the ways of the Children of Israel. Jesus, finding the Jews in the grip of vanity and false piety, arose to teach better morals. He likened God to a loving father, and either spoke of himself as son of that celestial father or was so described by his disciples; another possibility is that the four Gospels distort or inflate what he said.

Six centuries later Mohammad arose in the Hejāz and appealed for reform. How did he differ from Moses and Jesus?

Simple-minded believers make miraculous action the criterion of prophethood. Islamic writers therefore ascribed hundreds, indeed thousands, of miracles to Mohammad. More remarkable than this is the attitude of a modern Christian Arab scholar named Haddād. In his learned and well researched book *The Qor'ān and the Bible*, he quotes numerous Qor'ānic passages as evidence that no miracles were ever performed by Mohammad, and then naively states that miracles are proofs of prophethood and that the miracles of Jesus and Moses prove that they were prophets. All the cited miracles fall into the category of unverifiable imaginings or hallucinations. If Jesus had really restored life to a dead human body, no one in the contemporary Jewish community would have hesitated to bow down to him and believe in him. If God had wanted all the people to believe in one of His servants and to benefit from that person's teachings, surely it would have been simpler and wiser for God to make all the people good, or to endow that person with power over the people's minds rather than with powers to resurrect the dead, stop the flow of rivers, prevent fire from burning, and the like.

The problem of prophethood must therefore be approached from another angle. It should be seen as a sort of mental and spiritual genius peculiar to an extraordinary individual.

Among military leaders there have been individuals such as Cyrus, Alexander, Caesar, Nāder, and Napoleon who had a genius for planning and winning wars, though they had nothing to teach to their fellow men. In the fields of science and art, men such as Aristotle, Ebn Sinā, Nasir od-Din Tusi, Edison, Einstein, Leonardo da Vinci, Beethoven, Homer, Ferdowsi, 'Abu'l-'Alā ol-Ma'arri, Hāfez, and hundreds of others have brightened the course of civilization with discoveries, inventions, and master-pieces of art and thought. Why should not a human being possess similar genius in the spiritual field? There are no rational grounds to preclude the emergence of individuals who in the depths of their minds conceive the idea of the Absolute Being and by force of meditation gradually attain a sort of discovery or revelation which moves them to teach and guide others.

A process of this kind had begun in Mohammad's mind during his childhood and had prompted him to meet and talk with Christian monks and priests on his Syrian journey instead of spending all his time on commercial business. On his way back, through the lands of Medyan and the 'Ād and Thamud, he had heard the legends of the local people. In Mecca itself he had exchanged visits with followers of the scriptural religions. He had sat for hours in Jabr's shop near the hill of Marwa, and had been in constant touch with Khadija's cousin Waraqa b. Nawfal, who is said to have translated a part of the New Testament into Arabic. All these experiences are likely to have turned the ever-present disquiet in his inner mind into turmoil.

There is a reference in the Qor'ān to Mohammad's long and frequent talks with Jabr. The Qorayshites alleged that Mohammad had learned the words of the Qor'ān from Jabr, who was a foreigner. The answer is given in verse 105 of *sura* 16 (*on-Nahl*): "And We know that they say, 'It is only a human who is teaching him.' The speech of the person at whom they hint is outlandish, whereas this is clear Arabic speech." The biographies of the Prophet mention several other followers of the scriptures and possessors of knowledge with whom he exchanged visits before the start of his mission, e.g. 'Ā'esh, the sage of the Howayteb tribe, Salmān ol-Fārsi, and Belāl the Abyssinian. Abu Bakr also had discussions with him at that time and agreed with him.

From the accounts of Mohammad's appointment given in the biographies and certain Hadiths, and from the evidence of certain Qor'ānic verses, any thoughtful student can penetrate to the facts. All these sources indicate that a process of inner turmoil and absorption in an idea culminated in Mohammad's seeing an apparition, which was revealed in the first five verses of *sura* 96 (*ol-'Alaq*): "Recite in the name of your Lord who created, created mankind from a clot of blood! Recite! And your Lord is bounteous, He who taught by the pen, taught mankind what they did not know."

The Prophet Mohammad at the time of his appointment was forty years old, of medium stature, with a pale complexion tending to redness, black hair, and black eyes. He seldom joked and laughed, and whenever he laughed he held his hand over his mouth. He walked with a heavy and unhurried tread, and never looked to one side or the other. Although it seems probable, on the evidence of certain passages, that he had taken part in some of his community's ritual ceremonies, he had never joined in the amusements of the Qorayshite youths or in any sort of frivolity. He had won a reputation, even among his adversaries, for honesty. Since his release from pecuniary worries through his marriage to Khadija, he had devoted much time to spiritual matters. Like most of the *hanifs*, he regarded Abraham as the perfect model of devotion to God, and he of course loathed his own people's idolatry. In the opinion of Tāhā Hosayn, the majority of the Qoraysh chiefs had really ceased to believe in the idols of the Ka'ba, but were trying to maintain a show of respect because idolatry still prevailed among the Beduin and the cult brought them financial and social advantages.

Mohammad was careful and deliberate in his use of words. He was shy, according to one source "shier than a young virgin." His eloquence was powerful and always free from tautology and prolixity. He had long hair covering almost half of his ears and he usually wore a white headdress. He usually sprinkled perfume on his hair and beard. He was temperamentally disposed to modesty and kindness. When he shook hands with someone, he never withdrew his own hand first. He personally mended his clothes and shoes. He mixed with subordinates and once accepted an invitation from a slave, with whom he sat on the ground and ate dates. When preaching he sometimes raised his voice, particularly when condemning evil deeds, and at such times his eyes reddened and his face flushed.

Another of Mohammad's qualities was courage. During battles he leaned on a bow and heartened the Moslems to fight. At times when fear of the enemy gripped the warriors of Islam, he walked to the fore and came closer to the enemy than anyone else. Despite this, he only once killed with his own hand, and that was when he parried an assault with a fatal blow.

The following are a few of his reported sayings:

"If a person associates with a wrongdoer whom he knows to be a wrongdoer, that person is not a Moslem."

"If a person fills his stomach when there is someone hungry nearby, that person is not a Moslem."

"Good morals are one half of religion."

"The best *jehād* (holy war) is to say a word of truth to a wrongdoer."

"The strongest of you are those who control their anger."

## HIS APPOINTMENT

Mount Herā is a rocky, arid height three miles north-east of Mecca. On its almost inaccessible slopes are some caves to which ascetic *hanifs* used to make their way for spells of retreat and solitary meditation.

Mohammad had been doing this for some time. A strong desire to get away from the din of life and be alone had often drawn him to the place. Sometimes he took a stock of food and did not come home until it was finished; sometimes he went in the early morning and came home in the evening.

One day, in the year 610, when Mohammad was due back in the evening, he did not come, and Khadija grew anxious and sent someone to search for him; but after a while Mohammad appeared in the doorway, trembling and looking pale. Then he said, "Wrap me up!" They did so. Later, when his strength returned and the agitation passed, he told Khadija about the experience which had brought him to this state.

The following account by 'Ā'esha is quoted in the reliable Hadith collections of Bokhāri, Moslem b. ol-Hajjāj, Abu Dā'ud ot-Tayālesi, Ebn 'Abd ol-Barr, Nowayri, and Ebn Sayyed on-Nās, and in the *Mosnad* (Compilation) of the famous theologian Ahmad b. Hanbal (164/780–241/855):

"The start of the revelation was a holy vision as bright as daybreak which came to the Prophet. At sunset on a day which he had spent in the cave on Mount Herā, an angel appeared before him and said to him, 'Recite!' The Prophet answered, 'I cannot recite.'"[21]

According to this account, Mohammad described his experience to Khadija in these words:

"He (the angel) took me and pressed me down so hard that it took away my strength. When I revived, he again said 'Recite!' and I repeated 'I cannot recite.' He again pressed me down until I became powerless, and then released me and said, for the third time, 'Recite!' Again I repeated, 'I cannot.' Once more he pressed me down and released me. Then he said 'Recite in the name of your Lord who created, created mankind from a clot of blood! Recite! And your Lord is bounteous, He who taught by the pen, taught mankind what they did not know.' Then the angel vanished, and I revived again and walked home."

Later Mohammad told Khadija that he had been in fear for his life. How should these words be interpreted? What had caused him to become so afraid? Had he supposed that he was losing his senses, that he had been touched by sorcery or stricken by an incurable sickness? Some such cause can be inferred from Khadija's consoling reply: "The Lord would never deprive you of His care when you are so honest, so good to the poor, so hospitable, so affectionate to your family, and so helpful to the afflicted."

After this conversation and Mohammad's recovery, Khadija went out of the house in haste to tell Waraqa b. Nawfal what had happened. Always a loather of the Meccan idolatry, Waraqa had long been urging Mohammad to shun Qorayshite follies and to practice spiritual meditations. He told Khadija, "Probably this event shows that God cares for him and has appointed him to guide his people."

There is nothing of the supernatural in 'Ā'esha's account. Everything in it is reconcilable with the general findings of psychology.

A strong wish can make its object appear real and concrete. Formed in nearly thirty years of meditation, strengthened by contacts with followers of the scriptural religions, and supercharged by ascetic retreats to Mount Herā, Mohammad's wish acquired the shape of a vision or, in mystic terminology, an illumination. In personified form, a call for action rang out from the depths of his subconscious mind. Fear of taking action weighed so heavily on him as to cause prostration and fainting. No other explanation of the angel's pressing him until he became powerless is conceivable. The angel personified the aspiration long latent in the depths of his inner being.

This analysis, though hypothetical, is supported by another report, according to which Mohammad told Khadija: "While I was sleeping, he (the angel) brought to me a piece of brocade, in which there was a book, and said 'Recite!' I awoke, and a book seemed to have taken shape in my heart." The fatigue of a day of intense meditation sent him into a trance-like sleep in which his latent aspiration came to light, but the task daunted him.

In 'Ā'esha's account, the wording is as follows: "Then God's Apostle returned with his heart throbbing. He went to Khadija and said, 'Wrap me up!' They kept him wrapped up until the trembling ceased." His trembling had evidently been induced by extreme fear or anguish. This condition is known to occur in persons who lead a double life – an ordinary life combined with a shadowy, phantom-filled, and shoreless inner life.

After this event, Mohammad twice again went into retreat in the cave on Mount Herā; but now no vision came, no angel appeared, no voice rang out.

Was the whole experience no more than a dream and a delusion? Were the message of appointment to prophethood and the prediction of Waraqa b. Nawfal vain talk? From then onward corrosive doubt beset Mohammad's mind and so nearly prevailed that he more than once thought of suicide, of throwing himself over a cliff; but Waraqa and Khadija were always able to calm him and give him hope.

The length of the period in which Mohammad received no message and heard no voice from the unseen (in Islamic historical terminology, the interruption of the revelation) is given in different accounts as three days, three months, or three years. It lasted until *sura* 74 (*ol-Moddather*) came down. Then the revelation again ceased.

The cause of the interruption of the revelation is not difficult to find. After the vision or illumination, the burning thirst of his questing soul subsided. The manifestation of his long cherished inner wish quenched the flames. Naturally doubt and despair set in. Further meditation was necessary to rekindle the fire. Only then could the inner Mohammad hidden under his outwardly dormant self wake and stir again.

'Ā'esha's factual account of the Prophet's appointment has been quoted above. Not much more than a century after his death, reports of a very different type were in circulation. By that time fancy had begun to intrude upon fact, and as the years advanced myth-making and miracle-mongering became more and more widespread and extravagant. Ebn Es-hāq's biography of the Prophet, which survives in the recension of Ebn Heshām, has already been mentioned. Ebn Es-hāq died in 150/767 and wrote sometime before that date. A few lines from the work will be quoted to give objective readers food for thought:

"In the days before the appointment, whenever Mohammad walked beyond the houses of Mecca to relieve nature's demands, and as soon as the houses disappeared behind the bends in the path, a voice saying 'Peace upon you, O Apostle of God!' rang out from every rock and tree that he passed. But when the Apostle looked to one side or the other, he did not see anybody. There were only rocks and trees around him."

Rocks are of course inanimate, and trees do not have vocal cords with which to utter feelings and thoughts. The story is so repugnant to reason that many later theologians and writers on the life of the Prophet disbelieved it and maintained that the voices were voices of angels. It never occurred to their brains that the voice might have been the voice of Mohammad's own soul. Years of meditation and absorption in an idea naturally tend to concretize

26

that idea. In a totally committed mind, the idea might well resound like a voice.

In any case, these theologians who, in their anxiety not to impugn Ebn Heshām's veracity, ascribed the voices to angels, failed to discern the obvious corollary of their assertion. If angels had greeted the Prophet, surely they would have greeted him publicly. In that case, all the people would have believed in him, and God's purpose of bringing the Arabs to Islam would have been fulfilled without any trouble.

Admittedly theologians in that phase of history could not be expected to recognise that the voice (if genuine) was the voice of Mohammad's own soul; but they might surely have given some thought to another question. If the Prophet had heard such a voice when he was out of the town and alone, how could anyone else have known about it? He did not talk about it himself; there is no authenticated and reliable Hadith on the subject. Clearly it was a figment of the imaginations of myth-makers and miracle-mongers.

Ebn Es-hāq did not tell lies in the sense of deliberately concocting untruths. He must have heard the story from someone and have accepted it unquestioningly because it accorded with his own faith and feelings. He probably never asked his informant or himself whether any other people had heard the rocks and trees greet the Prophet or whether there was any evidence that the Prophet himself ever claimed to have heard them. The only recorded words of Mohammad about his appointment are in 'Ā'esha's account, which has been quoted above.

Human beings tend to be captive to their acquired beliefs and submissive to their bodily appetites and instincts. When this is the case, their rational faculty is dimmed. Instead of thinking clearly, they ignore facts which may dent their convictions or conflict with their wishes, and grasp at straws which give semblances of reality to their suppositions and hopes. This tendency has been the root cause of the spread of superstitions and illusions.

## AFTER HIS APPOINTMENT

The start of the preaching of Islam cannot be precisely dated, because the revelation was interrupted for an uncertain length of time after the notice of appointment given to Mohammad, when he was forty years old, in the first five verses of *sura* 96. Moreover the preaching was for some time conducted in secret and among a restricted circle. The seven, or ten, *suras* next revealed after *sura* 96 indicate that the preaching encountered derision and rejection and that Mohammad had moods of hesitancy and irresolution.

Unfortunately the Qor'ān was badly edited and its contents are very obtusely arranged. All students of the Qor'ān wonder why the editors did not use the natural and logical method of ordering by date of revelation, as in 'Ali b. Abi Tāleb's lost copy of the text. This would have made the contents more meaningful and given future generations a better understanding of the rise of Islam and the inspirations and thoughts of its founder.

The initiative in the matter of editing the Qor'ān came from 'Omar. He went to see Abu Bakr after the latter had become caliph, and argued that the Qor'ān ought to be collected and arranged because too many disagreements over wordings and readings had arisen. The matter was urgent because animals had devoured copies on palm-fronds belonging to some of the Prophet's companions slain in battle at Yamāma. Abu Bakr demurred on the ground that if editing had been necessary, the Prophet would have taken action during his lifetime; but on 'Omar's insistence, Zayd b. Thābet, the last of the scribes who had written down the revelations, was summoned and instructed to collect the Qor'ān. At a later date, when 'Omar had become caliph, 'Othmān was put in charge of the work. He and his assistants ordered the *suras* according to their lengths and included many Meccan verses in Madinan *suras* and Madinan verses in Meccan *suras*.

Study of thematic continuities, historical contexts, and mentioned events has enabled Moslem and European scholars, particularly Th. Nöldeke, to attempt to rearrange the contents of the Qor'ān roughly in accordance with the meanings of the verses and the dates of revelation of the *suras*.[22]

In any case, the early Meccan *suras* tell a good deal about the struggles of Islam in its first years. In *sura* 93 (*od-Dohā*), after two invocations, come the words "Your Lord has not forsaken you, nor taken a dislike to you. The ending will be happier for you than the beginning. Your Lord will give to you, and you will be gladdened. Did not He find you orphaned and shelter you, find you astray and guide you, find you dependent make you self-supporting?"

What had happened that God should thus console and encourage Mohammad? Did this *sura*, with its third verse "Your Lord has not forsaken you, nor taken a dislike to you," come down at the end of the period of interruption of the revelation? That is how it is interpreted in the *Tafsir ol-Jalālayn*. If the interpretation is correct, *sura* 93 must be chronologically the second *sura* of the Qor'ān, though it is generally assigned to the eleventh place. The wording of *sura* 93 suggests that it was sent down to Mohammad to console and encourage him in the face of rejection by adversaries. Likewise in the first two verses of the immediately following *sura* 94 (*ol-Ensherāh*), which is reputed to be chronologically the twelfth, God asks, "Have not We cheered your heart and relieved you of your burden?" These and the remaining verses have virtually the same import as the preceding *sura*, and must likewise have been sent down to dispel Mohammad's anxiety and strengthen his resolve. From the objective viewpoint of psychology, the two *suras* may be interpreted as expressions of the will and hope in Mohammad's own inner mind.

After preaching Islam in secret and among a small circle for some time, Mohammad received a new command from God in verse 214 of *sura* 26 (*osh-Sho'arā*): "And warn your tribe, your nearest kin!" He summoned the Qoraysh chiefs to a meeting on the hill of Safā, and when all were assembled, besought them to embrace Islam. From their midst Abu Lahab stood up and shouted angrily, "Perish you, Mohammad! Did you invite us here for this?" The answer to Abu Lahab's challenge came in verse 1 of *sura* 111 (*ol-Masad*), in which the same Arabic word meaning "perish" appears: "Perish Abu Lahab's hands, and may he (himself) perish!" Abu Lahab was proud of his wealth and children. God said, "His wealth will not give him security, nor will the gains that he has made. He will roast in a flaming fire" (verses 2 and 3). Nor would his wife, Omm Jomayyel, who had strewn thorns in the Prophet's path, be left unpunished: "And his wife, the carrier of the firewood sticks, will have a rope of palm fiber on her neck."

Study of the events of the thirteen years after the appointment, and above all study of the Meccan *suras*, brings to light the epic of a man who stood alone against his tribe and stopped at nothing in his zeal to convince and overcome them. He even sent some of his followers to Abyssinia in quest of help from that country's ruler, the Negus. He never flinched before mockery and slander. When ol-'Ās b. Wā'el derided the Prophet (after the death of his son

29

Qāsem) for having no heir, verse 3 of *sura* 108 (*ol-Kawthar*) came down: "It is your derider who is sterile."

During the pilgrimage season, whenever Mohammad approached the chiefs of tribes visiting the Ka'ba and invited them to embrace Islam, his influential uncle Abu Lahab used to follow him and say to them before his face, "This nephew of mine is mad. So take no notice of what he says!"

*Sura* 52 (*ot-Tur*), which is one of the most vivid and melodious Meccan *sura*s, gives glimpses of Mohammad's disputation with his compatriots. "So remind (them)! By your Lord's grace, you are not a fortune-teller and are not mad. Or if they say, 'He is a poet, we shall wait and see what the uncertainty of fate has (in store) for him,' answer, 'Wait and see! I shall be one of those waiting with you'" (verses 29–31). "Or if they say, 'He has invented it' . . . let them bring a report like it if they are truthful'" (verses 33–34). Further examples of the disputation and of Mohammad's forcefulness in speech and argument are to be found in *sura* 20 (*Tāhā*).

Verses 5–9 of *sura* 25 (*ol-Forqān*) make clear what sort of accusation was hurled at Mohammad: "The unbelievers have said, 'This is only a lie which he fabricated and in which other people helped him.' They have committed wrong and falsehood. And they have said, 'It is fables of the ancients which he caused to be written down. They were being dictated for him in the morning and the evening.' Answer, 'It has been sent down by Him who knows the secret in heaven and on earth, and is forgiving and merciful.' And they have said, 'What is the matter with this apostle that he eats meals and walks through the bazaars? Why has not an angel been sent down to him to be a warner with him? Why is no treasure being thrown to him, or why does not he have a garden from which to eat?' And the wrongdoers have said, 'You are only following a man who has been touched by sorcery.'"

Many passages in the Meccan *sura*s depict the contention and the charges against Mohammad. He was said to be a madman possessed by genies, a sorcerer, and an ally of Satan. The Qor'ānic verses were said to be a sorcerer's incantations and spells. Sometimes it was said that his utterances must have been prompted by others because he did not know how to read and write. Milder critics said that he was a visionary obsessed with his wild dreams, or a poet expressing his dreams and notions in rhymed prose.

Also to be found among the Meccan *sura*s are verses which diverge from the main theme of disputation. They indicate that moods of despair beset Mohammad and sometimes weakened his resolve. It can be inferred that the idea of conciliating his opponents came to him during such a mood. Perhaps in return for an offer of friendship he might reach some sort of compromise with the polytheists. Verses 75–77 of *sura* 17 (*ol-Esrā*) refer to this idea: "They nearly tempted you away from what We have revealed to you, (hoping) that you might fabricate other (ones) against Us. Then they would indeed have accepted you as a friend. And if We had not strengthened you, you might almost have inclined to them a little. In that case We would have made you taste double (punishment) in life and double (punishment) in death. You would not have found a helper against Us then."

These three verses require careful study. Was there really a time when Mohammad felt worn out by the stubborn opposition of the Qorayshites and therefore thought of compromise or at least hoped for fraternization? Perhaps ... Human nature being what it is, such a reaction to difficulties and poor prospects would not be improbable. Furthermore certain Qor'ān-commentators state that the occasion of the revelation of these verses was an incident – the affair of the cranes – which is reported in many of the biographies and stories of the Prophet.

According to these accounts, the Prophet one day recited *sura* 53 (*on-Najm*) to some Qorayshites at a place near the Ka'ba. This beautiful *sura* is a fine example of his spiritual fervour and persuasive force. While he was speaking about his mission and the truth of his claim, the messenger angel brought an inspiration down to him, and he then mentioned the famous idols of the Arabs, asking "Have you thought about Lāt and 'Ozzā? And Manāt, the third one, the other one?" (*sura* 53, verses 19 and 20). The tone is almost contemptuous, implying that the idols are useless. After these verses came two more verses, which were excised from most of the early copies of the Qor'ān because it was thought that Satan put them into the Prophet's mouth and that the Prophet regretted having uttered them: "Those are the cranes aloft. So their intercession may be hoped for." Then he knelt down. The Qorayshite listeners also knelt down after seeing Mohammad make this gesture of respect to the three goddesses and hearing him acknowledge their ability to intercede or mediate.

Believers in the Prophet's absolute infallibility deny the possibility of any occurrence inconsistent with that principle. They therefore treated the story as a fabrication and went so far as to excise the two sentences from the Qor'ān. Nevertheless the evidence given in well-attested reports and in the interpretations of certain commentators makes it likely that the incident occurred. The two irreproachably pious authors of the *Tafsir ol-Jalālayn* consider it to have been the occasion of the revelation of verse 51 of *sura* 22 (*ol-Hajj*), which they interpret as a sort of divine consolation sent down to relieve the Prophet of the bitter remorse which he felt after his utterance of the two sentences. This verse reassures the Prophet as follows: "We never sent an apostle or prophet before you without Satan's casting something into his hope when he hoped. But God annuls what Satan casts. Then God confirms His signs. And God is (all-)knowing, (all-)wise."

The Qor'ān contains other passages with the same purport, and in several contexts makes it clear that the Prophet was not infallible. Some of the early scholars of Islam considered the Prophet to have been infallible only in the announcement of his prophetic mission. Given that the Prophet was not infallible, the incident can be explained without difficulty. Mohammad, when feeling wearied by the stubbornness of the opposition, saw signs of a wish for tolerance and friendliness on the faces of his listeners and then said a few soothing words to them. They were pleased, and together with Mohammad they knelt down. Soon afterward, however, when the crowd had dispersed and the episode was over, a voice rang out in the depths of Mohammad's soul to warn him against such appeasement and to remind him that for more than thirty years he had believed in One God and deplored his people's degrading polytheism. Then verses 75–77 of *sura* 17 successively came down to him. Their content fully accords with this hypothetical interpretation. The only other conceivable hypothesis would be that the whole incident was staged, in other words that Mohammad wanted to give the pagan Qorayshites to understand that although he had been ready for conciliation and friendship, God had forbidden him. Since Mohammad had a reputation for truthfulness and honesty, such a hypothesis would scarcely be credible.

# CHAPTER II

# *The Religion of Islam*

## THE SETTING

Religion in a meaningful sense has never taken firm root among the Beduin Arabs, who even today show little interest in spiritual and metaphysical matters. Living in an inhospitable land, they were poor and had no stable social institutions apart from a few customs and inhibitions. In temperament they were volatile, being quickly moved, for example, to ecstasy or rage by a verse of poetry; self-centered and vain, being always eager to boast about their idiosyncrasies, including their weak points and even their crimes and cruelties; and so ignorant that they were easy prey to illusion and superstition, being ready to see a demon lurking under every stone or tree. The aridity of their land had debarred them from agriculture, which was the basis of human civilization. According to one of their sayings, a cow's tail symbolized disgrace and a horse's forehead glory. Their only aim in life was to satisfy their immediate physical needs, and their only reason for praying to idols was desire for help in the pursuit of that aim. Aggression was normal and acceptable, provided of course that the other side was not well armed or prepared for self-defense. Often an act of violence was extolled and made the subject of a heroic poem. In cases of abduction of another man's wife, the Beduin poets lacked any sense of chivalry; they had no scruples about disclosing her secrets, describing her embarrassment, and assessing her looks.

In the minds of these people, a god was an artificial and conventional being. They did not believe in a god's objective and independent existence. To compete with a tribe possessing a famous idol, they would invent and venerate another idol for their own benefit. The Ka'ba was an important idol-temple, much visited by Beduin tribesmen and greatly respected as a holy place.

For this reason 'Abd od-Dār b. Hodayb of the Johayna tribe urged his people to build an equally fine temple in the Hawrā district so that the Beduin might be drawn to it instead of the Ka'ba. When his people rejected the proposal as too ambitious and risky, they were derided in a satirical poem preserved in the *Tankis ol-Asnām*[23] of Heshām b. Mohammad ol-Kalbi (ca. 120/737–204/819 or 206/821), a reliable early work which vividly portrays the religious ideas of the pagan Arabs. Some stories from it are quoted below as examples of their mentality:

"When Abraha (the Christian ruler of the Yaman after the Abyssinian conquest in the middle of the 6th century) had built a church called the Qelis of stone and expensive timber at San'ā, he swore not to relax his grip on the Arabs until they abandoned the Ka'ba and visited this church instead. So an Arab chief sent some men one night to defile the Qelis with dirt and excrement."

"The son of a murdered man wanted to avenge his father, but first went to consult an idol called Dhu'l-Khalasa. By means of divining arrows he asked whether he should track down his father's killer or not. The prognostic was negative, which meant that Dhu'l-Khalasa advised against this course. The Arab then turned his back on Dhu'l-Khalasa, saying 'If your father had been murdered like mine, you would never have forbidden me to avenge my father.' In the words of a pre-Islamic poet, 'If you had been wronged like me, O Dhu'l-Khalasa, if your old man was in the grave like mine, you would not forbid killing enemies by stealth.'"[24]

While other primitive peoples venerated the sun and moon and stars, the Beduin Arabs were obsessed with stones and had a custom of circumambulating them. At every halt on a journey across the desert, an Arab traveler's first action was to find four stones; he would put the nicest one on the ground and walk around it, and then use the three others as supports for his cooking pot. Sacrificial slaughter of sheep, goats, and camels had to be done in front of a stone and in such a way that the blood would stain the stone red.

It has already been said that the ancient Arabs were not serious in their idolatry, but merely ignorant and credulous. In this connection another story from the *Tankis ol-Asnām* is worth quoting:

"An Arab took his camels to an idol called Sa'd to get them blessed. The camels shied away from the stone, which was stained red with the blood of sacrificed animals. This annoyed the Arab so much that he threw a pebble at the idol's head, shouting 'May you be deprived of the blessing of the people's praise!' The incident is recalled in these verses:[25]

'We came to Sa'd to collect our fortunes.
But Sa'd dissipated them. So we shall have nothing to do with Sa'd.
Is not Sa'd just a stone on a rise in the ground?
He cannot be asked to lead astray or to guide aright.'"

A similar impression of the Beduin character emerges from study of the events of the first years of the Prophet's career at Madina. The tribes of the neighboring districts were drawn to the Moslems by fear or by hope of booty, but shied away or switched to the other side whenever the Moslems suffered a reverse such as the defeat at Mount Ohod. Mohammad was well aware of their mentality and ways. The subject frequently comes up in Qor'ānic verses and above all in *sura* 9 (*ot-Tawba*), which is chronologically the last *sura* of the Qor'ān and may be regarded as the Prophet's testament: "The Beduin Arabs are the stubbornest in unbelief and hypocrisy, and the most likely to ignore the limits of what God has revealed to His Apostle" (verse 98). For this reason they were wishing that God "might have revealed it to some non-Arab" (*sura* 26, *osh-Sho'arā*, verse 198). At least in the greater part of Arabia, superstition was endemic and prayers were addressed to idols for help in meeting normal and casual needs.

This was not the case in the Hejāz, however, or at least not at Mecca and Yathreb (known after the *hejra* as Madina). The inhabitants of those two towns, particularly Yathreb, had been influenced by the beliefs of Jews and Christians. The word Allāh, meaning The God, was in use among them. They considered themselves to be descendants of Abraham, and were more or less acquainted with the legends of the Children of Israel and stories of the Old Testament. The story of Adam and Satan was generally known to them. They believed in the existence of angels and imagined them to be daughters – a fallacy to which the Qor'ān several times alludes, e.g. *sura* 53 (*on-Najm*), verse 21: "Do you have males (i.e. sons) and does He have females?"

Furthermore these town-dwellers had adopted several Jewish practices such as circumcision, ritual ablution, avoidance of

35

menstruating women, and observance of a rest-day, for which they chose Friday instead of Saturday.

Thus in the Hejāz the preaching of Islam was not wholly novel or alien to the social environment. Not only were there some clear-thinking individuals who shunned idolatry; the idolaters themselves had begun to see glimmers of light. This also is mentioned several times in the Qor'ān, e.g. in *sura* 43 (*oz-Zokhrof*), verse 87: "And if you ask them who created them, they say Allāh;" in *sura* 29 (*ol-'Ankabut*), verse 61: "And if you ask them who created the heavens and the earth and subdued the sun and the moon, they say Allāh."

The Qorayshite polytheists saw their idols as symbols of forces and as means of approach to the deity. This concept is mentioned in *sura* 39 (*oz-Zomar*), verse 4: "And those who choose friends other than Him say, 'We only worship them so that they may bring us nearer to Allāh.'"

Nevertheless Islam did not prosper at Mecca. After thirteen years of the Prophet Mohammad's preaching, and after the revelation of the wonderful Meccan *sura*s, so little success was achieved that the number of the converts in the town is generally reckoned at no more than one hundred. Mohammad's constant struggle during every day and night of those thirteen years failed to break the tenacious resistance of the Qorayshites. Among those whom he won over to Islam were a few men of substance such as Abu Bakr, 'Omar, 'Othmān, Hamza b. 'Abd ol-Mottaleb, 'Abd or-Rahmān b. 'Awf, and Sa'd b. Abi Waqqās. The rest were mostly either from the lower class or not wealthy, and therefore had no prestige and influence in Meccan society.

Waraqa b. Nawfal, who did not formally become a Moslem but always supported Mohammad, advised him to win over Abu Bakr because Abu Bakr was a highly respected man whose acceptance of the faith would help to advance the cause. It was because of Abu Bakr's conversion that 'Othmān b. 'Affān, 'Abd or-Rahmān b. 'Awf, Talha b. 'Obaydollāh, Sa'd b. 'Abi Waqqās, and Zobayr b. ol-'Awwām became Moslems.

In the preaching of Islam an essential factor was the Prophet Mohammad's perseverance, which in itself is evidence of his fidelity to his lofty aim. He was never deflected by inducements, threats, taunts, or persecutions of his uninfluential followers. At the same time Mohammad was resourceful and ready to use all available means. In the fifth year of his mission he sent some of his followers to Abyssinia in the hope that the Christian king of that country would make some move to help a man who had revolted against idolatry. This alarmed the Qoraysh chiefs, who sent a delegation to the Negus in the hope of persuading him to ignore the Moslem emigrants and hand them over as undesirables and rebels.

In the early phase of the preaching of Islam, the Qorayshites probably felt little concern and were content to do no more than scoff at Mohammad and his claim. They called him a madman, a poet, a ranter, a fortune-teller, a man possessed by genies or in league with Satan. As time went on, however, Mohammad's persistence and his success in winning over some respected notables began to make them anxious. The reasons for the gradual exacerbation of Qorayshite hostility to the Prophet are clear. Quite correctly the Qoraysh chiefs reckoned that if the Prophet's cause won success, their own livelihood would be undermined. The Ka'ba was the pilgrimage center of the Beduin tribes, drawing thousands every year. It had made Mecca the meeting place of Arab poets and orators, and had given it an annual fair and a bazaar frequented by people from all over Arabia. The livelihood of the Meccans and the prestige of the Qoraysh chiefs depended on this coming and going. The Beduin came to visit the Ka'ba, which was an idol-temple. If the new religion required destruction of the idols, they would not come any more.

Fifteen years later, when Islam had triumphed, the Moslems of Mecca were similarly anxious about their livelihood. Qor'ānic verses, revealed to the Prophet after his conquest of the town in 8/630, expressly debarred polytheists from the Ka'ba. The anxiety was allayed by the revelation of verse 28 of *sura* 9 (*ot-Tawba*): "If you fear impoverishment, God will enrich you from His bounty," i.e. will compensate you for the loss of business.

When the Qoraysh chiefs observed Mohammad's persistence in his preaching, and above all became better aware of the danger which it posed, they proceeded to more positive steps. They first approached the now elderly Abu Tāleb, whose advice would in their reckoning be likely to influence his nephew. They asked him to make Mohammad stop preaching, and promised in return to appoint Mohammad to a post at the Ka'ba. After Abu Tāleb's failure to dissuade his nephew from preaching, almost all the Qoraysh chiefs decided to boycott the Banu Hāshem. For some time members of the Hāshemite clan suffered great hardship from the ban on business with them, until finally certain individuals, moved by Arab feelings of honor, helped them out of their predicament.

After this affair, and especially after Abu Tāleb's death, no hope of silencing Mohammad remained. The Qoraysh chiefs then resolved on drastic action. Three possible courses lay open: to imprison him, to exile him, or to kill him. From their discussion of these alternatives they concluded that killing Mohammad would be the wisest course provided that the hands of all should be stained with his blood and that no particular clan should be exposed to Hāshemite vengeance. This plan was conceived in the twelfth or thirteenth year of Mohammad's mission. It prompted his decision to leave Mecca and emigrate to Madina.


# MIRACLES

Many Iranians have been reared on a diet of myth and are ready to believe that any *emāmzāda*,[26] of however doubtful ancestry, can at every moment perform a miracle. If they were to read the Qor'ān, they would be surprised to find no report of a miracle in it at all. They would learn from twenty or more Qor'ānic passages that whenever the Prophet Mohammad was asked by doubters to perform a miracle, he either stayed silent or said that he would not do so because he was a human being like any other, with no function except to communicate, to be a "bringer of good news and a warner."

The most explicit of these passages is in *sura* 17 (*ol-Esrā*), verses 92–95: "And they have said, 'We shall not believe you until you make a spring gush from the earth for us, or have a garden of palms and vines and make rivers gush from the midst of it, or cause the sky to drop on us in pieces as you claim (will happen), or bring God and the angels as a guarantee, or have a house adorned with gold, or ascend to heaven; and we shall not believe in your ascension until you bring down a written document for us to read.' Say (to them), 'Glory be to my Lord! Am I anything but a human, a messenger?'"

In the next two verses (96 and 97), surprise at the demands of these doubters is expressed: "And the only thing that stopped the people from believing, when the guidance came to them, was that they said, 'Has God sent a human as a messenger?' Say (to them),

'If there were angels walking safely on the earth, We would send an angel from heaven down to them as a messenger.'"

These two verses are entirely intelligible and logical. From among the people a man who could see and think more clearly had come forth and begun to show them the absurdity and folly of their superstitious beliefs and dissuade them from cruel and harmful customs. The soundness and lucidity of his advice are beyond question. The reason for the growth of opposition to him is also plain. Most of the people were strongly attached to habits of thought and behavior, however stupid, which had been inculcated into them since childhood. The same phenomenon is all too apparent in the supposedly rational and enlightened twentieth century. All the more intelligible is the reluctance of the people in that distant age to follow a man bent on upsetting their ancestral ways. When he claimed to speak on God's behalf, it was only natural that they should demand proof, because he himself had acknowledged various miracles of past prophets, repeating statements of followers of various religions about their prophets. There is a Persian saying to the effect that praise of another's ability implies one's own inability. The Qorayshites thought that if Mohammad's turn had come, he too ought to perform a visible miracle. They were not willing to obey an equal. For this reason they were asking (*sura 25, ol-Forqān*, verses 8 and 9), "'What is the matter with this apostle that he eats meals and walks through the bazaars? Why has not an angel been sent down to him to be a warner with him? Why is no treasure being thrown to him, or why does not he have a garden from which to eat?' And the wrongdoers have said, 'You are only following a man who has been touched by sorcery.'"

The Prophet Mohammad did not reply to these demands and carping criticisms. In the face of all the clamor for a miracle, he remained silent. A little later there is a reference to one of the reproaches when God assures him (in verse 22 of the same *sura 25*), "Every apostle whom We sent before you ate meals and walked through bazaars." The theme recurs in *sura 15 (ol-Hejr)*, verses 6 and 7: "And they said, 'O man to whom the reminder (i.e. scripture) has been sent down, you are possessed by a genie (i.e. mad)! Why do you bring us no angels, if you are speaking the truth?'" Likewise in *sura 21 (ol-Anbiyā)*, verses 3 and 5, "The wrongdoers have whispered to each other, 'Is this man anything but a human being like you? Are you going to succumb to sorcery with your eyes open?'" ... "Or rather they have said, 'Odds and ends of dreams. No, he has fabricated it. He is a poet. Let him bring us a sign, like the men of old who were sent as messengers!'"

A sufficient answer was given to them by verses 7 and 8 of *sura* 21, in which God tells Mohammad, "Before you, We only sent men whom We were inspiring." The word used for men means humans, not angels. Then Mohammad is instructed to advise the people, "Ask the possessors of the reminder, if you do not know!" Again on the subject of previous prophets, he is informed, "We did not give them bodies that do not eat. And they were not immortal."

Altogether more than twenty five passages in the Meccan *suras* refute the argument that Mohammad, if a prophet, ought to perform a miracle and ought not to be a human. Mohammad's response was either silence or assertion of his humanity. Although he received inspiration from God, he was a mortal man like any other. One clear statement of this fact comes in *sura* 10 (*Yunos*), verse 21: "And they say, 'If only a sign from his Lord had been sent down to him.' Say (to them), 'The unseen belongs to God alone. So wait! I am one of those waiting with you.'" Like the rest of the people, he had no knowledge of God's inscrutable purposes. In *sura* 13 (*or-Ra'd*), verse 8, the question about Mohammad's prophethood is answered with the statement that his only function is to transmit God's commands, while the question about the lack of a miraculous sign is not specifically answered: "The unbelievers say, 'Why has not a sign from his Lord been sent down to him?'" (God tells Mohammad), "You are only a warner, and every nation has a guide."[27] The words imply, however, that performing miracles is not one of the Prophet's functions.

Another passage in answer to the same argument of the polytheists repeats that the Prophet is a warner and that God alone performs miracles, but goes on to present the revelation of the Qor'ān as a miracle. In verse 49 of *sura* 29 (*ol-'Ankabut*), Mohammad is instructed to answer the question "Why have no signs (i.e. miracles) from his Lord been sent down to him?" with the words "Signs belong to God alone, and I am only a plain warner;" but in verse 50 God asks, "Is not it enough for them that We have sent the book down to you to be recited to them? In it are a mercy and a reminder to a people who believe." In *sura* 67 (*ol-Molk*), verse 25, the polytheists ask, "When will this promised (resurrection) be, if you are speaking the truth?" and the Prophet is instructed, in verse 26, to reply, "The knowledge belongs to God. I am only a plain warner." In *sura* 79 (*on-Nāze'āt*), verses 42–44, again on the subject of the resurrection day, the denial of prophetic knowledge is even more explicit: "They ask you about the hour, the time when the anchor will be dropped. What competence have you to speak of it? To your Lord belongs the final (hour) of it. You are only the warner to those who are afraid of it."

The persistence of the polytheists in demanding miracles, and their sworn promises that in the event of one they would believe, gradually engendered hopes in the minds of the Moslems and even in the depths of Mohammad's inner soul that God might send a miraculous confirmation of Mohammad's prophethood which would awe every objector into belief. The matter was resolved by the revelation of verses 109–111 of *sura* 6 (*ol-An'ām*): "And they swore solemn oaths to God that if you would bring them a sign, they would believe in it. Say (to them), 'Signs are from God alone.' And how are you to know that, if any came, they would not believe?" God then tells the Prophet, "We shall confuse their hearts and eyes, as (when) they disbelieved in it in the first place, and leave them to wander blindly in their waywardness. Even if We sent angels down to them and let the dead speak to them and assembled everything against them, right in front, they would not believe unless God so willed. But most of them are ignorant."

These three verses require analysis and study.

(1) The polytheists had sworn that if any of the miracles which they were demanding of the Prophet should occur, they would then believe; and God had commanded the Prophet to reply that miracles were not in his power but only in God's. This clear affirmation of the inability of any human being, even a prophet, to take supernatural action means that the laws of nature are immutable and that actions or phenomena contrary to those laws are impossible. Fire, for example, can never lose its capacity to burn.

(2) The Prophet asked himself how he was to know that, in the event of a future miracle, the polytheists would not believe? This question prompts a counter-question: can it be taken for certain that if a miracle had already occurred, the polytheists would have believed? In view of the human tendency to marvel at an abnormal deed and to admire its doer, they would of course have been likely to submit. The Qor'ān-commentators, however, attribute the non-occurrence of a miracle to God's foreknowledge that the polytheists would never believe.

41

(3)   God states that He would confuse (i.e. misguide) the hearts
and eyes of the polytheists because they had disbelieved in signs
which He had previously sent down. This statement prompts the
question whether Almighty God really causes mischief by depriving people of ability to see the truth. If He does, what can be
expected of mankind, and what use is there in sending prophets to
mankind? It is not clear, however, what earlier signs are meant.
They might be acts of earlier prophets or acts of the Prophet
Mohammad. About the earlier prophets, little is known for
certain. About the Prophet Mohammad, the Qor'ān attests that he
always answered the demands for a miracle with the assertion that
he was only a bringer of good news and a warner. Perhaps the
statement that previous signs had been disbelieved refers to the
verses of the Qor'ān; but if so, it was not a sufficient answer,
because the polytheists were refusing to believe in the divine
revelation of those verses to Mohammad unless he brought a proof
similar to the proofs brought by Jesus, Moses, Sāleh, and other
prophets whose miracles are cited in the Qor'ān itself.

(4)   In the last verse of the passage, God states that the polytheists would not believe even if angels were sent to them and dead
men came to life and spoke to them. They had been asking
Mohammad to prove his case by bringing angels from heaven to
earth or by resurrecting a dead man as Jesus had done, and
Mohammad had been hoping for some such occurrence. Then
God told him that even so they would not believe.

(5)   Such being the case, certain questions arise. If these
people's future unbelief and persistence in polytheism had already
been preordained, what useful purpose had been served by God's
appointment of a man to preach to them and guide them aright?
Can a useless action be attributed to God who is wise, omniscient,
and infallible? Formalists, who reject the application of reason to
religious questions, interpret the statement as an ultimatum or test
intended to make humans aware that they are wicked and deserve
punishment in the next life. This interpretation, however, is
inconsistent with the immediately following words "unless God so
willed" in the same verse 111. The inescapable conclusion is these
people were not going to believe because God did not wish them to
believe, and this is confirmed by the clear statement "We shall
confuse their hearts and eyes" in verse 110. Earlier in the same *sura*
6 it is stated, in verse 107, that "If God had so willed, they would
not have been polytheists." God must therefore have willed that

they should be polytheists. Surely Almighty God's humble creatures cannot change His will. Not even Mohammad could dissuade from polytheism those whose polytheism was caused by
God's will. The idolaters in question were not to blame. Why,
then, were they threatened with punishment after death? If the
divine will is the prerequisite of a people's religious belief, equity
and logic indicate that the same divine will is concerned with the
people's guidance and felicity. In that case there would be no need
for appointments of prophets, demands for miracles, and apologies for absence of miracles.

From the train of thought in these and other verses it can be
inferred that the Prophet's initial response to the demands of the
polytheists for a miracle had been tolerant and evasive. This is
certainly the impression given by *sura* 81 (*ot-Takwir*), which with
its melodiously rhythmic rhymed prose is one of the most
expressive and poetic of the Meccan *suras* and a shining example of
prophetic eloquence. The Prophet manifestly avoids a direct reply
to the polytheists and, instead, presents his own claim in vivid and
fervent language, speaking of course on behalf of God. After
eighteen invocations in the first eighteen verses, the polytheists,
who had spoken of Mohammad's utterances as fabrications of a
fortune-teller or illusions of an epileptic, are addressed as follows:
"They are the words of an honored messenger (the angel Gabriel)
who has power, is poised beside the Lord of the Throne, must be
obeyed, moreover is trustworthy. And your comrade is not possessed by a genie. He saw him (Gabriel) on the clear horizon. He
does not withhold (messages from) the unseen. They are not words
of a Satan who ought to be stoned" (verses 19–25).

The great majority of the Meccans wanted a miracle from
Mohammad before they would think of becoming Moslems, and
God referred to this fact when He said that they would not believe
even if He sent down angels or let the dead speak to them. Ten or
twelve years later, when the sword of Mohammad and his followers began to gleam, they professed the faith and "entered God's
religion in troops" (*sura* 110, *on-Nasr*, verse 2). Abu Sofyān, one of
Mohammad's stubbornest opponents and a participant in several
battles against the Moslems, embraced Islam in the year 9/631.
After Mohammad's conquest of Mecca at the head of several
thousand men, 'Abbās b. 'Abd ol-Mottaleb led Abu Sofyān to the
presence of the Prophet, who exclaimed, "Woe on you! Surely
you now understand that there are no gods except the One All-

knowing Provider!" "Yes," answered Abu Sofyān, "I am gradually moving toward that belief." Then the Prophet asked, "Do
you still deny that Mohammad is God's apostle?" Abu Sofyān
muttered, "I need to think more about that point." 'Abbās said to
him, "You had better become a Moslem straightaway, Abu
Sofyān! Otherwise the Prophet will order them to behead you here
and now." So in desperation Abu Sofyān professed Islam in the
midst of the encamped Moslem warriors. On the advice of 'Abbās
b. 'Abd ol-Mottaleb, the Prophet reassured Abu Sofyān by ordering that his house should be a place of asylum as safe as the
Ka'ba. "Whoever enters his house," the Prophet said, "shall be
safe." Later in the same year, when the Moslems defeated the
Hawāzen tribe and captured a vast amount of booty, the Prophet
conciliated Abu Sofyān and other leaders of the Qoraysh with such
princely gifts that the chiefs of the Ansār (the Prophet's Madinan
supporters) made loud complaints. Another instance is the conversion of Wahshi, who after killing Hamza b. 'Abd ol-Mottaleb at
the battle of Ohod in 3/625 had mutilated his body. The Prophet
had been so angered that he had vowed to avenge his beloved and
courageous uncle; but when Wahshi was brought to the Prophet's
presence and made a profession of Islam, the Prophet accepted it.

Manifestly the motive for such conversions was fear. Nevertheless the Prophet let them pass.

The foregoing comments on the three verses in *sura* 6 are not
mere conjectures or hypotheses; they are substantiated by other
Qor'ānic passages which show that Mohammad experienced a
mood of uncertainty when no sign from God came to confirm his
mission. The most explicit passage is in *sura* 10 (*Yunos*), verses 94
and 95: "And if you are in doubt concerning what We have sent
down to you, ask those who have been reciting the book (i.e.
scripture) before you! The truth has come to you from your Lord.
So do not be one of the doubters! Do not be one of those who call
God's signs (i.e. revelations) lies! You would then be one of the
losers." To explain these verses, there is no need to visualize a
scene where they were recited for the purpose of convincing
doubters or waverers by disclosing that the Prophet had felt
similar doubt until God removed it. A much more likely explanation is that the two verses are the voice of Mohammad's own
conscience or inner mind speaking to him at the time when he lost
hope of a miracle.

Other verses as well as these convey similar meanings. From

several passages in the Meccan *suras* it can be seen that Mohammad underwent a sort of inner spiritual crisis. In *sura* 11 (*Hud*),
verse 15, a note of reproach in God's words to him is discernible:
"So perhaps you are neglecting some of the things that are revealed
to you, and (are feeling) heart-sore about it, because they say, 'If
only a treasure had been sent down to him or an angel had come
with him.' You are nothing but a warner." In other words,
whatever the people might say, his sole function was to preach.

In verse 35 of *sura* 6, Mohammad incurs a different rebuke:
"And if their recalcitrance weighs heavily on you, then, if you
could search for a tunnel into the earth or a ladder up to heaven and
come back to them with a sign! Whereas if God had so willed, He
would have gathered them onto the right path. So do not be one of
the ignorant!"

In another context, the same concern reappears in *sura* 4
(*on-Nesā*), verse 152, where the subject is the attitude of the
possessors of scripture. It seems that the Jews also had demanded a
miracle from Mohammad and that the verse was revealed to
placate them. "The possessors of scripture ask you to bring a book
down from heaven for them. They asked Moses for more than
that, for they said, 'Show us God in the open!' So the thunderbolt
caught them because of their wickedness. Then they turned to the
calf, (even) after the proofs had come to them. We pardoned them
for that, and gave Moses a clear authority."

In verse 61 of *sura* 17 (*ol-Esrā*), the absence of miracles is
explained as follows: "Nothing has prevented Us from sending
signs except that the people of old called them lies. We gave the
she-camel to (the people of) Thamud as a visible (sign), and they
wronged her. Whereas (now) We only send signs to frighten."
According to the comment on this verse in the *Tafsir ol-Jalālayn*,
the prophet Sāleh was sent to the ancient Arab tribe of Thamud,
and they did not believe. God then performed on Sāleh's behalf the
miracle of causing a live she-camel to issue from a rock; but the
Thamudites killed the she-camel and persisted in their disbelief,
and God punished them for it by causing a thunderbolt to destroy
them. If God had performed a miracle on Mohammad's behalf and
the people had similarly persisted in their disbelief, they also
would deserve destruction; but God wished to give them a respite
pending the completion of Mohammad's task.

The next verse (*sura* 17, 62) is interesting and thought-provok-
ing: "And when We told you that your Lord surrounds (i.e.

controls) the people and devised the vision (i.e. of the night journey) which We showed to you, (it was) only as a trial for the people, and likewise the accursed tree in the Qor'ān. We frighten them, but it only hardens them in great waywardness." The implication of the opening words is that since God controls the people, Mohammad should not be afraid but should speak out. The vision was manifested to test the people, because they had scoffed at Mohammad, and a number had renounced Islam after he had told them about it. The three Qor'ānic mentions of the accursed *zaqqum* tree (in verses 60, 43, and 52 of *sura*s 37, 44, and 56) were also intended to frighten and test the people, but had in fact made them even more wayward; the Arabs had begun to ask mockingly how a tree could grow in hell fire.

Ultimately the discourse moved away from the manifestation of miracles and passed to the threat of hell, as for example in verse 60 of the same *sura* 17: "There is no town that We shall not destroy before the resurrection day, or severely punish." It is certainly strange that God, who is just and merciful and declares in verse 13 of *sura* 32 "If We had so willed, We would have given every soul its guidance", should nevertheless threaten those whom He chose not to guide with destruction in this life and severe punishment after death. Instead of such severity, would not a miracle have been better? All the people would then have embraced Islam, and much warfare and bloodshed would have been averted.

A different explanation of the lack of a miracle is given in *sura* 6 (*ol-An'ām*), verse 37: "And they have said, 'Why has no sign from His Lord been sent down to him?' Say (to them), 'God is able to send down a sign.' But most of them do not know."

Do the contents of this verse have rational consistency and logical sequence? The deniers were clamoring for a miracle and were told that God is able to cause miracles. But God's ability to do so was not in question; it was because they acknowledged this ability that they were making their demand. God, being omnipotent, ought to have caused a miracle, but no miracle had occurred. According to the verse, most of them did not know. What was it that they did not know? They must have known that God is omnipotent; otherwise they would not have demanded a miracle. The relevance of the reply to the people's demand is obscure. The explanation given in the *Tafsir ol-Jalālayn* is that "most demanders of miracles do not know that they will deserve destruction if a miracle occurs and they still disbelieve."

This prompts two questions. Firstly, why should miracle-demanders disbelieve after the occurrence of a miracle? Secondly, is it desirable that stupid and obstinate persons, who even after the occurrence of a miracle persist in disbelief, should be destroyed? Was the destruction of the forty eight pagan Meccans slain at the battle of Badr a loss to the world, or was it not?

# THE MIRACLE OF THE QOR'ĀN

It was noted in the preceding section that the Prophet Mohammad's attitude to the demand for a visible miracle was negative and that his reply to the polytheists was that he only brought good news and warnings.

Altogether different was his attitude to the Qor'ān. When the polytheists said that it was being invented by him or put into his mouth by other men, they were answered with a challenge (*sura* 11, *Hud*, verse 16): "Or do they say 'He has fabricated it'? Say (to them) 'Then bring ten *sura*s like it, fabricated ones, and appeal to anyone you can, apart from God, if you are honest!'"

Another allegation was that the Qor'ān consisted of old fables. "And when Our signs (i.e. Qor'ānic verses) are recited to them, they say, 'We have already heard (such things). If we wished, we could say (things) like this. These are only fables of the ancients'" (*sura* 8, *ol-Anfāl*, verse 31). According to the biographers, the man who said this was Nadr b. ol-Hāreth, who was later taken prisoner at the battle of Badr and beheaded on the Prophet's order by 'Ali b. Abi Tāleb. The reply came in verse 90 of *sura* 17 (*ol-Esrā*): "Say, 'If humans and genies were to combine to bring the like of this Qor'ān, they would not bring anything like it, however much they might support each other.'"

Mohammad saw the Qor'ān as the warrant of his prophethood. Moslem scholars are unanimous in regarding the Qor'ān as Mohammad's miracle. There has been much debate, however, on the question whether the Qor'ān is miraculous in respect of its eloquence or of its subject-matter, or of both. In general the Moslem scholars consider it to be miraculous in both respects. This opinion clearly stems from zealous faith rather than impartial study.

Non-Moslem scholars have found numerous grounds for questioning the intelligibility and eloquence of the Qor'ān, and

Moslem scholars have concurred in so far as they have found that the Qor'ān needs interpretation. A chapter in Soyuti's *Ketāb ol-Etqān*[28] is devoted to this subject. Not only the misarrangement of the contents in the 'Othmānic recension but also the language of the Qor'ān present difficulties.

Among the Moslem scholars of the early period, before bigotry and hyperbole prevailed, were some such as Ebrāhim on-Nazzām[29] who openly acknowledged that the arrangement and syntax of the Qor'ān are not miraculous and that work of equal or greater value could be produced by other God-fearing persons. He then argued that the Qor'ān is miraculous because it predicted the future, not in the oracular way of the fortune-tellers but with correct prescience of events which actually occurred. These opinions, as quoted by Ebn or-Rāvandi,[30] were taken as the pretext for the condemnation of on-Nazzām by the heresiologist 'Abd ol-Qāher ol-Baghdādi (d. 429/1037) in his *Ketāb ol-farq bayna'l-feraq* (book on differences between sects). According to ol-Baghdādi, the theses of on-Nazzām conflict with the clear statement in verse 90 of *sura* 17 that the Qor'ān is forever inimitable, even by humans and genies acting in combination.

Pupils and later admirers of on-Nazzām, such an Ebn Hazm[31] and ol-Khayyāt,[32] wrote in his defence, and several other leading exponents of the Mo'tazelite school shared his opinion. They saw no conflict between the theses of on-Nazzām and the statements in the Qor'ān. One of their arguments is that the Qor'ān is miraculous because God deprived the Prophet Mohammad's contemporaries of ability to produce the like of it; in other times and places the production of phrases resembling Qor'ānic verses is possible and indeed easy.

It is widely held that the blind Syrian poet Abu'l-'Alā ol-Ma'arri (368/979–450/1058) wrote his *Ketāb ol-fosul wa' l-ghāyāt*, of which a part survives, in imitation of the Qor'ān.

The Qor'ān contains sentences which are incomplete and not fully intelligible without the aid of commentaries; foreign words, unfamiliar Arabic words, and words used with other than the normal meaning; adjectives and verbs inflected without observance of the concords of gender and number; illogically and ungrammatically applied pronouns which sometimes have no referent; and predicates which in rhymed passages are often remote from the subjects. These and other such aberrations in the language have given scope to critics who deny the Qor'ān's eloquence. The problem also occupied the minds of devout Moslems. It forced the commentators to search for explanations and was probably one of the causes of disagreement over readings.

For example, in the first verse of *sura* 74, "O you who are clad in a cloak," the accepted reading of the word for "clad in a cloak" is *moddather*, but there was a widespread opinion that it should be *motadathther*; likewise in the first verse of *sura* 73, "O you who are wrapped in garments," the reading *mozzamel* prevailed over *motazammel*.

In verse 160 of *sura* 4 (*on-Nesā*), "But those among them who are well-grounded in knowledge, the believers . . . . . ., and the performers of the prayer, and the payers of the alms tax," the word for "performers" is in the accusative case, whereas it ought to be in the nominative case like the words for "well-grounded", "believers", and "payers". In verse 9 of *sura* 49 (*ol-Hojorāt*), "If two parties of believers have started to fight each other, make peace between them", the verb meaning "have started to fight" is in the plural, whereas it ought to be in the dual like its subject "two parties".

Verse 172 of *sura* 2 (*ol-Baqara*), which replies to Jewish protests against the change of the direction of prayer from Jerusalem to Mecca, is beautifully and impressively worded but contains a lexical difficulty: "Righteousness (*berr*) is not that you turn your faces to the east and the west, but righteousness (*berr*) is he who believes in God and the Last Day . . . . . . " The explanation given in the *Tafsir ol-Jalālayn* is that the word *berr* in the second part of the sentence means "possessor of righteousness". The great early grammarian Mohammad b. Yazid ol-Mobarrad (d. ca. 285/898) had timidly suggested that the word should be read as *barr*, which is an acceptable variant of *bārr* meaning "righteous (man)", but he had been accused of irreverence and reviled.

In verse 66 of *sura* 20 (*Tāhā*), where Pharaoh's people say of Moses and his brother Aaron "These two are sorcerers", the word for "these two" (*hādhāne*) is in the nominative case, whereas it ought to be in the accusative case (*hādhayne*) because it comes after an introductory particle of emphasis. 'Othmān and 'Ā'esha are reported to have read the word as *hādhayne*. The comment of a Moslem scholar illustrates the fanaticism and intellectual ossification of later times: "Since in the unanimous opinion of the Moslems the pages bound in this volume and called the Qor'ān are God's word, and since there can be no error in God's word, the report that 'Othmān and 'Ā'esha read *hādhayne* instead of *hādhāne* is wicked and false." The *Tafsir ol-Jalālayn* more temperately pretends that the dual suffix may be *āne* in all three cases and does not have to be *ayne* in the accusative and genitive. Yet the great early Qor'ān-scholar and philologist Abu 'Amr b. ol-'Alā (d. ca. 154/770) read *hādhayne*, as 'Othmān and 'Ā'esha had done.

A humane and salutary injunction in verse 33 of *sura* 24 (*on-Nur*) shows that a cruel and immoral abuse was practiced at that time: "Do not coerce your slave-girls into fornication, when they desire chastity, so that you may gain something extra in the life in this world! And when someone coerces them, God, after their coercion, is forgiving and merciful." Obviously the verse prohibits the vile practice of slave-owners who prostituted female slaves and pocketed the proceeds, and no less obviously the words "God, after their coercion, is forgiving and merciful" mean that God pardons slave-girls for having unwillingly committed fornication. The outward form of the words, however, is such that they can be taken to mean that God is forgiving and compassionate to men who prostitute their female slaves. The sentence is vague and does not adequately express the humane intention.

The views on the Qor'ān held by Ebrāhim on-Nazzām have already been mentioned, and it must be added that they were not his alone, but were also held by other scholars of the Mo'tazelite school such as Heshām b. 'Amr ol-Fuwati (d. ca. 218/833) and 'Abbād b. Solaymān (d. ca. 250/864). All were devout believers. They saw no inconsistency between their views and sincere faith.

The great and penetrating Arab thinker Abu'l-'Alā ol-Ma'arri considered some of his own writings to be on a par with the Qor'ān.

To sum up, more than one hundred Qor'ānic aberrations from the normal rules and structure of Arabic have been noted. Needless to say, the commentators strove to find explanations and justifications of these irregularities. Among them was the great commentator and philologist Mahmud oz-Zamakhshari (467/1075–538/1144), of whom a Moorish author wrote: "This grammar-obsessed pedant has committed a shocking error. Our task is not to make the readings conform to Arabic grammar, but to take the whole of the Qor'ān as it is and make Arabic grammar conform to the Qor'ān."

Up to a point this argument is justifiable. A nation's great speakers and writers respect the rules of its language in so far as they avoid modes of expression which are not generally understood and popularly accepted, though they may occasionally find themselves obliged to take liberties. Among the pre-Islamic Arabs, rhetoric and poetry were well developed and grammatical conventions were already established. The Qor'ān, being in the belief of Moslems superior to all previous products of the rhetorical genius, must contain the fewest irregularities.

Yet the Moorish author's censure of Zamakhshari is open to criticism on the ground that it reverses the usual argument. This is that the Qor'ān is God's word because it has a sublime eloquence which no human being can match, and that the man who uttered it was therefore a prophet. The Moorish author maintained that the Qor'ān is faultless because it is God's word and that the problem of the grammatical errors in it must be solved by changing the rules of Arabic grammar. In other words, while most Moslems answer deniers by citing the Qor'ān's eloquence as proof of Mohammad's prophethood, the Moorish author, having taken the Qor'ān's divine origin and Mohammad's prophethood for granted, held all discussion of the Qor'ān's wording and contents to be inadmissible.

At the same time the Qor'ān is indeed unique and wonderful. There was no precedent for it in the earlier literature of the ancient Arabs. In the Meccan *suras* we find fervently spiritual and movingly poetic passages, which attest Mohammad's gifts of thought and speech and give some idea of his power to persuade.

A good example is *sura* 53 (*on-Najm*), if we remove from it verse 33 which is Madinan and must for some unknown reason have been inserted into it by the caliph 'Othmān and his editors. With a graphic eloquence reminiscent of the Song of Solomon, but without mention of joys such as dalliance with maidens of Jerusalem whose breasts are as white as the goats on Mount Gilead, this *sura* jubilantly asserts Mohammad's apostleship and explains the nature of his prophetic illumination and visions. Although the assonance, rhythm, and beauty of the Arabic cannot be reproduced in another language, perhaps the following translation of the first eighteen verses will give some inkling of the ardor of Mohammad's visionary soul:

> "By the star when it sets,
> your comrade is not lost, not astray.
> and he does not speak at will.
> It is nothing but revelation being revealed,
> made known to him by one mighty in power,[33]

possessing great strength. He stood poised,
while on the highest horizon.
Then he approached and hovered.
He was the length of two bows away, or nearer,
and he revealed to his servant that which he revealed.
The heart did not falsify that which he saw.
Will you people dispute with him that which he saw?
And he saw him another time
beside the lote tree at the far end,
near which is the garden of refuge,
when the lote tree was covered with that which covers.
(His) eye did not shift, did not wander.
He saw some of the great signs of his Lord."

Various counsels to the people follow, and in verses 30 and 31 God addresses Mohammad: "So part company with those who have ceased to remember Us and who care only for the present life! That is the range of their knowledge. Your Lord knows well who have strayed from His path and who have found the right way."

There is a report that Omm Jomayyel, the wife of Mohammad's uncle Abu Lahab, went to the Prophet one day and said to him sarcastically, "We hope that your Satan has left you." This was during the interruption of the revelation, when Mohammad was so disappointed and distressed that he thought of throwing himself over a cliff. The incident is thought to have been the occasion of the revelation of the very melodious *sura* 93 (*od-Dohā*):

"By the morning,
and by the night when it is still,
your Lord has not forsaken you, nor taken a dislike to you.
The ending will be happier for you than the beginning.
Your Lord will give to you, and you will be gladdened.
Did He not find you orphaned and shelter you,
find you astray and guide you,
find you dependent and make you self-supporting?
So, as for orphans, do not oppress them,
as for beggars, do not spurn them,
and as for your Lord's bounty, speak about it!"

In all fairness the Qor'ān is a wonder. Its short *sura*s of the Meccan period are charged with expressive force and persuasive power. Its style has no precedent in the Arabic language. Its effusion from the tongue of an illiterate man with no education, let alone literary training, is a phenomenon which, in this respect, can justifiably be described as a miracle.

Some scholars have denied that the Prophet Mohammad was illiterate, arguing that the word *ommi* did not mean "illiterate" but meant "gentile" with reference to the pagan, non-Jewish and non-Christian Arabs. The word is used with this meaning in *sura* 62 (*ol-Jom'a*), verse 2, "It is He who appointed a prophet from among the gentiles," and in several more Qor'ānic passages (2, 73; 3, 19 and 69; 7, 156 and 158). Nevertheless, on the basis of both evidence and tradition, there is general agreement that the Prophet could not write, though perhaps in later life he could read a few words. In addition to explicit reports, there are two Qor'ānic references to the matter: in *sura* 29 (*ol-'Ankabut*), verse 47, "Before it, you did not recite from any book or write it down with your right hand;" and more clearly in *sura* 25 (*ol-Forqān*), verse 6, "And they say, 'Fables of the ancients which he caused to be written down. They were being dictated for him in the morning and the evening.'" The words indicate awareness of the polytheists that Mohammad could not read and write.

For those who consider the Qor'ān to be a miracle because of its contents, the difficulty is rather that it contains nothing new in the sense of ideas not already expressed by others. All the moral precepts of the Qor'ān are self-evident and generally acknowledged. The stories in it are taken in identical or slightly modified forms from the lore of the Jews and Christians, whose rabbis and monks Mohammad had met and consulted on his journeys to Syria, and from memories conserved by descendants of the peoples of 'Ād and Thamūd.

This fact does not, on a balanced assessment, detract from the Prophet Mohammad's greatness. An illiterate, uneducated member of a superstitious, immoral, and vituperative community, with no law except force and cruelty to hold it together, boldly arose to combat evil and idolatry and to propagate higher values through constant citation of the past experiences of other communities. His initiative is in itself proof of his innate genius and of his spiritual strength, moral conscience, and humane feeling. Hearing the words from this illiterate man's tongue in *sura* 80 (*'Abasa*) is like hearing the throb of his anxious heart. This very musical and intensely spiritual *sura* can no more be translated than a poem of Hāfez.[34] What follows is a very imperfect rendering of verses 16–33:

"Let mankind perish! They are so ungrateful.
From What does He create them?
From a seed that He creates and shapes.
Then He smooths their way,
then He makes them die and be buried,
then, when He so wills, He will make them rise again.
No! They have not done what He bade them.
Let mankind look at their food!
We poured down water,
then broke up the ground,
and made grain grow on it,
and vines, and reeds,
and olive trees, and date-palms,
and lush gardens,
and fruit, and herbage,
as provision for you and your livestock.
But when the trumpet-call comes ... "

With such beautiful and wonderfully spiritual sermons, Mohammad strove to guide his people to a better way.

In the field of moral teachings, however, the Qor'ān cannot be considered miraculous. Mohammad reiterated principles which mankind had already conceived in earlier centuries and many places. Confucius, Buddha, Zoroaster, Socrates, Moses, and Jesus had said similar things.

The Qor'ān also contains laws and ordinances which Mohammad, as Islam's legislator, enacted. It must always be borne in mind that most of the Qor'ānic laws and ordinances were formulated in response to random incidents and petitions from aggrieved persons. That is why there are some inconsistencies in them and why there are abrogating and abrogated ordinances. Nor should it be forgotten that Islamic jurisprudence is the product of long effort by Moslem scholars and was formulated during the first three centuries of the Islamic era. The Qor'ānic laws are brief and were insufficient for the needs of the huge Moslem community which came into being in the century and a half after the Prophet's lifetime.

Fasting came to Islam from Judaism through the channel of the pre-Islamic Arab practice of a fast on the tenth day of the month of Moharram, which was known as the day of 'Āshūrā and corresponded to the Jewish Yom Kippur. After the Prophet Mohammad's emigration to Madina and the change of the prayer-direction from

Jerusalem to Mecca, the duration of the fast was lengthened from one to ten days, namely the first ten days of Moharram; and after the final breach between the Moslems and the Jews, the whole month of Ramadān was reserved for fasting.

Prayer is found in all religions, the utterance of appeals and praises to a deity being an essential component of every religious way of life. In Islam, prayer is the first duty of a Moslem and is performed in a peculiarly Islamic manner which became established through force of custom; there are no detailed instructions on the subject in the Qor'ān.

During the thirteen years of the Prophet Mohammad's mission at Mecca and the first year and a half of his mission at Madina, the Moslems prayed in the same direction as the Jews, namely facing toward the "Furthest Mosque" (i.e. temple site) at Jerusalem.

Through the institution of the Islamic pilgrimage to Mecca, several national customs of the Arabs are known to have been endorsed and perpetuated. All the ceremonies of the *hajj* (pilgrimage in the month of Dhu'l-Hejja) and the *'omra* (supererogatory or lesser pilgrimage), such as the wearing of a seamless white robe, the kissing or touching of the black stone, the running between Safā and Marwa, the halt at 'Arafāt, and the pebble-throwing (symbolic stoning of the Satan), had been practiced in the pre-Islamic period and were retained with only a few modifications.

The pagan Arabs, while circumambulating the Ka'ba, used to call out to Lāt, 'Ozzā, Manāt, or any other idol that their tribe revered, "Here I am at your service (*labbayka*), O Manāt!" or whichever. Under Islam, the call to an idol was replaced by the call to God (*Allāhomma*), and the formula became *labbayka Allāhomma labbayka!*

The pagan Arabs had banned hunting in the month of the pilgrimage, but the Prophet maintained this ban only in the days of pilgrimage when the pilgrims are in the state of consecration (*ehrām*). The pagan Arabs had sometimes circumambulated the Ka'ba in the nude; Islam forbade this and required the wearing of seamless robes. The pagan Arabs had an inhibition against eating the meat of sacrificed animals; the Prophet made this permissible.

It is known that after the conquest of Mecca and the toppling of the idols of the Qoraysh, the Moslems refrained from running between Safā and Marwa because in the old days each of those hills had been the site of a stone idol, and the motive of the pagan pilgrims in running between them had been to win good fortune

(*baraka*) by kissing or touching those idols. The Prophet Mohammad, however, received a revelation (*sura* 2, *ol-Baqara*, verse 153),
which not only sanctioned the running between Safā and Marwa
but also declared those hills to be God's waymarks.

Abu'l-Fath Mohammad Shahrestāni (479/1086–548/1153)
writes in his valuable book on religions and sects (*ol-melal wa'n-
nehal*) that many of the duties and rites of Islam are continuations
of practices which the pagan Arabs had adopted from the Jews.
Already in pre-Islamic times, marriage to the mother, daughter, or
father's wife was prohibited and marriage to two sisters was
disapproved. Ablutions after defilements and after contact with a
human corpse, rinsing the mouth, sniffing water up the nostrils,
anointing the hair of the head, using the toothpick, washing after
defecation, plucking out the hair of the armpits and shaving the
pubic hair, circumcision, and amputation of the right hands of
thieves were all practiced by the Arabs before Islam and had
mostly come to them from the Jews.

Among the duties of Moslems are two which are peculiar to
Islamic law, namely service in holy war (*jehād*) and payment of
alms-tax (*zakāt*). The reason why no comparable obligations are
imposed in any other legal system is that other legislators did not
have the same purpose as Mohammad. His purpose was to
organize a state. No state can be organized and maintained without
an army and without financial means.

The peculiar and unprecedented Islamic law of holy war must
be regarded as a product of Mohammad's far-seeing and realistic
mind. When the spiritual message of the beautiful Meccan *suras*
proved ineffective, the only remedy that he could find was the
sword.

Maintenance of a combat-ready army, in which every man fit to
fight must serve, is expensive. Booty and property seizure can be
useful and may spur soldiers to fight, but a more secure and
permanent source of income is necessary. This is provided in
Islamic law by the alms-tax.

Mohammad's constructive thinking always had the new community's circumstances and needs in view. All his steps were
meant to promote its good. Among them was the prohibition of
intoxicants, another peculiarly Islamic law which was enacted
primarily in consideration of local social conditions. The Arabs
being a hot-blooded, excitable, and undisciplined people, mischief
and disorder often occurred when they indulged in alcoholic

drinks, which were in demand and available. The prohibition was enacted in three stages:

First, by verse 216 of *sura* 2 (*ol-Baqara*): "They are asking you about strong drink and casting lots with arrows. Say, 'In them are great sin and also benefits for the people. The sin in them is greater than the benefit.'"

Next, by verse 46 of *sura* 4 (*on-Nesā*), which was revealed on the occasion of a man's coming to the prayer at Madina in a drunken state: "O believers, do not come near the prayer while you are drunk!"

Finally, by verses 92 and 93 of *sura* 5 (*ol-Mā'eda*), in which the prohibition is made absolute: "O believers, strong drink, casting lots with arrows, images, and divining arrows are foul things, among the works of the Satan. So keep away from them! Then, perhaps, you will become more prosperous" (verse 92).

Both in verse 216 of *sura* 2 and in verse 92 of *sura* 5, drinking of intoxicants is linked with gambling; and in the last passage erection of images and divination by means of arrows, which was thought to procure the help of the idols, are also banned. In the following verse 93, strong drink and gambling are the subject, and the reason for their prohibition, which was probably revealed after a nasty incident, is explained as follows: "The Satan only wants to sow enmity and hatred among you through strong drink and casting lots with arrows, and to distract you from remembrance of God and from prayer. So will you be abstainers?" This verse lends substance to the view that liquor-drinking and gambling often caused strife and disorder among the Arabs.

In regard to polygamy, divorce, adultery, fornication, sodomy, and many other matters, the Qor'ānic commandments are either modifications of Jewish laws or reforms of previous Arab practices.

These observations do not alter the fact that the Qor'ān is a miracle – not a miracle befogged by centuries of myth and only credible to feeble minds, but one that is living and meaningful.

Neither the Qor'ān's eloquence nor its moral and legal precepts are miraculous. The Qor'ān is miraculous because it enabled Mohammad, single-handedly and despite poverty and illiteracy, to overcome his people's resistance and found a lasting religion; because it moved wild men to obedience and imposed its bringer's will on them.

Mohammad expressed pride in the Qor'ān, taking it to be the

warrant of his prophethood because it was revelation from God and he was the medium of its transmission.

The Arabic word *wahy*, which is usually translated into English as revelation or inspiration, occurs more than sixty times in the Qor'ān, in most contexts with the basic meaning of putting something into a person's mind, and in some contexts with the connotation of a fleeting hint. For this reason the Prophet was anxious, after each revelation, that a scribe should write it down forthwith. There are references to his haste in the Qor'ān, for example in verse 113 of *sura* 20 (*Tāhā*), "Do not hurry with the Qor'ān before its revelation to you is completed!", and in verses 16–19 of *sura* 75 (*ol-Qiyāma*), "Do not quicken your tongue with it to hurry with it! For Us is the collection of it and the recitation of it. When We have recited it, follow the recitation of it! Moreover for Us is the wording of it."

These mentions of the Prophet Mohammad's haste allude to the mental state which the receipt of revelation induced in him. The light which shone in his soul on these occasions was not a normal experience. According to a statement by Abu Sa'id ol-Khodri (a Madinan supporter of Mohammad and a source of many reports) quoted in the *Sahih* (Hadith compilation) of Moslem b. ol-Hajjāj (d. 261/875), the Prophet used to request: "Do not write down anything that I say except the Qor'ān! If anyone has written down words of mine other than the text of the Qor'ān, let him erase them!"

The important and remarkable point is that the Prophet Mohammad fell into an abnormal state when an inspiration came to him. An intense inner exertion seems to have been required. In the *Sahih* of Bokhāri, a statement by the Prophet's wife 'Ā'esha is quoted: "The Prophet was asked by Hāreth b. Heshām, 'What are the inspirations like?' He answered, 'The strongest of them are like the sound of a bell which rings in my mind after being silent. Sometimes an angel appears in human form and disappears as soon as I grasp the subject.'" 'Ā'esha added, "During inspirations sweat poured from his brow, even on cold days." In confirmation of 'Ā'esha's statement, Bokhāri quotes Safwān b. Ba'li (whose father accepted Islam after the Moslem conquest of Mecca) as saying: "Ba'li wished to observe the Prophet during an inspiration. One day a man wearing a perfumed cloak inquired of the Prophet whether he would be in the state of consecration necessary for performance of the '*omra* (lesser pilgrimage) if he wore that cloak. A state of inspiration came over the Prophet. 'Omar signalled to Ba'li to come in. Ba'li went in and saw the Prophet looking like someone asleep, snoring, and with his blessed complexion flushed. After a while the Prophet came out of that state and summoned the inquirer. He told him to rinse the perfume out of his cloak three times and then consecrate himself for the 'omra in the same way as for the hajj."

# MOHAMMAD'S HUMANITY

The prophets were ordinary commoners. Otherwise, in Your bounty,
You would have poured the elixir onto the copper of their being.

Mawlavi Jalāl od-Din Rumi[35]

All the early scholars of Islam acknowledged that the Prophet Mohammad was an ordinary human being except in respect of his spiritual distinction. This fact is attested by verse 110 of sura 18 (ol-Kahf): "I am only a human like you. It is being revealed to me that your God is One God."

None of the Sonnite scholars considered perfect knowledge and sinlessness to be essential attributes of the Prophet Mohammad. They saw his prophethood as a special gift from God in the sense that God selects for the prophetic task a man who is gifted with human qualities such as knowledge and virtue in an extraordinarily high degree, or rather who becomes gifted with such extraordinary qualities at the time of his appointment to guide the people.

The Sonnite scholars thought that we place our faith in a person because we believe him to be the bearer of revelation. They did not argue that we know a person to be a prophet because God has set him on a higher plane of knowledge and morals. Their opinion is based on several Qor'ānic verses, e.g. sura 42 (osh-Showrā), verse 52: "And in this way We have revealed a spirit to you through Our command. You did not know what the book (i.e. the Qor'ān) and the faith are. But We have made it a light by which We guide those among Our servants whom We so will." The same point is implied in the preceding verse, and very clearly and vividly conveyed in verse 50 of sura 6 (ol-An'ām), which is a reply to those who had asked the Prophet for a miracle: "Say (to them), 'I do not tell you that I possess God's treasures. I do not know the unseen. I do not tell you that I am an angel. I only follow what is revealed to me.'"

In *sura* 7 (*ol-A'rāf*), verse 188, Mohammad is instructed, "Say (to them), 'I get no profit for myself, nor loss, except what God wills. If I knew the unseen, I would have gained much advantage and would not have been touched by adversity. I am only a warner and bringer of good news to folk who believe." This verse also is a reply to the polytheists, who had been asking why Mohammad did not engage in trade and make big profits if his claimed communications with the unseen world were true.

The Qor'ānic verses on this subject are explicit and clear, and the Hadith and the contents of the reliable biographies confirm that the Prophet Mohammad never laid claim to either sinlessness or knowledge of unseen things. He was well aware of his human frailties, and he openly and frankly admitted them. According to a well attested Hadith, he had this to say about an attempt by some polytheists to fluster him with irrelevant questions: "What do these folk expect from me? I am one of God's servants. I only know what God has taught me."

Mohammad's truthfulness and honesty are made admirably clear in verses 1–11 of *sura* 80 (*'Abasa*), which are manifestly a divine rebuke to him:

> "He frowned and turned away
> when the blind man came to him.
> How can you know? Perhaps he will become pure (in heart),
> or will remember, and the remembrance will benefit him.
> But the man who claims to have no need (of God's help),
> to him you pay attention.
> It will not be your fault if he does not become pure.
> But the man who comes to you, running (with great effort)
> and fearing (God),
> You disregard him.
> Never again! This is a reminder."

The Prophet had formed a very human ambition to convert some rich and powerful men to Islam. Perhaps it was a justifiable aim, because the polytheists had boastfully asked, "Which of the two parties has the higher standing, carries the more weight in a discussion?" (*sura* 19, *Maryam*, verse 74). In any case, Mohammad's wish to win over some notables was only natural. One day when he was in conversation with a member of this class and doubtless engrossed in the effort to persuade, a blind man named 'Abdollāh b. Omm Maktum, who had embraced Islam, approached him and said, "Teach me some of what God has taught you!" The Prophet paid no heed to the blind man's request and went home. Then this noble *sura* was sent down to the Prophet, manifestly as a rebuke to him. Afterwards, whenever he met 'Abdollāh b. Omm Maktum, he gave a warm welcome to the man for whose sake God had reprimanded him.

In *sura* 40 (*ol-Ghāfer*, also called *ol-Mo'men*), verse 57, the Prophet is bidden, "Be patient! God's promise is true. Pray for forgiveness of your sin, and praise your Lord in the evening and the early morning!" This verse attributes sinfulness to Mohammad by commanding him to pray for forgiveness of his sin. The belief in the Prophet's absolute infallibility held by Moslems of later times is therefore in direct conflict with the text of the Qor'ān.

The theme recurs in a variant form in the first three verses of *sura* 94 (*ol-Ensherāh*): "Have not We cheered your heart and relieved you of your burden, which weighed (so heavily) on your back?" The word *wezr* (burden) is replaced by *dhanb* (sin) in the first two verses of *sura* 48 (*ol-Fat-h*): "We have given you a clear victory so that God may forgive your earlier and later sin, and bestow the fullness of His bounty on you, and guide you onto a right path."

Taken together, these explicit and incontrovertible Qor'ānic passages prove that the Prophet Mohammad, far from claiming the infallibility and superhuman rank later attributed to him by others, knew himself to be prone to sin. For anyone willing to study and to think, this greatly enhances Mohammad's spiritual stature.

In matters such as religious and political beliefs and social customs, which lack the certainty of mathematics and the relative demonstrability of the natural sciences, human beings are always disinclined to use their rational faculty. Instead, they first acquire a belief and then rack their brains for arguments with which to support it. The *'olamā* of Islam were no exception to this rule. In their zealous devotion, they began with belief in the Prophet's infallibility and then, in the hope of proving it, tried to explain away clear Qor'ānic statements.

The eager sophistry of the Qor'ān-commentators in this matter brings to mind a story about Sahl Tustari (a renowned early Sufi preacher from Shushtar in Khuzestān, d. 273/886). One of his disciples came and told him, "The people say that you can walk on water." Sahl answered, "Go and ask the muezzin! He is an honest man." The disciple went and asked the muezzin, who answered, "I do not know whether or not Sahl can walk on water. But I do know that when he walked up to the pool one day to perform the ritual ablutions, he fell in and would have drowned if I had not pulled him out."

One aspect of this matter, which no unbiassed seeker of the truth can deny, is the abundance of the documentary evidence. Goldziher[36] considered that the Hadith compilations and the early biographies of Mohammad depict the founder of Islam with a precision and clarity not to be found in the historical documentation of the other world religions, and that without exception they show him to have possessed human frailties.

In these sources, no attempt to dehumanize Mohammad is made; on the contrary, he is placed on a par with the believers and those around him. For instance, it is related that in the war of the trench at Madina in 5/627 he dug in the same way as everyone else on the Moslem side did. On the subject of life's pleasures, he is quoted as saying, "I am fond of three things in your world: scent, women, and above all prayer." Some of the Prophet's reported doings were scarcely consistent with asceticism and world-renunciation.

Notwithstanding the testimonies of the Qor'ān, the Hadith, and the biographies, Mohammad was quickly dehumanized. The process began as soon as he passed from the scene. On the day after his death, 'Omar (or perhaps another leading companion) threatened with drawn sword in hand to cut the throat of anyone who said that Mohammad was dead, and Abu Bakr protested, quoting the Qor'ānic words "You are mortal and they are mortal" (sura 39, oz-Zomar, verse 31). How right Abu Bakr was!

The greater the distance in time and space from the Prophet's death in 11/632 and from Madina, the more the Moslems let their imaginations run loose. They exaggerated and rhapsodized so much that they forgot two premises which are stated in the five daily prayers as well as in many Qor'ānic verses, namely that Mohammad was God's servant and God's messenger. Instead, they turned him into the ultimate cause of the creation, saying "But for you, the universe would not have been created." One zealous writer, Shaykh Najm od-Din Dāya (d. 654/1256), went so far as to assert in his book *Mersād ol-'Ebād* that the omnipotent Creator, who could make all things exist by uttering the single word "be", first had to bring the light of Mohammad into existence and then, after casting a glance at the light and thereby causing the light to sweat with embarrassment, was able to create the souls of the prophets and angels from the sweat beads.

Mohammad 'Abdollāh os-Sammān, a modern Egyptian biographer of the Prophet, has written: "Mohammad, like the other prophets, was human. His birth, life, and death were like those of other human beings. His prophethood did not place him apart from mankind. Like everyone else, he could be angered, pleased, saddened, and gladdened. He was once so annoyed with Aswad b. 'Abd ol-Mottaleb b. Asad that he cursed him, saying 'May God blind him and make his son an orphan!'"

Mohammad 'Ezzat Darwaza, a modern Palestinian author, has written a book on the Prophet's life in which he takes care not to express opinions of his own unless they are supported by Qor'ānic evidence. His sincere devotion to the Prophet and to Islam shines in every page of this impressive two-volume work. He regretfully concludes that the Moslem exaggerators (*gholāt*), among whom he mentions Qastallāni (851/1448–923/1517),[37] went completely astray and indulged in fantasies for which he (Darwaza) could find no basis in the Qor'ān or the authentic Hadiths and early reports. These zealots believed, without any justification, that God created mankind so that Mohammad might be born into the human race, and that Mohammad was therefore the cause of mankind's creation; they even maintained that the tablet, pen, throne, and stool, and the skies, earth, genies, humans, paradise, and hell, in short all things, were brought into existence through the light of Mohammad. They forgot the clear words of verse 124 of *sura* 6 (*ol-An'ām*): "God knows best where to place His message." They ignored Islam's fundamental principle that God alone determines the world of being.

The same enlightened Palestinian Moslem writer also notes that in several Qor'ānic passages all the prophets are stated to have been ordinary mortals whom God appointed to guide mankind. In the words of verses 7 and 8 of *sura* 21 (*ol-Anbiyā*), "Before you We only sent men whom We were inspiring. Ask the possessors of the remembrance (i.e. Jews and Christians), if you do not know! We did not give them bodies that do not eat. And they were not immortal." The same point that prophets do not differ from the rest of mankind except in their selection by God to convey His messages is reiterated in the following passages which Mohammad 'Ezzat Darwaza quotes. "Say, 'Praise be to my Lord! Am I other than a human, a messenger?' And the only thing that prevented the people from believing when the guidance came to them was that they said, 'Has God sent a human as a messenger?'" (sura 17, ol-Esrā, verses 95 and 96). "And they have said, 'What is the matter with this apostle that he eats meals and walks through the bazaars?'" (sura 25, ol-Forqān, verse 8). "We shall narrate the best of stories to you in Our revelation of this Qor'ān to you, even though you were formerly one of the heedless" (sura 12, Yusof, verse 3). "We did not grant immortality to any human before you. So if you will die, are they immortal?" (sura 21, ol-Anbiyā, verse 35). "And Mohammad is only a messenger. Messengers have come and gone before him" (sura 3, Āl 'Emrān, verse 138). "You did not know what the Book and the faith are" (sura 42, osh-Showrā, verse 52). "Say (to them), 'I am not something new among the prophets. Nor do I know what will be done to me and to you. I only follow what is revealed to me, and I am only a clear warner" (sura 46, al-Ahqāf, verse 8).

Indications of Mohammad's humanity and of his human feelings and failings can be found in all the well attested reports. For several days after the raid on the well of Ma'una, when seventy Moslems were killed, he began the morning prayer with the words "O God, trample on the Modar!" (i.e. the North Arabian tribes). After the defeat in the battle of Mount Ohod, in which his uncle Hamza b. 'Abd ol-Mottaleb was killed, an Abyssinian named Wahshi cut off Hamza's nose and ears, and Abu Sofyān's wife Hend ripped open Hamza's stomach and chewed his liver. The sight of Hamza's mutilated body angered the Prophet so much that he shouted vindictively, "By God, I am going to mutilate fifty Qorayshites." This event and similar incidents illustrate the cruelty and malice of the ancient Arab mind.

The social environment was one in which even an aristocratic woman would rip a dead man's stomach, take and chew the liver, and throw it away when it did not taste nice. During the battle, Hend and several other women of the Qorayshite aristocracy went into the midst of the Meccan fighters to encourage them with feminine charms and promises.

There is a report in Ebn Heshām's biography of the Prophet[38] that some men of the Bajila tribe who had fallen ill came to Madina

64

and asked him to help them. He replied that drinking camel's milk would cure them, and sent them out of the town to his herdsman. After drinking some camel's milk, they recovered. Then they killed the Prophet's herdsman, stuck thorns into his eyes, and made off with the camels. The Prophet was greatly angered by the news and immediately sent Korz b. Jāber in pursuit of them. After they had been caught, they were brought before the Prophet. He ordered that their hands and feet should be cut off and their eyes taken out, and this was done.

One of the Prophet's sayings quoted in Bokhāri's *Sahih* is "I am a human, very prone to anger and sorrow, just as all people become angry." Numerous reports confirm this.

Abu Rohm ol-Ghefāri, a companion of the Prophet, related that once when he was riding beside the Prophet on a raid, his mount accidentally brought him so close to the Prophet that his thick club knocked the Prophet's shin and caused him pain. The Prophet glowered and struck Abu Rohm's foot with his whip. Abu Rohm, according to Bokhāri's account, was very upset because he feared that a revelation about him and his misbehavior might come down.

The Prophet, in the last months of his life, appointed Osāma b. Zayd commander of the force which was to invade Syria. Not unnaturally the choice of a twenty-year-old youth to lead an army in which senior companions such as Abu Bakr were to serve evoked murmurs of discontent and disapproval, even among the Prophet's closest associates. On learning of these murmurs, the Prophet was so annoyed that he dragged himself from his sickbed to the mosque, and after conducting the prayer, he went up onto the pulpit and asked angrily, "What are these complaints about my appointment of 'Osāma?"

During the Prophet's terminal illness, Maymuna, one of his wives, prepared a medicine of which she had gained knowledge in Abyssinia, and it was poured into his mouth while he was unconscious. He suddenly awoke and shouted angrily, "Who did that?" They answered, "Maymuna prepared the medicine and got your uncle 'Abbās to pour it into your mouth." The Prophet then ordered that the medicine be poured into the mouths of all those present except 'Abbās. So even Maymuna, who was fasting, drank some of the medicine.

The Prophet Mohammad's psychological reactions and human emotions come to light in many reported incidents of the twenty three years, and especially the ten Madinan years, of his mission:

for example, in the affair of the lie concerning 'Ā'esha, in his self-imposed avoidance of Māriya the Copt, and in his haste to marry Zaynab and bring her to his house as soon as the waiting period after her divorce expired.

Yet despite the existence of all these testimonies and the absence of any Qor'ānic attributions of supernatural power to Mohammad, as soon as he was dead, pious Moslem miracle-mongers began to say that he had performed all sorts of impossible marvels. The greater the distance in time and space, the more the mass of fiction grew, even though many of Islam's best scholars knew it to be incredible and considered it to be unworthy. A few examples will suffice.

Qādi 'Iyād (476/1088–544/1149), an Andalusian judge (*qādi*), theologian, poet, and genealogist, wrote a book in praise of the Prophet entitled *Ketāb osh-shefā be-ta'rif hoquq Mostafā*. Contrary to what might be expected, the book is not about Mohammad's spiritual and moral strength and political skill. Its contents make the reader wonder how a learned and presumably not unintelligent man could ever have thought of writing such stuff about the Prophet. For example, on the purported authority of the Prophet's servant and prominent traditionalist Anas b. Mālek[39,] Qādi 'Iyād credits the Prophet with a miraculous sexual potency which enabled him to have daily intercourse with all his eleven wives and reputedly equalled the potency of thirty ordinary men. Again claiming the authority of Mālek b. Anas, Qādi 'Iyād makes the Prophet say, "I have four superiorities over other men: generosity, courage, frequency of copulation, and frequency of *batsh*" (an Arabic word meaning to strike down an enemy). The last point conflicts with the evidence of the sources that Mohammad only once killed a man in battle. Even if the statement stemmed from Mālek b. Anas, anyone with any sense would disbelieve it. The truth is that the Prophet never boasted about himself. In the Qor'ān there are no mentions of his generosity and courage, but only the words "You have moral strength" in *sura* 68, *ol-Qalam*, verse 4. If Qādi 'Iyād had boasted about his own munificence and valor, there might conceivably have been some justification; but he had no right to put into another man's mouth dishonorable boasts about sexual prowess and about killing people, especially when that man was the Prophet who had never said any such things. While ignoring the facts, Qādi 'Iyād obviously voiced his own secret lusts and ambitions. In his feverish zeal to dehumanize Mohammad, he goes so far as to make the Prophet's urine and feces speak and to state that, in the opinion of certain 'olamā, they were non-pollutant. To this he adds an idiotic story that Mohammad's maid-servant Omm Ayman drank his urine one day as a cure for dropsy, and that the Prophet then told her that in the rest of her life she would never again suffer from stomach ache. Most absurd of all is Qādi 'Iyād's assertion that when the Prophet went out of Mecca to relieve his bowels, the stones and trees walked up and formed a hedge around him so that he would not be seen. Any reader of this nonsense is bound to ask why Qādi 'Iyād's zeal to make Mohammad inhuman went no further. Would it not have been more sensible to say that the Prophet had no need to eat and excrete like other men? In that case there would have been nothing for walking stones and trees to conceal.

Such ravings are not peculiar to Qādi 'Iyād. Dozens of writers about the Prophet, such as the earlier mentioned Qastallāni, have repeated hundreds of similar silly stories which can only expose Mohammad's unique personality to disparagement and ridicule. The Prophet has even been made to say, "God put me into Adam's loins when He created Adam, then into Noah's loins, and then into Abraham's loins. I remained in pure loins and wombs until I was born of my mother." This suggests that other humans suddenly came into existence from under bushes. Obviously every human has had the potentiality of existence before acquiring its reality through being conceived and born.

Again according to Qādi 'Iyād, whenever the Prophet passed a place, the stones and trees would walk up and say, "Peace be upon you, O Apostle of God!' Perhaps animals, being mobile and endowed with throat, larynx, and tongue, could have come and uttered a greeting; but how could inanimate objects, lacking brain, vision, and will, have recognised a prophet, let alone greeted him? Some will say that it was a miracle; but what answer have they to the question why no miracle occurred when the Qorayshite poly-theists refused to believe without one? The sort of miracle that those Qorayshites demanded of Mohammad was relatively minor, only to make water flow from a rock or to turn a stone into gold. If stones uttered greetings to the Prophet, why did a stone strike him on the mouth and injure him at the battle of Mount Ohod? No doubt the miracle-mongers would answer that this particular stone was an infidel.

In numerous books, by both Sonnite and Shi'ite authors, it is stated that the Prophet Mohammad had no shadow and could see behind himself as well as in front. Sha'rāni[40] (d. 972/1565) goes further and writes in his book *Kashf ol-ghomma*: "The Prophet could see in all four directions and perceive things at night just as well as in daytime. When he walked with a tall man, he looked taller, and when he was seated, his shoulders were higher than those of the other men."

The writers of such stuff were too simple-minded to be able to measure the greatness of a man like Mohammad by any but outward, physical standards, and too obtuse to know that only spiritual, intellectual, and moral strength can give a person superiority over others. Even so, it is remarkable that none of the miracle-mongers asked why no miracle to help the Prophet's cause ever occurred. Nor did they ask why the Prophet could not read and write. Instead of making the Prophet shadowless and taller by a head and shoulders than other men, would not they have done better to make him write down the Qor'ān with his own blessed hand instead of hiring a Jewish scribe? Most remarkable of all is the fact that these miracle-mongers were Moslems who read the Qor'ān and knew Arabic well enough to understand its meanings, but still remained captive to illusions directly conflicting with explicit Qor'ānic texts and eager to present those illusions as established facts.

The Qor'ānic verses which state that Mohammad was a human being with all the normal human instincts and emotions are perfectly clear and cannot be explained away. In verse 131 of the Meccan *sura* 20 (*Tāhā*), the Prophet is told: "Do not stretch your eyes (i.e. look enviously) at what We have given certain couples among them to enjoy – the flower of life in the lower world – so that We may test them thereby! Your Lord's provision is better and more enduring." Likewise in verse 88 of *sura* 15 (*ol-Hejr*), which is also Meccan: "Do not stretch your eyes at what We have given certain couples among them to enjoy! Do not grieve over them! And lower your wing (i.e. be meek) to the believers!" From the wording of these two verses it is obvious that some sort of envy had crept into Mohammad's soul. Perhaps he had been wishing that he might enjoy the advantages of possessing wealth and sons, as the chiefs of the Qoraysh did.

The great majority of the Prophet's opponents were wealthy men, naturally averse to change and anxious to silence any voice capable of upsetting their established position. It was equally natural that discontented groups should gather around Mohammad. In these circumstances the Prophet had felt depressed and had wished that he could win over some influential rich men. He had fixed his hopes for Islam on them. But God forbade him to pursue that course. This is made clear in verses 33 and 34 of *sura* 34 (*Sabā*): "We have never sent a warner to a town without its wealthy men saying, 'We disbelieve in the message that you have been sent with.' They have said, 'We possess more property and more children. We are not in distress.'"

In *sura* 6 (*ol-An'ām*), verse 52, the Prophet is addressed in words which cannot fail to impress the percipient reader: "Do not drive away those who appeal to their Lord in the morning and the evening, longing for His face! You are not liable for anything in their account, and they are not liable for anything in your account. If you drive them away, you will be one of the oppressors." The reproachful tone of the verse is very significant as evidence of the Prophet's human nature and human behavior. The polytheists had been saying that they would not join Mohammad because his followers were men of no substance, and he had probably felt a temptation to appease the rich and even to despise his own poor flock. This supposition is supported by verses 27 and 28 of *sura* 18 (*ol-Kahf*): "Make yourself be more patient with those who appeal to their Lord in the morning and the evening, longing for His face! Do not avert your eyes from them, longing for adornment in worldly life! And do not obey anyone whose heart We have made neglectful of remembering Us, who pursues his own pleasures, whose way is extravagance! Say, 'The truth is from your Lord. Let those who so wish believe and those who so wish disbelieve!' We have prepared a fire for the oppressors." According to the *Tafsir ol-Jalālayn*, the occasion of the revelation of this verse was the refusal of 'Oyayna b. Hesn (a tribal chief) and his men to accept Islam unless Mohammad would get rid of his impecunious followers.

The same meaning of the Prophet's fallibility and therewith entirely normal humanity is very clearly conveyed in verses 75, 76, and 77 of *sura* 17 (*ol-Esrā*). Although the accounts of the occasion of their revelation differ, all confirm the meaning of the text: "They nearly tempted you away from what We have revealed to you, (hoping) that you might fabricate other (ones) against Us. Then they would indeed have accepted you as a friend. And if We had not strengthened you, you might almost have inclined to them a little. In that case We would have made you taste double (punishment) in life and double (punishment) in death. You would not have found a helper against Us then." According to some of the commentators, these verses were revealed after the Prophet's meeting with certain Qorayshites (mentioned above on p. 31) when he recited the *Surat on-Najm* and said the words, which he later rued, "They are the cranes aloft. So their intercession may be hoped for." Abu Horayra[41] and Qatāda[42] are reported to have said that the three verses were revealed after some negotiations between the Prophet Mohammad and the Qorayshite chiefs, who had demanded that he should recognise them as the masters, or at least cease to show disrespect for them, and had promised in return to leave him in peace, to enter into friendly relations with him, and to stop beating poor, homeless Moslems and throwing them out onto the sun-scorched rocks. Evidently the Prophet either yielded or softened to such an offer when it was first made, but changed his mind when the time for action came. Perhaps he was prompted to do so by his own inner soul, the same soul which had moved him to think about spiritual matters for so many years and then to start work on the eradication of polytheism and idolatry; for the proposed compromise would be likely to diminish or destroy the impact of his preaching. Perhaps he was told by devout, unbending believers such as 'Omar and by brave, militant believers such as 'Ali and Hamza that a compromise of whatever sort would be a blunder and a defeat. In any case, the words of these three verses prove that the Prophet Mohammad shared in the human characteristic of susceptibility to temptation.

This is confirmed in other Qor'ānic passages. Among them are verses 94 and 95 of *sura* 10 (*Yunos*): "And if you are in doubt concerning what We have sent down to you, ask those who have been reciting the book (i.e. scripture) before you! The truth has come to you from your Lord. So do not be one of the doubters! Do not be one of those who have called God's signs lies! You would then be one of the losers." Again in *sura* 5 (*al-Mā'eda*), verse 71: "O Apostle, transmit what has been sent down to you from your Lord! If you do not, you will not have transmitted His message. And God will protect you from the people."

How ought these verses to be interpreted by a Moslem who believes in God and acknowledges the Qor'ān to be God's word? What is the meaning of these stern admonitions to the Prophet?

Surely the only explanation can be that human weakness and frailty had begun to get the better of the Prophet. He must have been afraid of the people until God told him not to fear because he would be protected against molestation by the people. Certain Qorayshites, particularly Walid b. ol-Moghira, 'Ās b. Wā'el, 'Adi b. Qays, Aswad b. 'Abd ol-Mottaleb, and Aswad b. 'Abd Yaghuth, had deeply distressed the Prophet with their mockery of him and his teachings. Perhaps, in the depths of his soul, he had begun to regret his mission and even to harbor thoughts of giving it up and leaving the people to their own devices. Otherwise he would surely not have received God's command in *sura* 15 (*ol-Hejr*), verses 94 and 95: "Say out loud what you have been ordered (to say), and keep away from the polytheists! We have given you sufficient (protection) against the mockers." Three closely following sentences in the same *sura* spell out the matter and confirm the suggested interpretation: "We know that your heart is grieved by what they say. Proclaim the praise of your Lord! Be one of those who bow down, and serve your Lord! Then the certainty will come to you." Some commentators have taken the word *yaqin* (here translated as certainty) to mean the inevitable destiny of death; their presumption of Mohammad's infallibility has obviously prevented them from acknowledging his vulnerability to doubt and led them to invent this and other interpretations at variance with Qor'ānic wordings. The meaning of the three verses is perfectly clear; Mohammad was suffering from severe depression which made him have doubts, even about his own authenticity, but prayer and praise to God would restore his certainty, i.e. his confidence in his mission.

In *sura* 33 (*ol-Ahzāb*), verse 1, Mohammad is expressly bidden: "Fear God, and do not obey the unbelievers and the hypocrites!" The *Tafsir ol-Jalālayn* interprets the first verb as "continue to fear." Another commentary asserts that both commands, though addressed to the Prophet, are meant to be for the whole Moslem community. The zeal of such commentators is greater than their accuracy, because in verse 2 of the same *sura* God commands the Prophet: "Stick to what is revealed to you from your Lord!" The two verses clearly indicate that Mohammad reacted to his disappointment in a natural, human way by wondering whether to submit to the demands of his adversaries, and that God sternly forbade him to do so; in more scientific language, he was suffering from exhaustion and depression, but was restrained from surrender and brought back to his course by his inner strength of will.

If this explanation is ruled out, the only other possibility would be that the Prophet wanted to make a show of appeasement by pretending willingness to relent and compromise over the demands of his adversaries, but God forbade him to do so. In view of Mohammad's political astuteness, such a hypothesis might be arguable, but in view of his truthfulness, single-mindedness, and moral strength, it would scarcely be probable. Mohammad believed in what he said; he believed that he was inspired by God.

 To conclude this chapter, it will be fitting to quote a story from the Cambridge *Tafsir*[43] (an early Qor'ān commentary in Persian) as an illustration of Moslem thinking in the first centuries of Islam and its remoteness from the facts of the time when the Qor'ān was revealed. The story (on p. 295 of vol. 2 of the Tehrān printed edition) is as follows: "After the revelation of the *Surat on-Najm* (*sura* 53, which opens with the words 'By the star when it sets'), `Otaba b. Abi Lahab sent a message to the Prophet saying that he did not believe in the stars in the Qor'ān. The Prophet took offence and cursed him, praying, 'O God, may one of Your beasts of prey overpower him!' 'Otaba , on hearing of it, was frightened. At that time he was travelling in a caravan. When the caravan stopped at Harrān, 'Otaba lay down and slept in the midst of his friends. God sent a lion, which took 'Otaba from the midst of his friends and tore all his body but did not eat any of that accursed, unclean thing. So all the people knew that the lion had not taken him to eat him but to fulfill the Prophet's prayer." It never occurred to the fabricators of this story that the Prophet, instead of cursing 'Otaba , could have besought God to show mercy to him and convert him to Islam. Is not Islam faith in the Lord of the Worlds, the Compassionate, the Merciful?

At Madina, however, Islam was not only faith in God; it also became the basis of a new legal system and of an Arab state. Islam's rules and obligations were all laid down during Mohammad's stay at Madina in the last ten years of his prophetic career. The first step was the change of the direction of prayer from Jerusalem to Mecca.

One result of this step was that the Jews were thereafter separately taxed from the Moslems. Another was that the Arabs of Madina got rid of their inferiority complex and that the Beduin Arabs began to acquire a sort of national fervor; for the Ka'ba, the idol-temple which the tribes had revered, was thereafter the house of Abraham and Ishmael, the ancestors of all the Arabs.

Likewise in the matter of fasting, the example of the Jews was discarded. First the fast was extended from the tenth day of the month of Moharram, which was the Jewish practice, to a number of days; later the whole month of Ramadān was reserved for it.

The rules on marriage, divorce, menstruation, kindred and affinity, inheritance and polygamy, on penalties for fornication, adultery and theft, on retaliation, blood-money, and other criminal matters, and on civil matters such as defilements, food prohibitions, and circumcision, stemmed with some modifications mainly from Jewish law or pre-Islamic Arab custom and were all enacted at Madina. Other rules on civil and personal matters, though colored by Jewish and pagan Arab ideas and practices, were unquestionably measures taken for adjustment of the social and commercial order.

# CHAPTER III

# *Politics*

## THE EMIGRATION

History always moves one, but here and there in its pages we find days which become fixed in our minds as starting points of great events or transformations. One of these is the day, recorded as the 12th of the third month (Rabi' ol-Awwal) corresponding to 24 September 662 in the Gregorian Christian calendar, on which the Prophet Mohammad arrived in the town then known as Yathreb.

The main reason why the early Moslems saw Mohammad's emigration (*hejra*) as marking an era was simple religious enthusiasm. The ancient Arabs did not really possess an era, though after the defeat of the Abyssinian force which threatened Mecca in the Year of the Elephant[44] (probably 570 A.D.), some of them reckoned dates from that point.

Another reason for the identification of the new era with the *hejra* was that it enabled individuals to boast of the earliness and courageousness of their adherence to the Prophet's cause, and members of the Aws and Khazraj tribes to stress the importance of the protection which they had given to him.

The day from which the start of the era was reckoned was in fact not the twelfth day of the month of Rabi' ol-Awwal, but the first day of the first month, namely Moharram, of the same year, corresponding to the Gregorian date 16 July 622.

It certainly did not occur to the minds of Arabs living in that year that the twelfth day of Rabi' ol-Awwal was the first link in a chain of events destined to cause unprecedented change in their way of life. Nobody in the contemporary world dreamed that a collection of desert-dwellers, who had played no significant part in the history of civilization and whose more advanced tribes had attached themselves to the Roman and Iranian empires and were proud of their vassalage to the Caesar and the Khosraw, would soon become the masters of a great part of the lands of old civilization.

Migration from one region to another was not abnormal among the Arabs. The outstanding example had been the migration of South Arabian tribes to the northern borderlands of the peninsula after the bursting of the dam at Ma'reb[45] in the Yaman. In comparison with this, the move of Mohammad and his companions from Mecca to Yathreb was an unimportant affair involving a small number of people – a few emigrants from oppression by Qorayshite polytheists.

Yet this seemingly unimportant affair led within a decade to a complete upheaval. Ten years later the few men who had left Mecca to join Mohammad, some clandestinely as fugitives, others openly as travelers, would be the masters of Mecca while all their opponents would be on bended knees. The idols would be smashed and the traditional cult of the Ka'ba, managed by the Qorayshites and providing the wealth and prestige of their chiefs, would be uprooted. Abu Sofyān, the successor to Abu Lahab and Abu Jahl, would surrender for fear of his life, and all the diehards would profess belief in One God.

The genesis of a great event from a chain of small events has not been uncommon in history. Good examples are the French revolution, the Russian revolution, and the Mongol invasion of Iran.

Mohammad had clashed with the chiefs of the Qoraysh ever since he began to preach. Perhaps he had not at first expected that his teachings, being basically rational and similar to those of the other two Semitic religions, would encounter such persistent opposition; perhaps he had overlooked the important point that widespread acceptance of his teachings would necessarily undermine the supremacy of the Qoraysh and the power and wealth of their chiefs. In any case their hostility was a fact, and he was obliged to start thinking of ways and means to overcome it. Already before his departure to Yathreb he had taken two steps to this end.

The first step was the dispatch of a number of Moslems to Abyssinia in two successive groups. Evidently these Moslems, who were poor and had no protectors, suffered persecution by the Qorayshites and received advice from the Prophet to go to Abyssinia; but it can be inferred from the identities of the members of the second, more numerous group, which included his cousin Ja'far b.

Abi Tāleb, and from the instructions given to them, that a political purpose underlay this move. Hope of support from the Negus must have arisen in Mohammad's searching and resourceful mind. The Negus, being a Christian ruler, would be naturally opposed to idolatry, and on being informed of the anti-polytheist revolt of a party of monotheists at Mecca and of the persecution inflicted on them, might well be ready to send a force to Mecca to protect them. This would explain the inclusion of Jaʿfar b. Abi Tāleb, who being of a respected family had not personally suffered persecution. At the same time the Qorayshites sent ʿAmr b. ol-ʿĀs and ʿAbdollāh b. Abi Rabiʿa to Abyssinia with presents for the Negus, hoping to dissuade him from any intervention which the Moslem emigrants might propose and if possible also to secure their extradition.

The second step was Mohammad's journey to Tā'ef[46] in 620 A.D. Having lost his uncle and protector Abu Tāleb and then his helpmate Khadija, he was exposed to more open hostility than before. He had hopes of support from the Banu Thaqif tribe, to whom he was related on his mother's side. At Tā'ef, which was the tribe's center, the Banu Thaqif were held in high respect. All the people of Tā'ef were envious of Mecca's privileged position and of the Qoraysh tribe's prestige among the Beduin; they naturally wanted to make their own town the meeting place of the Arabs and to avoid submission to Qorayshite hegemony. This was not wishful thinking but proven fact, because the Prophet could remember a visit from some Thaqif chiefs who had said that the people of Tā'ef would probably become Moslems if he would make it the sanctuary and holy city of the new religion. The Banu ʿĀmer tribe, also influential at Tā'ef, had earlier made a similar proposal to him, requesting that in the event of the success of his cause and the implantation of Islam through their help, he should make them the noblest Arab tribe instead of the Qoraysh. Clearly the purpose of the Prophet's journey to Tā'ef was to explore the ground. If the Banu Thaqif were really willing to support him, it might be possible to humble the Qoraysh. This was why he traveled to Tā'ef secretly with no companion except his manumitted slave and adopted son Zayd b. Hāretha. His hopes were disappointed, however, because the Thaqif chiefs decided not to support him.

Beduin Arabs have never taken much interest in spiritual matters. Even today, nearly fourteen centuries after Mohammad's mission, they tend to view religion as a means of worldly gain. The

Banu Thaqif were too concerned about their livelihood to think of disregarding immediate material interests for the sake of promised future salvation. Tā'ef was the summer resort of Mecca, and its people made profits from Meccan visitors and business connections. The Qorayshites were taking action against Mohammad and would be antagonized by any support for him. It would therefore not be wise to rate his unproven promises higher than the practical requirements of Tā'ef's security and prosperity. On such a calculation of profit and loss, the chiefs of Tā'ef not only refused support but also showed malice to Mohammad. They assaulted him, insulted him, and even rejected his last request to them, which was that they should refrain from disclosing his unsuccessful journey and thereby emboldening the Qorayshites. As a result, the Meccan opposition to him became much more virulent after his return. Finally a number of leading polytheists met in the hall of the assembly (*dār ol-nadwa*) to discuss ways and means of putting an end to Mohammad's activity, which posed such a threat to their standing and wealth. Of the three suggested alternatives of deporting, imprisoning, or killing him, they decided on the last.

Besides Tā'ef, one other town in the Hejāz rivaled Mecca in economic and social importance. This was Yathreb, known also as ol-Madina (an Aramaic word, probably introduced by the local Jews, meaning "the city").[47] Mecca, with its temple of the favorite idols of the Arabs, was certainly the religious center most visited by the Beduin tribes, and the Qorayshites, as custodians of the Ka'ba and purveyors of the needs of the visitors, could naturally claim to be the noblest Arab tribe; but the oasis town of Yathreb, with a flourishing agriculture, which Mecca wholly lacked, in addition to a substantial commerce, and with a relatively considerable degree of literacy in its population thanks to the presence of three Jewish tribes, had attained a higher cultural and social level. Nevertheless Yathreb was generally placed second among the Hejāzi towns after Mecca.

The other element in Yathreb's population consisted of two feuding Arab tribes, the Aws and the Khazraj, each of which had friendly ties with one or two of the Jewish tribes. The Aws and Khazraj were Qahtāni Arabs, i.e. of Yamani origin, and this was another source of rivalry with the Qoraysh tribe, which was 'Adnāni, i.e. North Arabian.

On account of sloth and inexperience of agriculture and commerce, and Awsites and Khazrajites were not as prosperous as

their Jewish neighbors, and they often worked for Jewish employ-
ers. Thus in spite of their alliances with particular Jewish tribes,
they resented the economic superiority of the Jews in general,
whom they saw as their masters.

News of Mohammad's emergence and preaching of Islam at
Mecca, and of the Qorayshite opposition to him and the subsequent tension, had spread all over the Hejāz and been heard with
interest at Madina. Reports by Yathrebi travelers to Mecca and
discussions held by some of them with Mohammad prompted a
number of Awsite and Khazrajite chiefs to think of fishing in the
troubled waters. If Mohammad and his companions could be
brought to Madina and an alliance could be made with him, several
difficulties might be overcome. The wall of Qorayshite solidarity
would be breached, because Mohammad and his companions were
themselves of the Qoraysh tribe. A joint alliance with Mohammad
and his companions might help the Aws and Khazraj tribes to end
the feud which had so long plagued them. Furthermore Mohammad had brought a new religion. If this religion took hold, the
Jews would no longer be able to claim superiority on the ground
that they possessed scriptures and were God's chosen people.
Collaboration with Mohammad and his companions would therefore be likely to strengthen the Aws and the Khazraj in relation to
the three Jewish tribes at Madina.

During the pilgrimage season of the year 620, six men from
Yathreb met Mohammad and listened carefully to what he had to
say. In the same season of 621, a twelve-man delegation met him at
ol-'Aqaba on the outskirts of Mecca. They found his teaching
salutary and his requirements not overexacting: the people must
eschew fornication, adultery, usury, and lying, and instead of man-
made idols must worship One God as the scripture-possessors
did. The twelve men pledged allegiance to Mohammad, and
after returning to Yathreb informed their kinsfolk that they had
become Moslems and were in favor of a pact with Mohammad.
Their action and their proposal met with widespread approval. In
the following year 622, a large delegation consisting of seventy
three men and two women went to meet Mohammad at the same
place and concluded the second pact of ol-'Aqaba with him.

The thought of emigration was not strange to Mohammad's
mind. It is mentioned, evidently with reference to the Moslems
who went to Abyssinia, in verse 13 of *sura* 39 (*oz-Zomar*): "Say, 'O
worshippers who believe, fear your Lord! For those who do good

in this world there will be a good (reward). And God's earth is wide.'"

The pact of ol-'Aqaba must have answered Mohammad's secret hopes. His mission at Mecca, now in its thirteenth year, had not won any shining success. There had even been some regrettable backslidings of converts who, with typical Arab fickleness, had wearied and renounced Islam when they saw that Mohammad's cause was not advancing, and above all when they found that being Moslem involved being humiliated and persecuted. They had also been prodded into desertion by rich, influential polytheists. His approach to the Banu Thaqif of Tā'ef had not only failed but had further exacerbated the Qorayshite hostility to him. Although his own clan, the Banu Hāshem, continued to protect him, they only protected him against personal injury and could not be expected to join in his struggle against the Qoraysh.

The alliance with the Aws and the Khazraj would transform the prospect. With their support it would be possible to challenge the Qoraysh. While Islam had not taken firm root in Mecca, it might well do so in Yathreb, if only because of the Awsite and Khazrajite jealousy of the Qoraysh.

A further consideration was the likelihood that at Yathreb, with its thriving trade and its agriculture, Moslem emigrants would be able to find work.

In the negotiations between the Prophet and the chiefs of the Aws and Khazraj at ol-'Aqaba, 'Abbās b. 'Abdol-Mottaleb, who had apparently not yet become a Moslem but was a protector of his nephew, is reported to have been present and to have made a speech urging them to be frank about their intentions. He bluntly told the Yathrebi representatives that they and Mohammad would probably be attacked by the Qoraysh and that they ought to promise the same protection to Mohammad as they would give to their own wives and children. In any case they should not mislead him with empty promises. To this one of the Khazrajite delegates, ol-Barā b. ol-Ma'rūr, replied heatedly that they were fighting men with no fear of war and would face up to all difficulties. An experienced and prudent Awsite delegate, Abu'l-Haytham b. Tayyehān, is reported to have said to Mohammad, "We have quite close relations with the Jews, which may be broken after the conclusion of a pact with you and your companions. Perhaps your cause will advance. In that case, would you make a compromise with your own tribe and forsake us?" According to Ebn Heshām's biography, the Prophet smiled and answered, "On the contrary. Blood, blood, destruction, destruction! I shall be yours and you shall be mine. I shall be at war with those at war with you and at peace with those at peace with you."

The repetition of the words "blood" and "destruction" brings to mind the statement of the famous French revolutionary Jean Paul Marat, "I want blood."

Also noteworthy is another phrase said to have been used by the Prophet Mohammad in his answer to Abu'l-Haytham: "war with the reds and the blacks among the people." Probably this meant war with people of all races, non-Arabs as well as Arabs.

These words must have expressed the Prophet's feelings, or in other words his inner desires.

The whole tenor of the answer to Abu'l-Haytham indicates that it was a cry from the heart concealed in the outward Mohammad, an articulation of a long dormant hope. The support of the Aws and the Khazraj would open the door to a brighter future; it would enable Mohammad to press on with the propagation of Islam, to strike at the Qorayshite intransigents, and to manifest his own hidden self. From chrysalis of the Mohammad who had preached with scant effect for thirteen years, the Mohammad who was to subdue all Arabia could now emerge.

# THE CHANGE IN MOHAMMAD'S PERSONALITY

Unimportant or seemingly unimportant events have often changed the course of history. They had decisive effects, for example, on the careers of Napoleon and Hitler.

The Prophet Mohammad's emigration to Yathreb was seemingly a minor local affair, but actually the start of a great transformation of Arab fortunes and world history. The ensuing developments provide a wide field of study for scholars seeking to ascertain the causes, correlations, and latent social factors.

Of all these problems, perhaps the most interesting and certainly the most striking is the change of the personality of one of the great makers of history. In this particular case, change of personality is an unsatisfactory term; emergence of Mohammad's inner self would be a more nearly accurate description. The *hejra* started a great historical transformation, but also followed from a transformation of Mohammad's personality which requires meticulous psychological and spiritual analysis.

Mohammad was devout and free from the vices of his time. He pictured the end of the world and the day of judgement as near at hand. With his thoughts fixed on the hereafter, he implored his Meccan compatriots to revere the Lord of the Universe, and condemned violence, injustice, hedonism, and neglect of the poor. Like Jesus, he was full of compassion. After the move to Madina, however, he became a relentless warrior, intent on spreading his religion by the sword, and a scheming founder of a state. A Messiah was transformed into a David. A man who had lived for more than twenty years with one wife became inordinately fond of women.

In the view of the English novelist H. G. Wells, human beings undergo constant change, but on account of the slowness and imperceptibility of the process we persist in imagining fifty-year-olds to be the same persons as they were in their twenties when in fact they have gradually but thoroughly changed. In so far as the vital faculties decline while the mental faculties are brought to their peak through experience, study, and reflection, this theory is sound. Normally the main difference between a twenty-year-old and a fifty-year-old is that the former has strong physical and emotional desires while the latter has had time to gain experience and learn to think.

Useful though this theory may be, it is not always right, and in the case of Mohammad it is wrong. After the move to Madina at the age of 53, i.e. at an age when most men's physical and emotional faculties are on the wane, a new Mohammad emerged. During his last ten years, which he spent at Madina, he was not the same man as the Mohammad who for thirteen years had been preaching humane compassion at Mecca. The Prophet bidden by God "to warn your tribe, your nearest kin" (*sura* 26, verse 214) reappeared in the garb of the Prophet intent on subduing his own tribe and on humbling the kinsmen who for thirteen years had mocked him. Shedding the gown of the warner to "the mother town (i.e. Mecca) and the people around it" (*sura* 42, verse 5), he donned the armor of the warrior who was to bring all Arabia from the Yaman to Syria under his flag.

The beauty and melody of the Meccan *sura*s, so reminiscent of the preachings of Isaiah and Jeremiah and evocative of the fervor of a visionary soul, seldom reappear in the Madinan *sura*s, where the poetic and musical tone tends to be silenced and replaced by the peremptory note of rules and regulations.

At Madina orders and rules were issued on the authority of a commander who could allow no infringement or deviation. The penalties prescribed for violation or negligence were very severe.

Ignaz Goldziher[48] attributed this abrupt metamorphosis to an inner drive which Adolf Harnack had described as at once the affliction of supermen and the source of their extraordinary energy. Such a drive makes great men immune to hesitancy, fatigue, and despair, and fearless of obstacles however grave. Nothing else can explain their achievement of feats beyond the power of normal men.

The following quotations will suffice to show that Mohammad's metamorphosis after the *hejra* is not only attested by the record of events but is also echoed in the different tones of the Meccan and Madinan *sura*s. In verses 10–12 of the Meccan *sura* 73 (*ol-Mozzamel*), the Prophet is bidden, "Be patient with what they say, and part from them courteously! Leave the deniers, the possessors of wealth, to Me, and give them a little respite! Fetters and hellfire are in Our hands." In the *Tafsir ol-Jalālayn* it is stated that this command to part from believers courteously was given before the command to fight and try to kill them; it would have been more fully true to say that the earlier command was given before the Prophet's rise to power with Awsite and Khazrajite help. Only when he could rely on the support of men of the sword was the command to fight unbelievers sent down to him in the Madinan verse 187 of *sura* 2 (*ol-Baqara*): "Kill them wherever you find them, and drive them out from wherever they drove you out, for persecution is worse than killing!"

In *sura* 6 (*ol-An'am*), the text of verse 108, which was revealed at Mecca, is as follows: "Do not curse those other than God to whom they pray! They will then resentfully curse God from lack of knowledge. It will be like that because We make every community's practice (seem) fair to it. Later their return to their Lord (will take place), and He will explain to them what they have been doing." It is not clear whether this advice (with its plural verb) is addressed to the Prophet or to sharp-tongued zealots among his Companions such as 'Omar b. ol-Khattāb or Hamza b. 'Abd ol-Mottaleb. At Madina, however, particularly after the expansion of Moslem power, the mere cursing of the deities of the Qoraysh was no longer at issue; peaceful and affable contact with unbelievers was categorically forbidden. In the words of the Madinan *sura* 47 (*Mohammad*), verse 37, "So do not be weak and call for peace when you are uppermost! God is with you and will not deprive you of (the proceeds of) your deeds."

Sometimes two contradictory commands appear in the same *sura*. Although *sura* 2 (*ol-Baqara*) is considered to be the first in order of revelation after the *hejra*, it is likely in view of its length to have been sent down in parts over a period of one or two years. In its 257th verse, which evidently dates from the beginning of the period, comes the explicit statement: "There is no compulsion in religion. Right has been distinguished from wrong. Those who reject false deities and believe in God have grasped the firmest handle, which will never break." On the other hand in the 189th verse, which perhaps came down when the Moslem community was stronger or on the occasion of some incident, use of force is enjoined: "Fight them until there is no persecution and the religion is God's! And if they give up, let there be no enmity except to evil-doers!"

In *sura* 9 (*ot-Tawba*, also known as *ol-Barā'a*), which is chronologically the last *sura* of the Qor'ān, the command to use force is unqualified and peremptory:

(1)  "Fight those who do not believe in God and the last day . . . . . . !" (verse 29).
(2)  "It is not for the Prophet and the believers to pray for forgiveness of the polytheists . . . . . . !" (verse 114).
(3)  "O Prophet, struggle against the unbelievers and the hypocrites, and be harsh with them! Their refuge is hell. What a wretched destination!" (verse 74).
(4)  "O believers, fight the unbelievers who are near (kin) to you, and let them find harshness in you . . . . . . !" (verse 124).

The same command to use force comes with identical wording in the late Madinan *sura* 66 (*ot-Tahrim*), verse 9: "O Prophet, struggle against the unbelievers and the hypocrites, and be harsh with them. Their refuge is hell. What a wretched destination!"

Initially there had been no sanction for the use of force and harshness. Even in verse 40 of the Madinan *sura* 22 (*ol-Hajj*), in which holy war against the unbelievers was first authorized, the verb is not in the imperative mood: "Permission is given to those who fight because they have been wronged." In verse 41 the wrong done to the Moslems is specified: "Those who have been unjustly driven from their homes on the sole ground that they say, 'Our Lord is God.'" Zamakhshari commented that this first authorization of war on the polytheists came after more than seventy Qor'ānic verses in which violence is forbidden.

In justification of the license to wage war, the Prophet Mohammad put to use his innate understanding of human nature. The eloquent reminder of the forced departure of the Moslems from Mecca would stir them to seek vengeance on the Qoraysh. The same cogent rhetoric is used in another context, where the words are spoken by the Children of Israel but the lesson is for the Moslems: "Why should not we fight in God's cause when we have been driven out of our homes and away from our children?" (sura 2, part of verse 247). Although the war was for God's cause, remembrance of personal loss would stir the Moslems to fight for revenge.

There had been no question of war while the Prophet remained at Mecca. Verse 67 of sura 6 (ol-An'ām) shows that the Prophet then used to meet and talk with polytheists and that they sometimes treated him discourteously and mocked him: "And when you see them launch out against Our signs (i.e. Qor'ānic verses), turn away from them until they launch out on some other subject! And in case the Satan may make you forget, do not, after (this) reminder, sit with evil-doing people!"

As regards the possessors of scriptures, in verse 45 of the Meccan sura 29 (ol-'Ankabut) God instructs not only the Prophet but also, since the verb is plural, the Moslems, as follows: "Argue with possessors of scriptures, other than evil-doers, only by means of (arguments) that are better! And say, 'We believe in what has been sent down to us and sent down to you. Our God is the same as your God, and we have surrendered to Him.'"

Amicable behavior toward possessors of scriptures is recommended in several other Meccan and early Madinan verses. "Say to those who have been given scripture and to the common people,[49] 'Have you surrendered (to God)?' If they have surrendered, they are rightly guided, and if they have turned away, your duty is only to convey the message" (sura 3, Āl 'Emrān, part of verse 19). "Those who believe, and those who are Jewish, Christian, and Sabaean, all who believe in God and the last day and who do right, will have their reward from their Lord. They need not fear or grieve" (sura 2, ol-Baqara, verse 59, and almost identical

84

words in *sura* 5, *ol-Mā'eda*, verse 73). The contexts indicate that these verses were revealed in the first or second year after the *hejra*.

In the course of the Madinan decade, however, and especially after the conquest of Mecca, changes occurred, and finally *sura* 9 (*ot-Tawba*) came down like a thunderbolt onto the heads of the scripture-possessors. These people, who at Mecca had on God's advice been politely answered and not threatened (any more than the common people) with future punishment for failure to embrace Islam, because the Prophet's function was solely to convey the message to them, were ordered in the year 10 A.H. to choose between the alternatives of conversion, payment of tribute and acceptance of inferior status, or condemnation to death. The edict comes in verse 29 of *sura* 9: "Fight those who do not believe in God and the last day and do not prohibit the things which God and His apostle have prohibited! And (fight) possessors of scriptures who do not accept the religion of truth (i.e. Islam) until they pay tribute by hand, being inferior!" With the passage of the years, these scripture-possessors had become the "worst creatures" (*sura* 98, verse 5).

Mohammad's announcement of this edict after the elimination of the Madinan Jews, the seizure of the Jewish villages of Khaybar and Fadak, and the conquest of Mecca, indicates that with Islam in power, polite and rational discussion with dissentients was no longer deemed necessary. The language of future discourse with them was to be the language of the sword.

# THE ESTABLISHMENT OF A SOUND ECONOMY

After the move to Yathreb, the Prophet Mohammad arranged covenants of brotherhood between his local supporters (*Ansār*) and the gradually arriving Meccan Moslem emigrants (*Mohājerun*), whereby the former lodged the latter in their homes as adoptive brothers. Although the Mohājerun intended to work and did in fact open shops in the bazaar and find jobs as agricultural laborers, their position was neither easy nor secure. Being committed to struggle against the Qorayshites, they needed more dependable livelihoods which would enable them to stand on their own feet. The Prophet, who did not himself take an employment but subsisted on the generosity of the Mohājerun and the Ansār, went through a hard time, often having to retire to bed with no supper or to assuage his hunger with no more than a few dates.

Thus the small Moslem community faced a vital problem: how to acquire a less precarious and more self-sufficient economic base. The steps taken to solve this problem are discussed below.

Among the contemporary Arab tribes, the traditional method of self-enrichment was attack on another tribe and seizure of its animals and other possessions. For the Moslems then living at Madina no alternative was discernible. They therefore took up raiding. The Arabic word *ghazwa* (raid) meant a sudden attack on a caravan or another tribe for the purpose of seizing property and women and thereby easing the hard task of survival in Arabia.

News reached the Prophet that a Qorayshite caravan led by 'Amr b. ol-Hadrami was proceeding from Syria to Mecca with a large cargo of goods. He sent a band of Mohājerun under the command of 'Abdollāh b. Jahsh to attack the caravan. They lay in ambush near a stopping place called (on-)Nakhla and took the approaching caravan by surprise, killing its leader and capturing two other men before their safe return to Madina with the entire cargo in their possession. The successful venture is known in Islamic history as the Nakhla raid.

This action caused a great stir, because it was the first Moslem raid and because it took place on the first day of the month of Rajab, one of the four months (Moharram, Rajab, Dhu'l-Qa'da, and Dhu'-l-Hejja) in which fighting was forbidden by ancient Arab custom. Cries of indignation against the breach of the ban rang out from the Qoraysh and not unnaturally were echoed by other tribes. This unfavorable aspect of the matter seems to have worried the Prophet, who showed some coolness to 'Abdollāh b. Jahsh and his men, and some uncertainty about the future course to be followed. 'Abdollāh b. Jahsh claimed that the attack had taken place on the last day of the month of Jomāda oth-Thāniya, in which case a solution might be found; but there was also the problem of the booty, which would provide needed financial resources for the Prophet's followers and therefore ought not to be relinquished in response to hollow Qorayshite protests. Probably some of his companions pointed out to him that the accomplished fact could not be undone and that any sort of disavowal would be tantamount to acknowledgement of Moslem guilt and enemy innocence. The importance of the booty for improving the situation of the Mohājerun must also have been present to their minds.

A definite and precedent-setting solution came to hand when verse 214 of *sura* 2 (*ol-Baqara*) was sent down: "They are asking you about the forbidden month, (about) fighting in it. Say, 'Fighting in it is a great (evil), but turning (men) away from God's path, disbelieving in Him and the Mosque of the Sanctuary, and expelling its people from it are greater (evils) in God's sight. Persecution[50] is a greater (sin) than killing. They will not stop fighting you until they estrange you from your religion, if they can.'"

After the Nakhla raid, further attacks on Qorayshite caravans and unfriendly tribes met with success and helped to make the financial position of the Moslems more secure. This raiding opened the way for the acquisition of power by the Prophet Mohammad and his companions and for their eventual domination of all Arabia; but the immediate step which secured the economic base and strengthened the prestige of the Moslems was their seizure of the property of the Jews of Yathreb.

Three Jewish tribes, the Banu Qaynoqā', the Banu'n-Nadir, and the Banu Qorayza, lived at Yathreb. They had prospered in both their agricultural and their commercial and craft-industrial pursuits, and thanks to their religious schooling and relative literacy had attained a higher cultural level than the two other local tribes, the Aws and the Khazraj. Many Awsites and Khazrajites were employed by Jews as agricultural laborers and as watchmen of shops and warehouses. These two tribes consequently had feelings of inferiority and jealousy toward the Jewish tribes. As already mentioned, the main reason why the Aws and Khazraj approached Mohammad and concluded the pact of ol-'Aqaba with him was their desire to overcome the Jewish dominance and get rid of their own inferiority complex. The Prophet, after his arrival at Madina, at first maintained a prudent discretion. He not only avoided controversy with the Jews, who were powerful as well as rich; he also made a sort of non-aggression pact (the *'Ahd ol-Mowāda'a*) with them which further provided for mutual co-operation in certain circumstances. It laid down that individual Moslems and Jews should continue to belong to their respective religious communities; that in the event of aggression by the Qoraysh or any other tribe, the Moslems and the Jews should jointly defend Madina; and that each party should bear the cost of its own military operations against hostile tribes.

In addition to this, there was a bond of common feeling between

87

the Moslems and the Jews. Both abhorred polytheism and idolatry. Both bowed their heads in the same direction when they prayed.

As long as the Moslems were weak, no incidents arose. Not until a year and a half after the *hejra* did the Prophet Mohammad change the direction of Islamic prayer from the Furthest Mosque (at Jerusalem) to the Ka'ba (at Mecca). This step evoked protests from the Jews, and in answer to them verse 172 of *sura* 2 was sent down: "Righteousness is not that you turn your faces toward the east and the west, but the righteous man is he who believes in God and the Last Day and in angels, scripture, and prophets, and gives wealth, however cherished, to kinsfolk and orphans, to the poor and homeless, to beggars, and for (the manumission of) slaves."

For the Jews this decision was an alarm signal. Their anxiety was sharpened by a succession of small raids and by the attacks on Meccan trading caravans, which culminated in the victory of Mohammad's followers at the battle of Badr (in March 624). They faced Awsites and Khazrajites who were no longer impecunious and generally glad to work for them, but had now combined under Mohammad's flag to form a strong, united front called Islam. For this reason certain leaders of the Jews such as Ka'b b. ol-Ashraf betook themselves after the battle of Badr to Mecca, where they expressed sympathy with the defeated Qorayshites and urged them to make war against Mohammad and his followers. There is a reference to the matter in verse 54 of *sura* 4 (*on-Nesā*): "Have not you seen how those who have been given a share of scripture place their trust in demons and false deities and say to the unbelievers, 'These are better guided than the believers'?" The verse is a clear rebuke to people claiming to possess scriptures which condemn polytheism and idolatry, yet willing to fraternize with polytheists and to deem them better than Mohammad's monotheistic followers.

At this juncture a trivial incident in the bazaar of Madina led to a fight with the Banu Qaynoqā' and a siege of their street. A woman of the Ansār went to the shop of a goldsmith of the Qaynoqā' tribe. He started to flirt with her, and she spurned him. In order to hit back and demean her, he surreptitiously pinned the back of her skirt to her blouse with a thorn, so that when she stood up the lower part of her body was exposed and the people burst out laughing. Her shrieks of protest about this indecent act prompted a Moslem man to go to her rescue. This man killed the goldsmith, and the Jews then rushed to the help of their coreligionists and killed the Moslem. A riot ensued, and the Moslems complained to the Prophet. With his authorization they besieged the street of the Banu Qaynoqā', blocking their access to food supplies. After fifteen days the Banu Qaynoqā' surrendered on the offered terms, which were that their lives would be spared, that they must emigrate from Yathreb, and that they must deposit all their belongings except things portable by beasts of burden at a certain place for distribution among indigent, homeless Mohājerun.

This event strengthened the economic position of the Moslems and dismayed the other Jewish tribes. The turn of the Banu'n-Nadir came next. They were in an angry mood because one of their chiefs, the already mentioned Ka'b b. ol-Ashraf, had been assassinated on Mohammad's order. When the Prophet, accompanied by some of his followers, went to the street of the Banu'n-Nadir to judge a dispute about blood money, they plotted to revolt and kill him. He gave orders to fight them, and the Moslems blockaded their street, preventing any delivery of food to them. The Banu'n-Nadir, however, were better armed than the Banu Qaynoqā', and perhaps with the latter's fate in mind had taken more precautions. They fought back stubbornly and valiantly. The siege lasted so long that the Prophet began to fear that the Moslems might succumb to the usual Arab inconstancy and wearily go back to their homes. He therefore ordered that the palm grove belonging to the Banu'n-Nadir should be burned down.

Since date palms, like camels and sheep, are a basic source of food and wealth in Arabia, the protests of the Banu'n-Nadir did not pass unheard. "How is it", they asked the Prophet Mohammad, "that when you claim to be a doer of good, an opponent of evil and destruction, you cruelly destroy a productive resource?" Nevertheless Mohammad did not flinch. In reply to the clamor and in justification of the deed, he cited verses 3, 4, and 5 of *sura* 59 (*ol-Hashr*) which was sent down on this occasion: "If God had not prescribed eviction for them, He would have punished them in this lower world. And they will have the punishment of fire in the world to come. That is because they broke away from God and His Apostle, and if people break away from God, then God is stern in retribution. When you cut down some palms and left others standing on their roots, it was with God's permission and in order that He might disgrace the sinners."

Underlying these verses is the principle that the end justifies the means. Inhumane though it is, this principle was taken for granted by the contemporary Arab tribes. The Prophet again acted on it in the war with the Banu Thaqif and siege of Tā'ef in 8 A.H./630, when he ordered the burning of their vineyard. There was thus no lack of precedent for the action of the Omayyad troops who in 61/680 cut off the supply of water, even for the women and children, in order to force the Prophet's grandson Hosayn b. 'Ali into surrender.

Eventually the Banu'n-Nadir surrendered after twenty days. Through the intercession of some chiefs of the Khazraj, it was agreed that they should quit Madina with a safe conduct after depositing all their moveable property in a certain place for distribution among the Prophet's followers.

The only remaining Jewish group of any importance at Yathreb was the Qorayza tribe. After the war of the trench in 5 A.H./627, they too came to a bad end. It was alleged that they had agreed to provide help from within the town to the Qorayshite besiegers; but the Prophet had skilfully sown dissension among them, and they had not in fact helped Abu Sofyān's force. As soon as Abu Sofyān lost hope of taking Madina and abandoned the siege, the Moslems turned against the Banu Qorayza and blockaded their street for twenty five days. They then expressed readiness to accept the surrender terms which had been conceded to the two other Jewish tribes, namely cession of their belongings and departure with a safe conduct. The Prophet, however, being deeply aggrieved with them because they had been in touch with Abu Sofyān, would not consent. He may also have thought that their destruction would enhance the awesomeness of Islam and serve as a grim warning to others.

Fearing such a decision, and remembering how the intercession of Khazraj chiefs had saved the lives of the other two Jewish tribes, the Banu Qorayza sought the help of Aws chiefs. In response to pleas by the latter on their behalf, the Prophet Mohammad undertook to appoint an Awsite arbiter and to implement whatever sentence this arbiter might pronounce. He then appointed Sa'd b. Mo'ādh whom he knew to be on bad terms with the Banu Qorayza. His expectations of Sa'd were not disappointed. Sa'd ruled that all the Qorayza men should be beheaded, that the women and children should be sold as slaves, and that all their property should be divided among the Moslems.

These sentences were unjust, but could not be changed because both sides had sworn to accept Sa'd b. Mo'ādh's ruling. The primary consideration, however, was the need for drastic action, however cruel it might be, in order to establish a viable state. Trenches were dug in the bazaar of Madina for disposal of the decapitated bodies of the seven hundred (or according to some sources nearly one thousand) Jewish prisoners, who had surrendered in expectation of a safe conduct to leave the town.

In contravention of Sa'd's ruling, a Jewish woman, the wife of Hasan ol-Qorazi, was also beheaded. She was friendly with 'Ā'esha, with whom she sat and talked until the time came for her to go to her death. When her name was called out, she walked smilingly and cheerfully to the execution ground. Her offence was throwing a stone during the blockade of the Banu Qorayza's street. 'Ā'esha said of her, "I have never met a more beautiful, good-tempered, and kind-hearted woman. When she rose to walk to the execution ground and I told her that they would certainly kill her, she answered with a smile that staying alive did not matter to her."

# THE ADVANCE TO POWER

The record of the first decade after the *Hejra* presents a picture of the genesis of a state. At Mecca the Prophet Mohammad's mission had for thirteen years been devoted to preaching, counseling, warning people about the judgement day, and exhorting them to righteousness. At Madina the prophetic mission became institutionalized and was perforce devoted mainly to governing people and making them accept the new dispensation.

To this end every sort of expedient was considered permissible, regardless of consistency with the spiritual and moral precepts which were being taught.

Among the events of the period were political assassinations, raids which were manifestly unprovoked, and attacks on tribes who had not acted aggressively but were reported by spies to be restless or unsympathetic to the Moslems. All these steps were taken for reasons of state. The raids on Qorayshite trading caravans served the purposes of injuring the Qoraysh, acquiring booty, enhancing the military prestige of the Moslems, and intimidating potential opponents.

During the same relatively short period, most of the laws of

Islam were revealed and Islamic financial and governmental institutions were established.

No laws had been enacted in the course of the Prophet's mission
at Mecca. This was noted by Goldziher, who wrote: "The Meccan
revelations do not announce the introduction of a new religion.
Most of the Meccan verses of the Qor'ān are exhortations to piety,
to worship and praise of the One God, to charitable concern for
others, and to moderation in eating and drinking."

Only the following five principles had been ordained at Mecca:

(1)  belief in one God and in the appointment of prophets.
(2)  prayer.
(3)  almsgiving, at that time in the form of voluntary donation.
(4)  fasting, at that time in the same manner as the Jews.
(5)  pilgrimage, in the sense of visiting the Arab national shrine.

Soyuti remarked that there were no Islamic legal penalties in the
Meccan period for the simple reason that no laws had yet been
enacted. Ja'bari considered every *sura* which imposes an obligation
to be unquestionably Madinan. 'Ā'esha is reported to have said:
"In the Meccan Qor'ān, heaven and hell are the only subjects.
Permission and prohibition entered after the spread of Islam."

At Madina the times were different. Laws and regulations
enacted in the last decade of the Prophet's career not only gave
Islam a new legal stamp but also paved the way for the formation of
an Arab state.

The opening move was the change of the direction of the prayer
from the Furthest Mosque (*ol-Masjed ol-Aqsā*) at Jerusalem to the
Ka'ba at Mecca. One result was that the Jews were thereafter taxed
separately from the Moslems. Another was that the Arabs of
Madina cast off their inferiority complex and that the Arabs in
general were stirred to a sort of national fervor; for all the tribes
revered the Ka'ba, which from being an idol-temple became the
house of Abraham and Ishmael, common ancestors of every Arab.

Similarly in the matter of fasting, Islam's legislator ceased to
follow the example of the Jews and changed the duration of the fast
from the tenth day of the month of Moharram, which was their
practice, to a number of days in the month of Ramadān and later to
the whole of Ramadān.

Also dating entirely from the Madinan period are the rules on
marriage, kindred and affinity, polygamy, divorce, menstruation,

inheritance, punishment of adultery and theft, retaliation and compensation for murder and injury, and other civil and penal matters, together with the rules on matters such as defilement, circumcision, and food and drink bans. Although these rules were for the most part derived from either Jewish laws or pagan Arab customs, various changes and adaptations were made. Irrespective of their Jewish and pagan coloring, their purpose was unquestionably to establish order in the community and in the mutual relations of its members. The civilization of every community or nation is colored by elements from the civilizations of others.

In every religion there are rites which require some sort of organization and training. The details of their content and form are generally of little intrinsic importance. No thoughtful person, however, can discern any philosophical reason for pilgrimage (*hajj*) to Mecca and for the useless and meaningless rites which the pilgrims perform.

The Prophet Mohammad's decision to set out on a visit to the Ka'ba in 6 A.H./628 is puzzling. Did he really believe the Ka'ba to be God's abode? Or did he make this move in order to placate followers for whom Ka'ba-visitation was an ancestral tradition? Was his decision, which came unexpectedly in view of the resolve of the hostile Qorayshites to prevent Moslems from entering Mecca, and which led to the disappointing truce of Hodaybiya, a political stratagem designed to impress the Qoraysh chiefs with Moslem numerical and military strength and to draw ordinary, unfanatical Meccans to the new religion? How could the man who had introduced the new religion and laws and had repudiated all the beliefs and superstitions of his own people now revive the main component of the old tradition in a new form? Islam's zealous founder and legislator had above all insisted on pure monotheism, telling the people that belief in the One God is the only road to happiness and proclaiming that "the noblest among you in God's sight are the most pious among you" (*sura* 49, verse 13). Had he now succumbed to national or racial feeling? Did he want to make veneration of Ishmael's house a symbol of Arab national identity?

However that may be, the decision was so surprising and so inconsistent with Islamic principles that many Moslems were upset. Several believers objected to the running between Safā and Marwa because it had been a pagan Arab rite; but its retention was imposed by verse 153 of *sura* 2, "Safā and Marwa are among God's waymarks." According to well authenticated reports, 'Omar b.

ol-Khattāb, who was one of Mohammad's greatest and wisest companions, said that he would never have kissed the black stone if he had not personally seen the Prophet kiss it. Ghazzāli,[51] whose authority in Islamic matters deserves respect, wrote frankly that he could find no explanation of the *hajj* ritual but obeyed because it was an accomplished fact.

There is one verse in the Qor'ān which sheds some light on the matter and is perhaps an answer to questions about it. This is verse 28 of *sura* 9 (*ot-Tawba*): "O believers, it is a fact that the polytheists are unclean. Therefore they shall not approach the Mosque of the Sanctuary (i.e. the Ka'ba) after this year of theirs. If you fear poverty, God will enrich you from His bounty." According to the *Tafsir ol-Jalālayn*, this meant that God would compensate the Arabs with victories and receipts of tribute. The *sura* of Repentance (*ot-Tawba*) is chronologically the last in the Qor'ān, having been sent down in 10 A.H./631, well after the Moslem conquest of Mecca. The ban on visitation of the Ka'ba by non-Moslem tribes was likely to disquiet the people of Mecca, whose livelihood and flourishing trade depended on the coming and going of Arab tribes and groups. Although the Meccans were of the same tribe as the Prophet, most of them had only become Moslem under duress. If Mecca should lose its prosperity, there might be a risk of widespread apostasy. That risk would be averted by making pilgrimage to Mecca incumbent on Moslems.

This explanation is of course a mere hypothesis; to what extent it corresponds to the reality can never be known. In any case no rational or religious justification can be found for the retention of ancient pagan practices in the ritual of the Islamic *hajj*. This prompted the great and universally admired philosopher-poet of the Arabs, Abu'l-'Alā ol-Ma'arri,[52] to exclaim:

> People come from far corners of the land
> to throw pebbles (at the Satan) and to kiss the (black) stone.
> How strange are the things they say!
> Is all mankind becoming blind to truth?

The bans on wine-drinking and gambling, which were proclaimed at Madina and are peculiar to Islamic law, can readily be attributed to contemporary social conditions. Nor is it difficult to understand why at Madina the *zakāt* ceased to be voluntary alms-giving and was transformed into a system of income and property taxation appropriate for the fiscal needs of the newly founded state. At the same time, however, legal form was given to an obligation which has no parallel in other canons or statutes, namely the obligation of holy war (*jehād*).

At first war was only permitted; in the words of *sura* 22, verse 40, "Permission is given to those who fight because they have been wronged." Subsequently it was made obligatory through verbs in the imperative and emphatic moods. Many passages in *suras* 2 (*ol-Baqara*), 8 (*ol-Anfāl*), 9 (*ot-Tawba*), and other Madinan revelations enjoin use of force. It is a remarkable and significant fact that the Meccan *suras* contain no mentions of holy war or fighting polytheists, whereas the Madinan *suras* are so full of verses on the subject that this obligation appears to be more heavily stressed than any other. Two comments spring to the mind in this connection. One is that the Prophet Mohammad, being aware of the difficulty of controlling unruly Arabs and forming an Islamic state and society without recourse to the sword, probably chose that method because it was rooted in Arab custom and capable of influencing the Arab mind. The other is that the method necessarily involves trampling on the most precious of human rights, namely the right to freedom of thought and belief. This has evoked widespread criticism, which is not easily answerable. Is use of the sword to force people into profession of a doctrine or a religion meritorious? Is it compatible with ideals of justice and humanity?

Obviously injustice and evil have in varying degrees permeated many communities in different times and places; but to discerning minds there is no tyranny more cruel, irrational, and pernicious than a ruler's or a ruling group's denial of the people's freedom to think and to believe. Attempts by a ruler or government to suppress opposition, though inconsistent with humane principles, may be presented as moves in the struggle for political survival; but attempts to compel all the people to think and feel in the same way as the power-holders cannot in any circumstances be excused. History shows, however, that all nations have at times experienced oppression of this type. Disregard for human rights and individual personality is a very widespread and multiform phenomenon, by no means confined to ruling groups; it is also found among the masses, who can be as opinionated as any tyrant and equally intolerant of ideas and beliefs other than their own. Such fanaticism has been the source of dark phases in the life of mankind. It has impelled men to burn, behead, hang, mutilate, and immure their fellows, and not only this, but also to perpetrate wholesale massacres. In our own age there are the examples of Nazi and communist bloodshed on a vast scale.

The fact that freedom of thought and belief has been violated in many countries around the world is not in dispute. The question requiring study is whether such violation was consistent with the duty of the spiritual guide who had made known that "there is no compulsion in religion" (sura 2, verse 257), and that God had decided that "those who perished should perish by a clear sign, and those who survived should survive by a clear sign" (sura 8, verse 44). Had not God said to His Apostle, "We sent you only as a mercy to the world's peoples" (sura 21, verse 107), and "You have moral strength" (sura 68, verse 4)?

The occasion of the revelation of the Meccan sura 90 (ol-Balad) is said to have been the boastful behavior of a man named Abu'l-Ashadd, who possessed great bodily strength as well as great wealth. According to a report which has come down, he used to stand on a carpet at the 'Okāz fair and offer a huge reward to anyone who could pull it from under his feet; young men used to rush up and pull the carpet from all sides until it tore, but could never shift him from where he stood. Over against such vanity, the Surat ol-Balad movingly expresses the Prophet Mohammad's faith. Unfortunately its eloquence and euphony cannot be conveyed in another language. The following translation is an attempt to give the meaning of verses 4–18:

"We created mankind in trouble (i.e. helpless). Does he think that no one is stronger than he is? He says, 'I have spent vast wealth.' Does he think that no one has seen him? Have not we given him eyes and a tongue and lips, and shown him the two ways? Yet he has not scaled the pass. And do you know what the pass is? It is freeing a slave, or giving food in a day of famine to a kindred orphan or to a poor person in need. Then he would be one of those who believe and urge each other to forbearance and urge each other to mercy."

The apostle who had so movingly preached faith and compassion at Mecca gradually changed course at Madina and began to issue orders for war: "Fighting is prescribed for you" (sura 2, verse 212); "Fight those who do not believe.... !" (sura 9, verse 29); "If anyone desires a religion other than Islam, it will not be accepted from him" (sura 3, verse 79); "When you meet unbelievers, it is (a matter of) smiting necks. Then, after you have cowed them with much slaughter, fasten the bonds tight!" (sura 47, verse 4).

Dozens of equally stern verses were revealed at Madina. The value of iron, unmentioned at Mecca, is appraised as follows in verse 25 of the Madinan *sura* 57 (*ol-Hadid*): "And We sent down iron, (because) in it lie great power and benefits for the people, and so that God in the unseen world may know who support Him and His Apostles." At Mecca, so it seems, either iron had not existed or God in His omniscience had not given thought to means of identifying His and His Prophets' adversaries; for at Mecca God had commanded Mohammad to "summon (people) to your Lord's path with wisdom and good preaching, and argue with them by (using arguments) that are better! Your Lord knows well who have erred from His path, and He knows well who have been (rightly) guided" (*sura* 16, *on-Nahl*, verse 126).

Thus Islam was gradually transformed from a purely spiritual mission into a militant and punitive organization whose progress depended on booty from raids and revenue from the *zakāt* tax.

The Prophet's steps in the decade after the *hejra* were directed to the end of establishing and consolidating a religion-based state. Some of the deeds which were done on his command, such as killings of prisoners and political assassinations, have been adversely judged by foreign critics.

After the battle of Badr, the Prophet was uncertain what to do with the prisoners whom the Moslems had captured. Should he release them in return for ransoms which would be useful as pay for the warriors of Islam? Should he keep them as slaves? Or should he intern them? His realistic and far-sighted companion 'Omar, who must be regarded as one of the founders of the Islamic state, advised that they should be killed. In 'Omar's reckoning, release of the prisoners for ransoms would be unwise because they would rejoin the enemy and fight more bitterly, while enslavement or internment of them would involve too much expense on guarding because of the risk of their escape; but killing them would cow the tribes and enhance Islam's military prestige. The decision came when verse 68 of *sura* 8 (*ol-Anfāl*) was revealed: "It is not for a Prophet to have prisoners until he has spread fear of slaughter in the land. You people want casual gain (i.e. ransom payments) in this lower world, while God wants (happiness in) the next world (for you)."

Among the prisoners taken at Badr were two men named 'Oqba b. Abi Mo'ayt and on-Nadr b. ol-Hāreth. The Prophet, on seeing them, remembered their hostility and malice at Mecca and ordered that they should be beheaded. Nadr was the captive of ol-Meqdād b. 'Amr, who very much wanted some ransom money. Meqdād said to the Prophet, "This man is my prisoner, so I am entitled to him as my share of the booty." The Prophet asked Meqdād whether he had forgotten what this vile man had said about the Qor'ānic revelations. It was Nadr who had said at Mecca, "We have already heard (such things). If we wished, we could say (things) like this. They are only fables of the ancients" (sura 8, verse 31). Death was the penalty which Nadr finally paid for that utterance. Meqdād withdrew his claim, and Nadr was beheaded. At the next halt, 'Oqba was brought before the Prophet, and 'Āsem b. Thābet was ordered to put him to death. 'Oqba cried out, "What is to happen to my children?" The Prophet answered "Hellfire."

When Mecca was conquered, a general amnesty was proclaimed, but certain exceptions were made. The Prophet gave orders for the killing of six persons wherever they might be found, even in the sanctuary of the Ka'ba. They were Safwān b. Omayya, 'Abdollāh b. ol-Khatal, Meqyas b. Sobāba, 'Ekrema b. Abi Jahl, ol-Howayreth b. Noqaydh b. Wahb, and 'Abdollāh b. Sa'd b. Abi Sarh.

The last-named had for some time been one of the scribes employed at Madina to write down the revelations. On a number of occasions he had, with the Prophet's consent, changed the closing words of verses. For example, when the Prophet had said "And God is mighty and wise" ('aziz, hakim), 'Abdollah b. Abi Sarh suggested writing down "knowing and wise" ('alim, hakim), and the Prophet answered that there was no objection. Having observed a succession of changes of this type, 'Abdollāh renounced Islam on the ground that the revelations, if from God, could not be changed at the prompting of a scribe such as himself. After his apostasy he went to Mecca and joined the Qorayshites.

'Abdollāh b. ol-Khatal owned two slave-girls, named Fartanā and Qariba, who had sung satirical songs about the Prophet; both of them, as well as he, were put to death. Two more women, Hend b. 'Otba and Sārā, a freed slave of 'Amr b. Hāshem of the Banu 'Abd ol-Mottaleb, who had also caused great annoyance to the Prophet, were condemned to death; but Hend b. 'Otba, who was the wife of Abu Sofyān, finally professed allegiance and was spared.

'Abdollāh b. Abi Sarh was a foster-brother of 'Othmān. He took refuge with 'Othmān, who kept him hidden for several days until the commotion subsided, and then brought him to the Prophet and requested pardon for him. After a long silence, the Prophet said "Yes", meaning that he reluctantly accepted 'Othmān's intercession. Thereupon 'Abdollāh b. Abi Sarh professed Islam again, and 'Othmān and he departed. The Prophet, when asked the reason for the long silence, replied, "His Islam was not voluntary but from fear, so I was reluctant to accept it. I was expecting one of you to stand up and behead him." (This was because it had been proclaimed that his blood might be lawfully shed in any place where he might be found, "even if clinging to the covering of the Ka'ba"). One of the Ansār from Madina asked the Prophet why he had not winked, and received the answer that "God's Apostle cannot have false eyes", meaning that he could not falsely pretend silence while giving a sign with the eyes to kill. This same 'Abdollāh b. Abi Sarh was chosen during 'Othmān's caliphate to command the Arab invading force in North Africa; he acquitted himself so well that 'Othmān dismissed 'Amr b. ol-'Ās, the conqueror of Egypt, and appointed 'Abdollāh to the governorship.

The assassination of Ka'b b. ol-Ashraf of the Jewish tribe of the Banu'n-Nadir has already been briefly mentioned. After the battle of Badr, being alarmed by the growth of the Prophet's power, Ka'b went to Mecca where he expressed sympathy for the Qorayshites and urged them to keep up the fight. Later he returned to Madina and addressed amatory verses to Moslem women. This gave a pretext to the Prophet, who asked his followers, "Who will deal with Ebn ol-Ashraf for me?" A man named Mohammad b. Maslama stood up and volunteered. The Prophet said to him, "Do it if you can!" He then sent Mohammad b. Maslama on the task together with four other Awsites. One of them was Ka'b's foster-brother Abu Nā'ela, whose presence would ensure that Ka'b would not become suspicious and unwilling to step out of his fortified house on the outskirts of Madina. The Prophet accompanied them to the edge of the town, where he bade them farewell and prayed God to help them. The five men made their way by night to Ka'b's house. Ka'b, seeing Abu Nā'ela among them, stepped unsuspectingly out of his house to talk with them, and then set out with these glib friends toward the town. They kept him talking until, at a safe distance from the house, they pounced on him and, after a struggle, killed him. When they reached Madina, they found the Prophet awake and waiting for good news.

Sallām b. Abi'l-Hoqayq, another influential Jew and an old friend of the Awsites, had moved from Madina to Khaybar. Some Khazrajites asked the Prophet for permission to go and kill this leader of the Jews and ally of the Aws tribe. The Prophet gave permission and appointed 'Abdollāh b. 'Atik to lead the squad. They accomplished the task, and on their return informed the Prophet of this success, shouting joyfully "God is great."

After the elimination of Ka'b and Sallām, a squad under the leadership of 'Abdollāh b. Rawāha was sent to kill Yosayr b. Rezām, another Madinan Jew who had gone to Khaybar and was inciting the Banu Ghatafān, a big Beduin tribe, to fight Mohammad.

At Nakhla, Khāled b. Sofyān, a chief of the Hodhayl tribe, was provoking hostility to Mohammad among its people. The Prophet appointed 'Abdollāh b. Onays to go and deal with him. He too was successfully eliminated.

When Refā'a b. Qays started an anti-Moslem agitation in his tribe, the Prophet ordered 'Abdollāh b. Abi Hadrad to go and bring back his head. The killer fulfilled the task by first ambushing Refā'a and shooting him with an arrow, then knocking him down with an axe, and then cutting off his head, which he brought to the Prophet.

'Amr b. Omayya was commissioned to kill Abu Sofyān, but Abu Sofyān got word and eluded him. Instead, 'Amr killed a harmless Qorayshite and another man on his way back to Madina.

Abu 'Afak, a man of great age (reputedly 120 years), was killed because he had lampooned Mohammad. The deed was done by Sālem b. 'Omayr at the behest of the Prophet, who had asked, "Who will deal with this rascal for me?" The killing of such an old man moved a poetess, 'Asmā b. Marwān, to compose disrespectful verses about the Prophet, and she too was assassinated.

Two prisoners taken at Badr, Abu 'Azza ol-Jomahi and Mo'āwiya b. Moghira, had been freed on parole and allowed to live at Madina. After the Moslem defeat at the battle of Ohod, Mo'āwiya b. Moghira absconded and Abu 'Azza ol-Jomahi petitioned Mohammad for release. The Prophet ordered the immediate execution of Abu 'Azza and the capture and execution of Mo'āwiya b. Moghira. Both orders were carried out. Abu 'Azza's executioner was Zobayr b. ol-'Awwām.

One of the leading men of Madina was a Khazrajite chief, 'Abdollāh b. Obayy. He had professed Islam, but when the situation changed and he saw the growth of Mohammad's social and political influence, he became alarmed and ceased to manifest sincere faith. He was reckoned to be the chief of the hypocrites (*monāfequn*). Various intrigues took place and were disclosed to the Prophet. 'Omar eventually came to the conclusion that 'Abdollāh b. Obayy would have to be killed. On the other hand Sa'd b. 'Obāda, a Khazrajite and a leader of the Ansār, advised the Prophet to be lenient with him because "God, by sending you to us, saved us from his ambition to be our ruler. Otherwise we should have been on the point of giving him a crown and a signet."

Mohammad Hosayn Haykal,[53] the modern biographer of Mohammad, has written that the Prophet said to 'Omar at that time, "If I had acted on your advice and killed 'Abdollāh b. Obayy, his kinsmen would have retaliated to avenge him; but his conduct has been so objectionable that if I now give the order, even his kinsmen will carry it out." According to Haykal, 'Abdollāh b. Obayy's own son offered to kill him, if the Prophet so ordered, rather than let other men carry out the order, in which case the son would be obliged by Arab custom to take vengeance on the killers.

Soyuti states that 'Abdollāh b. Obayy's conduct was the occasion of the revelation of verse 90 of *sura* 4 (*on-Nesā*): "What is the matter with you people that, in regard to the hypocrites, you are two parties? God has set them back as they deserved. Do you people wish to guide a man whom God has led astray?" According to Soyuti, the Prophet in his exasperation with 'Abdollāh b. Obayy had asked the people whether anyone was willing to rid him of this man who was always gathering opponents in his house and trying to cause trouble.

In the event, 'Abdollāh b. Obayy was spared. He died in 9 A.H./631, and the Prophet conducted his funeral.

Sometimes killings which were really motivated either by desire to make a show of valor or by personal grudge were passed off as services to Islam. For example there was a Jewish shopkeeper at Madina who had Moslem customers and was on good terms with them. On the day when the Prophet gave the order to "kill every Jew whom you have captured," Mohayyesa b. Mas'ud ran out and killed the harmless shopkeeper, whose name was Ebn Sonayna. The only person who reproached Mohayyesa was his own brother.

When the campaign of 8 A.H./639 against the Romans was

being planned, news reached the Prophet that some men were gathering in the house of a Jew named Showaylem to discuss ways of opposing the enterprise. The Prophet ordered Talha b. 'Obaydollāh and some others to besiege and set fire to the house. Only one man was able to get out, and in doing so he broke his leg. There is a reference in verse 82 of *sura* 9 (*ot-Tawba*) to persons who did not wish to join in the campaign because of the heat: "And they have said, 'Do not march out in the heat!' Say, 'The fire of hell is hotter!'"

## PROPHETHOOD AND RULERSHIP

To form a picture of Mohammad in the role of Prophet, we must study the Meccan *suras*, particularly those such as 23 (*ol-Mo'menin*) and 53 (*on-Najm*) which radiate a Christ-like spirituality. To see him in the role of ruler, statesman, and legislator, we must turn to the Madinan *suras* such as 2 (*ol-Baqara*), 4 (*on-Nesā*), 47 (*Mohammad*), and above all 9 (*ot-Tawba*).

Three or four years after the *hejra*, and especially after the elimination of the Madinan Jews and the defeat of the Banu Mostaleq (a Beduin tribe occupying land to the west of the town), signs of rulership began to appear in Mohammad's conduct as well as his decrees.

There is a story in Ebn Heshām's biography of the Prophet that Safiya, the daughter of Hoyayy b. Akhtab of the Jewish Nadir tribe, dreamed that the moon came down onto her lap. When she told her husband, Kenāna b. Abi Rabi'a, about her dream, he angrily slapped her face, so hard that her eyes went dim, and shouted, "You hope to become the wife of the king of the Hejāz." As it happened, the Prophet, after conquering Khaybar, added this woman to the number of his wives.

Another report states that when a Jewish notable, 'Abdollāh b. Sallām of the Banu Qaynoqā', accepted Islam, the Jews said to him, "You know perfectly well that the prophethood belongs to the Children of Israel, not to the Arabs. Your new master is not a prophet. He is a king."

When Abu Sofyān accepted Islam under duress, he is reported to have said to 'Abbas b. 'Abd ol-Mottaleb, "Your nephew has a huge territory." 'Abbās answered him, "Yes. It is the realm of the prophethood."

'Omar b. ol-Khattāb, soon to become a great figure in the history of Islam, was a man whom the Prophet trusted and respected. It was because of 'Omar's sincerity and strength of character that Mohammad at the start of the prophetic mission was keenly anxious to bring him into the Moslem inner circle. The Prophet's assent to the truce of Hodaybiya in 6 A.H./628 was a bitter disappointment to 'Omar, who saw it as a humiliating reverse. What happened was that the Prophet with a large number of followers and Beduin set out for Mecca with the announced intention of performing the pilgrimage. The Qorayshites, on hearing the news, made military preparations to prevent their entry into Mecca. The Moslems then halted at Hodaybiya, about 6 km. from Mecca, and sent representatives to parley with the Qorayshite chiefs. Finally agreement was reached on a truce whereby the Moslems were to withdraw but would be permitted to visit the Ka'ba in the following year. 'Omar thought that the Qoraysh had made Mohammad accept all their demands, and told him so in such vehement words that the Prophet lost his temper and shouted "May your mother mourn for you!" Faced with the Prophet's wrath, 'Omar held his tongue.

The Mohammad who assented to the truce of Hodaybiya was no longer the Mohammad who ten or twelve years earlier had been so anxious to bring men like 'Omar and Hamza into Islam. The withdrawal and surrender to the Qorayshite demands were presented in a different light with the timely revelation of verse 1 of *sura* 48 (*ol-Fat-h*): "We have given you a manifest victory." Everyone now approved, and even 'Omar's indignation was soothed by the tactful Abu Bakr.

Although the truce of Hodaybiya was in some respects a reverse and therefore an occasion for protest by 'Omar, events proved it to have been an example of the Prophet's political sagacity. In all probability he agreed to it because he was not sure that the Moslems could beat the Qoraysh if fighting broke out. A temporary compromise and truce would be safer than a battle of uncertain outcome. A Moslem defeat would embolden the Qoraysh and bring to their side Beduin tribes resentful of his growing influence, as well as aggrieved Jews. The position of the Moslems would then be precarious. Prudent considerations such as these are likely to have passed through the Prophet's mind. In any case he was now less concerned with posing a challenge than with establishing a state. He probably accepted the Qorayshite

terms in confident expectation of sufficient growth of his power
and prestige to ensure that he and his followers could perform the
pilgrimage a year later without risk of trouble or defeat.

The hypothesis that the truce of Hodaybiya was an act of
prudent statesmanship is supported by analysis of the Prophet's
next enterprise. One of the risks of war with the Qoraysh was that
many Mohājerun, having kinsmen in Mecca or being susceptible
to Qorayshite influence, might not fight wholeheartedly. An attack
on the last stronghold of the Jews, namely the oasis of Khaybar,
would involve no such risk and would also offer morale-raising
prospects of booty.

Some sentences in *sura* 48 (*ol-Fat-h*) throw light on the matter:

> "God was well pleased with the believers when they were
> swearing loyalty to you under the tree, and He knew
> what was in their hearts" (verse 18).

At Hodaybiya, at a time when a battle with the Qoraysh seemed
likely, the Prophet had assembled the Moslems under a tree and
obtained their solemn promise to fight if the Qoraysh proved
obdurate. In Islamic history this is known as the Oath of Good
Pleasure (*Bay'at or-Redwān*), i.e. the oath with which God was
well pleased.

> "And He made them worthy of an imminent victory" (verse 18),
> "and much booty which they will take" (verse 19).
> "God promises you men much booty which you will
> take, and He will hasten it for you. And He
> kept the people's hands off you" (verse 20).

After concluding the truce, Mohammad hastened back from
Hodaybiya to Madina and stayed only a fortnight in the town to
mobilize troops before marching against Khaybar. He feared that
the Moslems might quarrel over the Hodaybiya truce terms, and
knew that at Khaybar they would be too busy taking booty to
worry any more about the alleged surrender to the Qorayshites.

It is clear from verse 15 of *sura* 48 that hope of booty from
Khaybar thrilled the Beduin so much that those who had shown
reluctance to confront the Qoraysh sought eagerly to join the
Moslem warriors in the attack on the rich oasis: "Those who
lagged behind will say, when you set out to take booty, let us

accompany you!" After this, in verse 16, God commands the Prophet, "Say to the laggards among the Beduin, 'You will be summoned against a people possessing great strength, to fight them unless they surrender. If you obey, God will reward you well. If you turn back, as you turned back before, He will punish you painfully.'"

The Khaybar oasis contained a number of castles. On the first day the Moslems attacked the castle of Sallām b. Meshkam and lost nearly fifty men before they took it. Abu Bakr led another detachment against the castle of Nā'om, but achieved nothing and was replaced by 'Omar, whose assault also failed; it was 'Ali b. Abi Tāleb who finally broke into this castle. Later the water-supply of the castle of Zabir was cut, and its occupants had to come out; they fought but eventually fled. Several more castles fell, one after the other, to the Moslems. Finally the Moslems reached the castles of os-Salālem and ol-Watih where the women and children had been concentrated. The Jews had to ask for a cease-fire, and the Prophet decided that their lives should be spared and that the cultivated lands of Khaybar should become the property of the Moslems but be left in the occupation of the Jews on condition that they should cede half of the annual produce to the Moslems.

Included in the Prophet's share of the booty was the Jewish woman Safiya, the daughter of Hoyayy b. Akhtab – the same woman who had been slapped by her husband for mentioning her dream of the moon's descent onto her lap. The Prophet married her on his way back to Madina.

The oasis of Fadak, east of Khaybar, was also inhabited by Jews. Warned by the example of Khaybar, they surrendered without fighting and agreed to cede half of their property. Not having been taken by force, this property was assigned to the Prophet.

The Jewish tribes living in the Wādi ol-Qorā and at Taymā, to the north of Madina, also surrendered. The terms required them to pay tribute in the form of a poll-tax (jezya).

These victories brought the whole of the northern part of the Hejāz under Mohammad's rule.

It must be added that in the Khaybar campaign Mohammad made good use of diplomacy. He first took care to win over the neighboring Beduin tribe of the Banu Ghatafān, who might otherwise have helped the Jews and greatly impeded the Moslems. He decided that half of the booty of Khaybar should go to the Banu Ghatafān.

These and other actions show that after the *hejra* the Prophet Mohammad was more occupied with politics than with preaching.

In the Moslem raids, the usual tactic was the ambush, which in many cases was mounted after a reconnaissance by carefully chosen spies. Several Qorayshite trading caravans were successfully spotted and attacked in this way. The raids served the dual purpose of inflicting financial damage on opponents and providing booty and encouragement for supporters.

The defeat of the Moslems at the battle of Mount Ohod near Madina in 3 A.H./625 was a severe shock but not a decisive blow. Instead of pushing on to Madina, the Qorayshite force under Abu Sofyān went back to Mecca after the battle. The Moslems would not have been beaten if they had adhered to the Prophet's strategy and stayed in their positions on the slopes of the mountain; but some of them greedily rushed down in the hope of seizing booty and suffered considerable losses.

Danger again faced the Moslems in 5 A.H./627 when allied Qorayshite and Beduin forces besieged Madina. This event is known in Islamic history as the war of the trench, because the Moslems, in anticipation of the siege, had with great effort dug a trench around the town. The use of trenches, hitherto unknown in Arab warfare, is said in some of the sources to have been suggested by Salmān ol-Fārsi, the first Iranian convert to Islam. The Qorayshites were again led by Abu Sofyān. None of the besiegers were able to cross the trench, but there was a risk that the Jewish Qorayza tribe inside the town might combine with them. If that had occurred, the Moslems might have been decisively beaten and the rise of Islam might have been cut short. Thanks to Mohammad's cunning, however, the danger was averted, and within a fortnight the Beduin and the Meccans retired. During the conflict, the Prophet employed a man of the Ghatafān tribe who had secretly become a Moslem to sow dissension between the Banu Qorayza and the besiegers. Since this man, named No'aym b. Mas'ud, had a long record of friendship with the Jews and was also on good terms with the Qorayshites, all the parties supposed him to be an opponent of Mohammad, and each was persuaded by him to suspect the other. After losing hope of any collaboration with the Banu Qorayza, the Qorayshite troops suffered hardship in a sudden tempest of cold wind and decided to return to Mecca.

It has already been mentioned that as soon as the siege and the Qorayshite threat to Madina were over, the Prophet Mohammad sent an armed band to the street of the Banu Qorayza. Since their refusal to collaborate with Abu Sofyān hàd been the main reason for the outcome of the war to the Moslem advantage, they might have been thought to deserve at least the Prophet's lenience. Nevertheless Mohammad decided to eliminate them because their continued presence within Madina would present a potential danger. Their destruction would spread fear of the power of Islam, provide booty for the Moslems, and make the Awsites and Khazrajites more firmly loyal to his flag.

The burning of the palm grove of the Banu'n-Nadir in 4 A.H./625 had been a dishonorable act by contemporary standards. It was done, regardless of protests, because it was the necessary means to the end of overcoming them. Qor'ānic verses (sura 59, ol-Hashr, 2–17) were sent down to justify the Prophet's conduct. The same destructive expedient was used in the Moslem blockade of the vineyard of the Banu Thaqif at Tā'ef in 8 A.H./630. First the delivery of food to the encamped occupants was stopped, but soon it became clear that they had a large stock of food and that a long siege would be necessary. For fear that the Moslem troops, in keeping with the fickle character of the Arabs, might then become tired or bored, the Prophet ordered them to burn down the vineyard. The vines were such an important source of income that the Banu Thaqif sent a messenger to the Prophet, begging him to desist from the destruction and offering the ownership of the entire vineyard to the Moslems.

Later in the same campaign, the Prophet abandoned the siege of Tā'ef and went to Mecca to distribute booty taken from the Hawāzen tribe. He then sent a message to Mālek b. 'Awf, one of the chiefs of the Banu Thaqif, offering to release his wife and children and give him a hundred camels if he would become a Moslem. Mālek b. 'Awf secretly left Tā'ef and professed Islam in the Prophet's presence.

All these reports come in early source-books and are well authenticated. The record of events in the first years of Islam gives ample evidence of the contemporary mentality and of the reasons for the progress of Mohammad's cause and the spread of the new religion.

The defeat of the Hawāzen, which took place soon after the conquest of Mecca and before the siege of Tā'ef, yielded a large amount of booty. When the time for its distribution came, the Moslems were overwhelmed by greed. They feared that their shares of it would be reduced by the Prophet's generosity to new converts; for he had given a hundred camels each to Abu Sofyān and his son Mo'āwiya, to ol-Hāreth b. ol-Hāreth, ol-Hāreth b. Heshām, Sohayl b. 'Amr, and Howayteb b. 'Abd ol-'Ozzā, and smaller presents to lesser Qorayshite notables, all of whom had only professed Islam under duress after the conquest of Mecca. The Prophet's Madinan supporters (Ansār) were particularly discontented, and their leader, Sa'd b. 'Obāda, informed the Prophet of their feelings. The Prophet then summoned the Ansār and reassured them with a speech which gives some idea of his diplomacy and skill in handling people. At the end of it he asked, "O men of my Ansār, is it not better that other men should take away camels and you should take back God's Apostle with you?"

The reports of Mohammad's deeds and words in the decade which he spent at Madina give plenty of evidence of his statesmanship. A percipient reader of the biographies of the Prophet will find perhaps a hundred times more examples than those chosen for mention here.

According to the *Tafsir ol-Jalālayn*, verses 106–108 of *sura* 4 (*on-Nesā*) were revealed on the occasion of the following incident. A man named To'ma b. Ebriq stole a suit of armor and hid it in the house of a Jew. The owner of the armor found it there, and To'ma, when suspicion fell on him, swore that he was not guilty of the theft and accused a Jew. To'ma's relatives laid the case before the Prophet, hoping to exonerate him and of course expecting that Mohammad would favor him against a Jew. Mohammad did nothing of the sort. In the award of justice, he put truth before partisanship, as verse 106 of the *sura* shows: "We have sent down the Book to you with the truth, so that you may judge between people by what God has manifested to you. Do not be an advocate for perjurors!"

Verse 9 of *sura* 49 (*ol-Hojorāt*) has a similar import and gives an indication not only of the Prophet's statesmanship but also of the contemporary social conditions and the beginnings of factionalism in Islam: "If two parties of the believers have started to fight each other, make peace between them! If one of them wrongs the other, fight against the one that is doing the wrong until it returns to God's authority! Then, if it returns, make peace equitably between them!" The verse is both clear and wise.

In the *Tafsir ol-Jalālayn* there is a report of an incident said to have been the occasion of the revelation of this verse. The story is quoted here as an illustration of the social conditions and the incipient fanaticism of some of Mohammad's supporters. "The Prophet was riding an ass and he passed 'Abdollāh b. Obayy. Just at that moment the ass staled. Ebn Obayy gripped his nose to avoid inhaling the smell. 'Abdollāh b. Rawāha (a leader of the Ansār), who happened to be there, said to Ebn Obayy, 'By God, the smell of the ass's stale is less displeasing to the Prophet than the smell of the scent you use.' These words provoked a brawl, with sticks and shoes as weapons, between Ebn Obayy's men and Ebn Rawāha's men."

In the conditions of the time, fear of the Prophet spread as his cause advanced.

After the conquest of Mecca, a poet named Bojayr b. Zohayr b. Abi Solmā wrote to his brother Ka'b, also a poet, that the Prophet was executing people at Mecca who had lampooned him or otherwise offended him, and that every poet who had done any such thing had now fled from Mecca. If Ka'b wanted to be safe, he had better go to the Prophet and apologize, because the Prophet was not killing those who repented of their past deeds. Otherwise Ka'b ought to get out and not let himself be seen anywhere around.

Ka'b b. Zohayr decided to profess Islam and save his life. He composed an ode in praise of the Prophet, known as the Ode of the Cloak (*Borda*) because the Prophet was so pleased when Ka'b recited it to him that he gave Ka'b his cloak.[54]

The people, being simple and unaccustomed to formality, at first behaved toward their leader in a familiar and unconstrained way. They thought that their only obligation was to obey the Qor'ānic commands and prohibitions. Otherwise they treated Mohammad as one of themselves. This state of affairs could not last. Orderly procedure and observance of something like the respect due to a head of a state became necessary. A number of rules for the believers, almost amounting to a code of etiquette, were set out in the first five verses of *sura* 49 (*ol-Hojorāt*) and some other Qor'ānic passages.

"O believers, do not push yourselves forward (i.e. speak or act first) in the presence of God and His Apostle!" (49, 1). Since nobody can speak or act first in God's presence, the rule can only mean "Do not voice an opinion or take an action without the Prophet's leave!"

"O believers, do not raise your voices above the Prophet's voice or shout in speaking to him, as some of you shout at each other!"

(49, 2). They should not behave as 'Omar, for example, had done when he loudly and publicly contradicted the Prophet over the Hodaybiya truce terms and addressed him as "Mohammad" instead of "God's Apostle."

"Those who lower their voices before God's Apostle are those whose hearts God has tested for piety. They will receive forgiveness and great reward" (49, 3). Clearly this form of courtesy had not been practiced by the Arabs but became appropriate after Mohammad's rise to power.

"Those who call you from the back of the apartments – most of them do not understand" (49, 4). The Arabs used to walk to the back of the Prophet's house, where the private apartments of his wives were situated, and shout "Mohammad" to summon him. The Prophet disliked this behavior, but rightly attributed it to their ignorance (or strictly speaking, God did, because the words are God's words). It had been natural and normal in the days when he joined his companions and supporters in tasks such as shoveling earth from the trench, but was unbecoming after his cause had triumphed.

"If they would wait until you come out to them, it would be better for them" (49, 5).

The most precise rule of etiquette for the believers came in verse 13 of *sura* 58 (*ol-Mojādela*): "O believers, if you wish to talk privately with the Apostle, offer a charitable gift before your private talk!" The Moslems must have found this burdensome, because the rule is relaxed later in the same verse: "If you cannot afford, God is forgiving and merciful."

The matter of access to the Prophet recurs in verse 53 of *sura* 33 (*ol-Ahzāb*): "O believers, do not walk into the Prophet's houses unless you are admitted for a meal! (And) without looking at its cooking pot![55] But if you have been invited, walk in, and when you have eaten, disperse without lingering for conversation! That would cause inconvenience to the Prophet, and he would be too shy (to tell) you. But God is not shy of the truth." The verse needs no comment and gives evidence of what used to happen. The Prophet's friends treated him with familiarity, dropped in without notice, waited for a meal to be brought for them, and stayed after the meal to chat with one another. Such things were unseemly when the Prophet was the head of a state. He needed a measure of seclusion from the people. To tell them would be embarrassing for him, but not for God who is above embarrassment. In other words,

God through the voice of His Apostle would teach the people correct behavior toward the head of the state.

This interpretation is supported by the next sentence of the same verse, though the subject is different: "And when you ask the women (i.e. the Prophet's wives) for a thing, ask them from behind a curtain![56] That is purer for their hearts and yours."

A story which appears in the Hadith compilations and is attributed to 'Ā'esha explains the sentence as follows: "The Prophet and I were eating a meal from a dish when 'Omar passed by. The Prophet invited him to join in the meal. While we were eating, 'Omar's finger touched my finger. 'Omar said, 'If only my advice had been heeded! No eye would then have seen you.' After that, the verse of the curtain was sent down."

According to a reported statement of 'Abdollāh b. ol-'Abbas, the reason for the revelation of verse 53 was that 'Omar had said to the Prophet, "Your wives are not like the wives of other men." Verse 32 of *sura* 33 begins with the words "O wives of the Prophet, you are not like any other women."

Why did the Prophet's wives differ from other women? Evidently because Mohammad was not in the same category as other men. Maintenance of his dignity required maintenance of the dignity of his wives. They would have to be secluded like oriental princesses. Verse 53 of *sura* 33 (parts of which have already been quoted) goes on to state in the last sentence: "It would not be (right) for you to offend God's Apostle by marrying his wives after him at any future time. That would be an enormity in God's sight." The reason why this sin would be such a major one was that Mohammad was sensitive about the matter. His wives, like those of ancient Israelite kings, must not be touched by other men even after his death.

A similar assumption of superiority over other people and lack of consideration for them is apparent in a different context. Verse 14 of *sura* 49, referring to events after the conquest of Mecca, states: "The Beduin have said, 'We believed.' Say (to them), 'You did not believe. Rather you should say, "We surrendered."'" Belief has not entered their hearts at all."

When the new converts protested that their acceptance of Islam had not been forced on them by coercion or war but was voluntary, verse 17 of *sura* 49 came down: "They count it as a favor to you that they have surrendered. Say, 'Do not count your surrender as a favor to me! On the contrary, God is conferring a favor on you, as He has guided you to the faith.'"

What a contrast there is between this cold, haughty tone and the glowing zeal, like that of Jeremiah, with which Mohammad had earlier condemned arrogance and enjoined charity! A good example is the Meccan *sura* 89 (*ol-Fajr*), which he is said to have recited to the people as he stood by the wall of the Ka'ba. Unfortunately this *sura* cannot be literally translated and its melodious assonances cannot be reproduced. Below is an inadequate rendering of verses 5–13 and 18–21:

"Have you not seen how your Lord dealt with 'Ād,
Eram of the pillars,[57]
the like of which was never created in the land,
and Thamud,[58] who carved the rocks in the valley,
and Pharaoh, the owner of the pegs,[59]
who were all arrogant in the land
and caused much corruption in it?
Your Lord inflicted a scourge of punishment on them.
Certainly your Lord is always watching."
. . . . . . . . . . . . . .
"No indeed! But you do not honor the orphan,
you do not bestir yourselves to feed the poor,
you eat (i.e. embezzle) inheritances greedily,
and you love wealth dearly."

At Madina the rules which were laid down had practical and disciplinary aspects. The waywardness of the Arabs needed to be curbed. This is very clearly shown by verse 96 of *sura* 4 (*on-Nesā*): "O believers, when you march forth (to war) in God's cause, make sure (of the facts) and do not say to anyone who gives you a peaceful greeting 'You are not a believer' (merely because) you desire casual gain in this lower world! God disposes of abundant booty. You were like that before, but God favored you. So make sure! God is aware of everything that you do." The occasion of the revelation of this verse is said to have been as follows. On a march, some of the Prophet's supporters encountered a shepherd of the Solaym tribe with his sheep. He greeted them by saying *salām* (peace), which was the password of the Moslems. Supposing that he had said it out of fear, they killed him and took his sheep as booty.

Some references to contemporary ways of behavior in *sura* 49 (*ol-Hojorāt*) have already been quoted. There is another in verse 11: "O believers, let no group of people deride (another) group who may perhaps be better than they are, nor women (other) women who may perhaps be better than they are! Do not find fault with each other, and do not call each other names! Rude names are sins after profession of the faith." This verse is said to have been sent down after members of the Tamim tribe had mocked some impecunious Moslems such as 'Ammār and Sohayb for being poor.

Dozens of Qor'ānic verses give instruction on morals and manners: what to do and what not to do, how to speak and when to be silent. They also give glimpses of Arab society as it was in the days of the Prophet.

## WOMEN IN ISLAM

"Look after women kindly! They are prisoners,[60] not having control of themselves at all." These words are reported to have been said by the Prophet Mohammad in a speech which he made at Mecca during his farewell pilgrimage in 9 A.H./631.

In pre-Islamic Arab society, the women did not have the status of independent persons, but were considered to be possessions of the men. All sorts of inhumane treatment of the women were permissible and customary.

Like any other chattel in a deceased man's estate, a woman was transferred to his heir, who could then make her his wife without settling any dower on her. If she was unwilling to become his wife, he could prevent her remarriage under she ceded to him whatever property she might have inherited; and if she refused to do so, he could detain her until her death when her property would pass to him. This cruel injustice was abolished by the revelation of verse 23 of *sura* 4 (*on-Nesā*): "O believers! It is not permissible for you to inherit women against their will. And do not detain them so that you may get some of what you have given them! (That is) unless they do something manifestly unchaste. And treat them properly!"

The statement that "men are the guardians of women" in verse 38 of *sura* 4 postulates inequality of men and women in civil rights. The words are followed by two brief explanations of men's superiority over women: "because of the ways in which God has favored the ones over the others, and because of what men have spent out of their wealth." The ways in which God has favored men over women are not specified.

According to the *Tafsir ol-Jalālayn*, the superiority of men lies in

113

their greater intelligence, knowledge and administrative ability. Zamakhshari,[61] Baydāwi,[62] and several other commentators go into more detail and construct metaphysical theories; they liken men's authority over women to that of rulers over subjects, and maintain that prophethood, prayer-leadership, and rulership are reserved for men because men are stronger, more intelligent, and more prudent.

In Islamic law, male heirs get more than female heirs, and men's evidence is more reliable than women's; to be exact, a man's inheritance share is twice a woman's share, and his evidence carries twice the weight of hers in the courts. The religious duties of holy war and of congregational prayer on Fridays are not incumbent on women. The right to divorce belongs to husbands but not to wives. Many functions, including utterance of the call to prayer, leadership of the congregational prayer, delivery of the Friday sermon, horse-riding, archery, and giving evidence in penal cases, are specifically reserved for men.

Readers will have observed the logical weakness of the arguments for male dominance. Nearly always the effect is misread for the cause. In reality, social conditions and customs were the cause of the reservation of many functions for men and the consequent low status of women. In contemporary opinion, however, the non-participation of women in those functions appeared to be the effect of female inferiority and incompetence. It is because Islamic law regards women as weak that female heirs and witnesses have half the worth of male ones. This lower worth is not a cause, but an effect, of the attribution of inferior status to women.

The facts are perfectly clear and cannot be explained away by specious arguments. In all primitive societies since the dawn of history, the men have borne the brunt of the struggle for means of living, and the women have therefore been relegated to the second rank or, in the words of the German philosopher F. W. Nietzsche, have been treated as second-class humans.

Among the ancient Arabs, the treatment of women as second-class humans had some more than ordinarily barbaric aspects. Through the Qor'ānic legislation, and by exhortation and admonition, the Prophet Mohammad blunted the edge of this savagery and endowed the women with a number of legal rights (specified for the most part in *sura* 4).

The arguments and theories of the Qor'ān-commentators have little or no value from a rational viewpoint, being basically attempts to justify Arab practices. For this the commentators can hardly be blamed, because they needed to show how God "has favored the ones over the others."

The second explanation of men's superiority in verse 38 of *sura* 4, namely that men spend some of their wealth on women, is logically sounder. The man shoulders the burden of the woman's expenses; therefore she is dependent on him; therefore she ought to comply with his commands and prohibitions. This is the reason why Zamakhshari, Baydāwi, and many other commentators think that the husband is the ruler or master and the wife is the subject or servant. The same conclusion can be drawn from the next sentence of verse 38 of *sura* 4: "Good women are submissive and keep secret that which God has kept secret." This means that a good wife is one who obeys her husband and keeps herself for him whenever he is absent. There is an implication that wives belong to husbands and should not forget it. *Sura* 4, however, prescribes rights and duties for both men and women; it shows how Islam's legislator helped the female sex by changing ancient Arab practices.

One example is the commandment to men in verses 24 and 25: "If you wish to replace a wife with another and have given a hundred-weight to one of them, do not take anything from it! Will you take it through slander and plain crime? How shall you take it when you have been intimate with each other and they got a concrete pledge from you?" A man wishing to divorce and remarry after enjoying his wife's services is forbidden to withhold any part of the dower, however large, which had been an agreed condition of their marriage. It can be inferred from the verse that an ancient Arab husband who repudiated his wife normally took back much or all of whatever dower he had given to her.

There is one passage, however, which apparently endorses a pre-Islamic Arab custom. This is the sentence at the end of verse 38 permitting a husband to beat his wife: "And those women whose insubordination you fear, admonish them, then leave them alone in the beds, then beat them!" Men with their greater bodily strength have certainly resorted to this unjust and unchivalrous expedient since the earliest times, and they still do so in the twentieth century. Nevertheless its authorization by the law of Islam provides ammunition for critics.

Every community's laws reflect its life-style, customs, and morals. In addition to the testimony of verse 38 of *sura* 4, there is historical evidence that the ancient Arabs considered the husband

115

to be the owner of his wife and fully entitled to inflict pain on her. Abu Bakr's daughter Asmā, who was the fourth wife of Zobayr b. ol-'Awwām (one of the Prophet's first ten converts and principal companions), is reported to have said, "Whenever Zobayr was angry with one of us, he used to beat her until the stick broke." The Islamic law on this subject has at least the merit of gradation. First admonition, next cessation of intercourse, and only in the last resort violence should be used to make the wife obey. In the opinion of several commentators and lawyers, the beating should not be so severe as to break a bone, because in that case the legal right to retaliation in kind and degree might be invoked. Zamakhshari, however, writes in his comment on the verse that "some authorities do not accept gradation of the punishment of the insubordinate wife but consider infliction of any of the three penalties to be permissible." This was of course the interpretation given to the words by fanatical Arab theologians such as Ebn Hanbal and Ebn Taymiya.[63] Nevertheless, the meaning of the words is clear and moreover confirmed by what follows in verse 39: "And if you fear a breach between the two, send an arbiter from his kinsfolk and an arbiter from her kinsfolk in case they desire reconciliation."

The forbidden degrees of kindred and affinity in marriage, specified in verse 27 of *sura* 4, are for the most part found in Jewish law and were also observed by the pagan Arabs, though with some exceptions. Verse 26 states, "Do not marry women whom your fathers married, unless it has already been done!" The ordinance and in particular the qualification indicate that this vile practice was current among the Arabs before Islam.

The prohibition of marriage to already married women in verse 28 of this *sura* is not novel. What is remarkable is the exception which the verse makes in favor of owners of female slaves. A female slave acquired by purchase or captured in war may be taken in marriage without moral compunction or legal impediment even though she already has a husband. An explanation is given in a report quoted by Ebn Sa'd:[64] "Some female captives fell into our hands in the fighting at Awtās (near Honayn), and as they had husbands, we refrained from intercourse with them and consulted the Prophet. Then came the revelation of the words (in verse 28), 'Also (forbidden to you) are married women, except any that your right hands have acquired.' Possession of those captives was thus made lawful for us."

Yet the same verse 28 gives evidence both of the Prophet's concern for women's rights and of the contemporary malpractices. The last three sentences state: "It is lawful for you, apart from that (i.e. that which is forbidden), to seek them with your wealth, taking them in marriage, not in prostitution. And to such women as you (thus) enjoy, pay them their rewards, an obligatory portion! There will be no sin for you in what you mutually agree after (payment of) the obligatory portion."

On the words "to such women as you (thus) enjoy, pay them their rewards" (i.e. dower) hangs the question whether temporary marriage[65] is permissible in Islamic law. The Sonnite scholars consider it impermissible because they think that the revelation of these words occurred after the Moslem conquest of Mecca and was valid for three days only, after which it expired. The Shi'ites, however, hold this form of marriage to be religiously sanctioned.

The social conditions and the importance of the pecuniary factor in the relations between men and women in those days are made plain in another Qor'ānic ordinance, which comes in verse 10 of *sura* 60 (*ol-Momtahana*): "O believers, when women who have professed the faith come to you as emigrants, test them! God will know about their faith. And if you find them to be believers, do not send them back to the unbelievers! They will be illicit for the unbelievers, and the unbelievers will be illicit for them. But repay them (i.e. the unbelievers) what they have spent (i.e. on those women)! Then there will be no sin for you in marrying them if you pay them their rewards. And do not hold fast to (marital) ties with unbelieving women! Ask for what you have spent, and let them ask for what they have spent!" Thus if a married woman became a Moslem and fled, her unbelieving husband lost his right to her; the Moslems must not send her back to him if he requested them to do so, but they ought to compensate him for his expenditure on her. Likewise if a Moslem's wife remained stubbornly polytheist and was thus a potential fifth columnist, he should not insist on keeping her but ought to return her to her kinsfolk conditionally on getting his expenditure on her back from them.

Further evidence of the Prophet Mohammad's humane concern to dissuade the Arabs from ill-treating their women is to be found in several passages in *sura* 2. One is in verse 231: "When you have divorced women and they have reached their term (i.e. the end of their waiting period[66]), retain them honorably or dismiss them honorably, but do not retain them by force in order to violate (their rights)!" This means that when a husband has pronounced the divorce of a wife, and when the end of the waiting period after which she can be remarried approaches, he must not try to force her into remarrying him. The decision for or against resumption of their marriage must be made honorably and amicably, and her rights must not be violated by threats such as to make her pay ransom money or to keep her locked up for a long time.

A further command on this subject comes in the following verse 232: "And when you have divorced women and they have reached their term, do not try to prevent them from remarrying their husbands if they have agreed together honorably!" The verse is said to have been sent down because of the violent behavior of Ma'qil b. Yasār who wanted to prevent his sister from remarrying the husband who had divorced her.

Another topic in *sura* 2 is seldom discussed and is not strictly relevant to the present subject, but will be mentioned here because it gives another glimpse of social conditions in the Prophet Mohammad's time and the sort of inquiry that was referred to him. Verse 222 prohibits intercourse with menstruating women and continues: "When they have become pure, approach them from the direction that God prescribed for you!" According to the *Tafsir ol-Jalālayn*, this means the same direction from which they had been approached when not menstruating, but a different and almost contradictory meaning seems to be conveyed by the immediately following words in verse 223: "Your women are a field for you. Approach your field by whatever way you wish!" The *Tafsir ol-Jalālayn* gives the meaning of "by whatever way you wish" as either "standing, sitting, or lying, from the side, from the front, or from behind", and states that the purpose of the revelation is to dispel a Jewish notion that when the woman has been approached from behind, the child is born left-handed or squint-eyed. In Soyuti's opinion, the words "from the direction that God prescribed for you" in verse 222 were abrogated by verse 223, and the abrogation occurred after a protest by 'Omar and a number of the Prophet's other companions. The possessors of scripture (i.e. Jews and Christians) lay on their sides with their women, and the Prophet's Madinan supporters (Ansār) had adopted this custom, which was more in accord with the concept of female modesty and seclusion. The Moslem emigrants (Mohājerūn) adhered to the customs of the Qorayshites and other Meccans, who liked to handle their women in different ways, such as throwing them onto their backs or their chests and approaching them from in front or from behind. When a Mohājer who had married a woman of the Ansār wished to handle her in this way, she refused, saying "We lie on our sides." The case was reported to the Prophet, and the verse giving discretion to men in this matter was sent down. According to Ebn Hanbal and Termedhi,[67] the meaning of the verse is "from in front or from behind, supine or prone", and its revelation took place after 'Omar had said to the Prophet one morning "I am done for", and in reply to the Prophet's question "How so?" had answered "I changed my approach last night but it did not work."

It can be seen from the verses of the Qor'ān and the teachings of Islam that the women had a very low status in ancient Arab society and were very cruelly treated by the men. For example, in verse 33 of *sura* 24 (*on-Nur*) owners of female slaves are forbidden to make pecuniary profit by hiring them out as prostitutes against their will: "And do not force your slave-girls into prostitution if they wish to keep themselves chaste, so that you may seek casual gain in this life below!" The verse is said to have been sent down because 'Abdollāh b. Obayy engaged in the vile business. There is evidence that he was not the only offender and that this cruel exploitation of female slaves by forcing them into prostitution and pocketing their receipts was quite a big industry at the time.

After the Moslem conquest of Mecca, a large delegation of Meccan women went to the Prophet to swear allegiance and profess Islam. This was the occasion of the revelation of verse 12 of *sura* 60 (*ol-Momtahana*), which made their admittance to Islam conditional on their belief and behavior: "O Prophet, when believing women come to you swearing allegiance to you, (it must be) on condition that they shall not ascribe any partner to God, shall not steal, shall not engage in adultery and prostitution, shall not kill their children, shall not tell the slanderous tales which they invent about what is between their arms and their legs (i.e. make false allegations about the paternity of expected children), and shall not disobey you on any matter of right custom. Then accept their oaths of allegiance, and pray for God's forgiveness of them!"

The importance of these conditions for admittance into Islam is self-evident. Among the wrong customs which the women were to drop were lamentations such as wailing, tearing the collar, plucking the hair, and scratching the face.

After the revelation of the list of conditions, Hend b. 'Otba, the wife of Abu Sofyān and mother of the future caliph Mo'āwiya, is

119

reported to have said that free women of noble birth never engaged
in adultery and prostitution.

One of the evil practices forbidden by Islamic teachings was
female infanticide. In the words of verses 8 and 9 of *sura* 81
(*ot-Takwir*), "the infant girl who was buried alive, for what crime
was she slain?"

The ancient Arabs valued sons and boasted of having them, but
reckoned daughters to be an encumbrance and a disgrace. They
were too ignorant to see that continuance of the human race
depends on the birth of girls. Their attitude is vividly depicted in
verses 60 and 61 of *sura* 16 (*on-Nahl*): "And when one of them
receives news of (the birth of) a female (child), his face goes black
as he chokes down his anger. He hides himself from people
because of the badness of the news that has been given to him,
(wondering) whether to keep it in disgrace or to bury it in the
ground."

# WOMEN AND THE PROPHET

Ignaz Goldziher remarked that no other religion's scriptures and
records contain anything like the frank and detailed information
which the Qor'ān, the Hadith, and the biographies give about the
career and private life of Islam's founder. The remark is made
appreciatively in Goldziher's valuable book *Le dogme et la loi de
l'Islam*, in the course of a chapter in which the historical and well
documented fact of the Prophet Mohammad's growing appetite
for women is mentioned. About the lives of Jesus and Moses, let
alone Abraham and Noah, whatever information we possess is
clouded by dusts of popular mythology and religious and racial
prejudice. About the life of Mohammad, hundreds of reports
which have not undergone tendentious deformation are available
to us in Qor'ānic verses, reliable Hadiths, and early biographies.
The most important of these sources is the Qor'ān, through which
knowledge of many contemporary events can be obtained both
directly, from certain verses, and indirectly, from the accounts of
occasions of revelations given by commentators. The number of
verses concerning the Prophet's private life is quite large.

All the commentators agree that verse 57 of *sura* 4 (*on-Nesā*) was
sent down after the Jews had criticized Mohammad's appetite for
women, alleging that he had nothing to do except to take wives.

The verse says, "Or do they envy the people for what God in His bounty has given them? We gave scripture and wisdom to Abraham's descendants, and We gave them a great realm." The Jews were jealous of Mohammad for God's gifts of prophethood and many wives to him. The second sentence replies to their argument that a genuine prophet would not take so many wives, and obviously refers to the prophets David and Solomon, who were supposed to have had ninety nine wives and a harem of one thousand women respectively, but had not suffered any consequent loss of prophetic status. These suppositions, like other stories of the kings of the children of Israel, were of course embroidered with the exaggerations of fable.

European critics have viewed this appetite for women as excessive and irreconcilable with the spiritual role of a man who preached moderation and renunciation. Some have surmised that Mohammad's fondness for women prompted those elements of the Islamic legislation which improved women's status and rights.

Such objections lose weight when the matter is considered from a purely rational, and not emotional, viewpoint. Mohammad was a human, and no human is without weak points. The sexual appetite is a necessary human instinct and an important factor in any person's thinking and behavior toward others; it is only reprehensible when it induces socially harmful behavior. Otherwise there is no point in discussing merits and demerits, or strengths and weaknesses, of a person's private life. The ideas of Socrates radiated from Athens to all of Greece and to all of mankind; the question whether he led a perverted private life is irrelevant unless he thereby did harm to society. Adolf Hitler could be called chaste because he either lacked or had only a feeble sexual instinct, but instead he had pernicious notions which plunged the world into bloodshed and ruin.

The Prophet Mohammad saw himself as a human who had submitted to God and undertaken to rescue his people from the sink of idolatry. His fondness for women and his marriages to many wives did not impair the validity of his mission or infringe the rights of other persons. The actions and ideas of great leaders of communities should be assessed in the context of the social environment and by the criteria of their benefit to the community and to mankind. Seen in this light, the denial of intellectual and religious freedom to others, which results from giving them only the choice between acceptance of Islam and payment of tribute on humiliating terms, is much more open to question.

Moslems also have made misappraisals, but of a very different kind. In order to glorify Islam's founder, they have said and written things which contradict clear verses in the Qor'ān and reports in the reliable early sources. The learned modern Egyptian author Mohammad Hosayn Haykal, who in his *Life of Mohammad* set out to examine matters with the methods of twentieth century scholarship, took such umbrage at the Western criticisms that in one chapter he even tried to defend the Prophet by denying that he had any great fondness for women at all. A passage from the chapter is quoted below:

"Mohammad had twenty years of conjugal life with Khadija and did not then desire to take another wife . . . . . . This was natural and inevitable. Khadija was a wealthy and distinguished woman who had married a poor, but hard-working and honest, employee. She had taken him into her house because, either by nature or by dint of his straitened circumstances, he was free from the frivolous and licentious proclivities of other Qorayshite youths. It was for these reasons that the mature and experienced Khadija devotedly cared for her husband, who was fifteen years younger than herself, and from her own resources helped him to achieve a prosperity in which he could forget his childhood experiences of hardship and dependence on his uncle. The peace and comfort of Khadija's house enabled him to ripen the thoughts which he had been nurturing for ten or twelve years. Khadija herself certainly concurred with his austere ideas, because as a cousin of Waraqa b. Nawfal she sympathized with ascetics (*hanifs*).[68] After Mohammad's appointment to the prophethood, she believed in the truth and divine inspiration of his vision, and became the first convert to Islam. Furthermore Khadija was the mother of the Prophet's four daughters, Zaynab, Roqayya, Omm Kolthum, and Fātema.[69] In such a situation, how could Mohammad take another wife while Khadija was living? Only after her death did he proceed to ask for the hand of 'Ā'esha, and as 'Ā'esha was then a seven-year-old child, to marry Sawda, the widow of os-Sakrān b. 'Amr." Haykal then states, in an evident attempt to absolve Mohammad of desire for women, that "Sawda possessed neither beauty nor wealth. The Prophet's marriage to her was an act of charity and helpfulness to the lonely widow of one of the Moslem emigrants to Abyssinia."

Surely Haykal would have done better to write that the Prophet married Sawda because, being a mature person, she was well fitted to do his housekeeping and look after his four young daughters; though this theory is open to the objection that the Prophet first thought of 'Ā'esha, a child whom he could not marry until two years later because she was so young, and then married Sawda because he could not live without a wife – a reason which is in no way blameworthy. Perhaps a further reason was the lack of any other available women at that time, when the Qorayshites would have been unwilling to give a daughter to Mohammad and the Moslems probably did not have any marriageable daughters. The time was the period of two or three years in which the Prophet remained at Mecca after Khadija's death.

After the move to Madina, however, opportunities arose and the Prophet Mohammad's strong appetite for women found ample scope. This fact cannot be denied and is sufficiently demonstrated by the following more or less complete list of his wives:

1　Khadija, daughter of Khowayled. She was a distinguished and wealthy woman, and Mohammad was her third husband. She bore him four daughters as well as two sons, named (ol-)Qāsem and (ot-)Tāher, both of whom died in infancy.

2　Sawda, daughter of Zam'a. She was the widow of a Meccan Moslem emigrant who had died in Abyssinia. M. H. Haykal's opinion that the Prophet married her out of compassion for a lonely Moslem widow has been discussed above.

3　'Ā'esha, daughter of Abu Bakr os-Seddiq. She was seven years old when she was betrothed and nine years old when she was married to the Prophet, the gap between them being more than forty years. Her age when he died in 11 A.H./632 was sixteen or seventeen years. She was the Prophet's favorite wife. She was also one of the persons who learned the Qor'ān by heart. She was considered an important source of information on words and deeds of the Prophet (*Hadith*) and customs of the Moslems (*Sonna*). After the assassination of 'Othmān, she opposed the accession of 'Ali b. Abi Tāleb to the caliphate and was one of the prime movers of the force which unsuccessfully challenged 'Ali at the battle of the camel in 36/656.

4　Omm Salama, the widow of a Meccan Moslem emigrant to Madina who had died of wounds suffered in the battle of Ohod.

5　Hafsa, daughter of 'Omar b. al-Khattāb. She too was married to the Prophet after she had been left a widow. There is evidence that this marriage had a pragmatic aspect.

6   Zaynab, daughter of Jahsh and former wife of the Prophet's adopted son Zayd b. Hāretha. This marriage can be counted as one of the Prophet's love-matches. There is a long narrative poem about Zayd and Zaynab. The Prophet's affection and care for Zaynab were such as to make her a rival of 'Ā'esha.

7   Jowayriya, daughter of ol-Hāreth b. Abi Derār, the chief of the Mostaleq tribe, and former wife of Mosāfe' b. Safwān. She had been taken prisoner at the time of the defeat of the Banu'l-Mostaleq in 5 A.H./627 and given to one of the Moslem warriors as his share of the booty. Her owner wanted to ransom her for a certain price, but she found the price too high and beyond her means. She therefore went to the Prophet's house to plead for his intercession to get the price lowered. What happened next has been told by 'Ā'esha: "Jowayriya was so beautiful and charming that anyone who caught sight of her was captivated. When I saw Jowayriya outside the door of my room, I felt worried because I was sure that God's Apostle would be carried away as soon as his eye fell on her. And so he was. After she had gained admission to the Prophet's presence and made her plea, he said that he would do something better for her; he would pay for her ransom himself and then ask her to marry him. Jowayriya was pleased, and she consented. As a result of her marriage to the Prophet, the Moslems freed many of the Mostaleq captives because they had become the Prophet's brothers and sisters in law. I can think of no other woman who did so much good and caused so many blessings for her own kinsfolk."

8   Omm Habiba, daughter of Abu Sofyān. She had been left a widow when her first husband 'Obaydollāh b. Jahsh died in Abyssinia.

9   Safiya, daughter of Hoyayy b. Akhtab and former wife of Kenāna b. Abi Rabi', one of the leaders of the Jews at Khaybar. After being taken prisoner, she was selected by the Prophet as his share of the booty. He married her on the eve of his return from Khaybar to Madina.

10   Maymuna, daughter of ol-Hāreth of the Helāl tribe. One sister of hers was married to Abu Sofyān, and another to 'Abbās b. 'Abd ol-Mottaleb. Maymuna was the maternal aunt of Khāled b. ol-Walid (the future conqueror of Syria); reportedly it was after her marriage to the Prophet that Khāled walked into the Moslem camp and professed Islam, and the Prophet made a gift of horses to Khāled.

11 Fātema, daughter of Shorayh.

12 Hend, daughter of Yazid.

13 Asmā, daughter of Sabā.

14 Zaynab, daughter of Khozayma.

15 Habla, daughter of Qays and sister of ol-Ash'ath b. Qays (a South Arabian chief, subsequently prominent in the conquest of Iran).[70]

16 Asmā, daughter of No'mān. The Prophet did not consummate this marriage.

17 Fātema, daughter of od-Dahhāk. This marriage was also left unconsummated.

18 Māriya the Copt, a slave-girl who was sent from Egypt as a gift to the Prophet.[71] She bore him a son, Ebrāhim, who died in infancy.

19 Rayhāna, like Māriya the Copt, fell into the Qor'ānic category of "those whom your right hands have acquired", i.e. she was a slave-girl with whom contractual marriage was unnecessary but concubinage was permissible. She was one of the captives from the Jewish Banu Qorayza and the Prophet's share of the booty taken from that tribe. She was unwilling to profess Islam and enter into a contractual marriage with the Prophet, preferring to retain the status of a slave in his house.

20 Omm Sharik, of the Daws tribe, was one of four women who gave themselves to the Prophet. In addition to contractual wives and concubines, there were some women in the Prophet's harem who fell into this third category. Marriage to contractual wives, up to the limit of four, requires formalities such as the provision of dower, the presence of witnesses, and the approval of the woman's father or other guardian. Concubinage with slave-women is permissible to Moslems if the woman's husband was a polytheist or other unbeliever. For the Prophet only, marriage to a woman who gave herself was permitted by the last part of verse 49 of *sura* 33 (*ol-Ahzāb*). The other three women who gave themselves to the Prophet were Maymuna, Zaynab, and Khawla.

Omm Sharik's gift of herself disturbed 'Ā'esha, because Omm Sharik was so beautiful that the Prophet immediately accepted the gift. In extreme jealousy and indignation, 'Ā'esha reportedly said, "I wonder what a woman who gives herself to a man is worth." The incident is cited as the occasion of the revelation of the last part of verse 49, which sanctioned Omm Sharik's gift and the Prophet's acceptance. On hearing this, 'Ā'esha was reportedly so impertinent as to say, "I see that your Lord is quick to grant your wishes."

Another well authenticated report, quoted by the "Two Shaykhs" (Jalāl od-Din ol-Mahalli and Jalāl od-Din os-Soyuti) in the *Tafsir ol-Jalālayn*, gives a different version of 'Ā'esha's row with the Prophet. According to this, it was after the affair of Omm Sharik and the revelation of verse 49 that 'Ā'esha indignantly said, "I wonder what a woman who gives herself to a man is worth." Verse 51 was then sent down to rebuke her, and it was after the revelation of verse 51 that she made her remark about the Lord's quickness to grant the Prophet's wishes.

Verse 49 of *sura* 33 defines the Prophet's rights in the acquisition of wives and concubines: "O Prophet, We have made lawful for you your wives to whom you have paid their rewards, those whom your right hand has acquired out of the booty which God gave you, daughters of your paternal uncles and aunts and daughters of your maternal uncles and aunts who emigrated with you, and (any) female believer if she gives herself to the Prophet (and) if the Prophet wishes to enter into marriage with her – for you only, not for (other) believers."

Verse 50 continues: "We know well what duties We have imposed on them in the matter of their wives and those whom their right hands have acquired. (This exemption is) in order that no blame shall fall on you. And God is forgiving, merciful."

'Ā'esha's protest against the last part of verse 49 brought down the warning in verse 51, which sets forth, or rather sets no limits on, the Prophet's powers over his wives, depriving them of any sort of right or redress against him: "You may postpone (the turns) of whomsoever of them you will, and you may take to bed whomsoever you will. And if you want (back) any of those whom you have laid off, it will not be a sin (held) against you. That is more likely to make them happy, not sad, and to make all of them content with what you give them. God knows what is in your hearts, and God is knowing, forbearing."

Zamakhshari, in his Qor'ān-commentary entitled *ol-Kashshāf*, explains the revelation of verse 51 as follows. The Prophet's wives, who were jealous rivals of each other, began to demand higher subsistence allowances. (This was after the massacre of the men of the Qorayza tribe, when the Moslems had acquired much booty and the Prophet's wives naturally hoped that part of his one fifth share of this booty might be spent on them). According to

'Ā'esha's account, which Zamakhshari quotes, the Prophet then boycotted his wives for one month until the revelation of verse 51 gave him a free hand in his relations with them. The wives became apprehensive and asked him to give them whatever personal attention and financial help he pleased.

This means that the wives acknowledged the Prophet's absolute discretion to deal with each of them in any way that he might choose. Zamakhshari in his detailed study interprets verse 51 as giving the Prophet freedom to approach, shun, retain, or divorce each or all of his wives and to marry other women of his community whenever he pleased. Furthermore, according to a statement by Hasan b. 'Ali which Zamakhshari quotes, if the Prophet wanted a woman's hand, no other man would have the right to pay court to that woman unless the Prophet changed his mind. Zamakhshari adds that at that time the Prophet had nine wives and was not taking turns regularly or at all with five of them, namely Sawda, Jowayriya, Safiya, Maymuna, and Omm Habiba, but was granting favor and regular turns to the other four, namely 'Ā'esha, Hafsa, Omm Salama, and Zaynab. 'Ā'esha is again quoted as saying, "There were few days when the Prophet did not call on each of us, but he showed special consideration to the one whose turn had come and with whom he would be spending the night. Sawda b. Zam'a feared that the Prophet might divorce her and therefore said to him, 'Do not keep my turn! I have given up hope of conjugal relations with you, and I cede my night to 'Ā'esha. But do not divorce me, because I would like to be counted as a wife of yours on the Judgement Day!'"

The point of the last part of verse 51 is that deprivation of conjugal rights would make the Prophet's wives happier. Even though the divine command had endowed him with absolute discretion and deprived them of any right to claim their due from him, the new dispensation was better for them because it would end their rivalry and make them contented in future.

Perhaps it was to soothe the hurt feelings and wounded pride of the wives that verse 52 of *sura* 33 was sent down, as the words certainly seem to be a message of consolation and reassurance to them: "It is not permissible for you (to marry) women hereafter, nor to replace them with (other) wives even if their beauty pleases you, with the exception of those whom your right hand has acquired. And God is watchful over everything."

This verse presents a problem, because in the words of 'Ā'esha, which every Hadith compiler quotes and deems authentic, "the Prophet did not die without all his wives being permissible for him" (i.e. all his marriages were permissible for him). In Zamakhshari's opinion, 'Ā'esha's words show that verse 52 was abrogated by custom and by verse 49 ("O Prophet, We have made lawful for you . . . . . . "). But an abrogating verse ought to come after the abrogated one. Nevertheless Soyuti, in his treatise on Qor'ānic problems entitled *ol-Etqān*, maintains that in this case the earlier verse abrogated the later one.

When the Prophet's marital privileges, specified in numerous verses of *sura* 33, are added up, their astonishing range becomes apparent. He could have more than four wives, the maximum allowed to other believers; he was permitted to marry first cousins who had emigrated to Madina with him; he could take as a wife, without payment of dower and presence of witnesses, any female believer who gave herself to him; he was exempt from the obligation of respect for the equal rights of co-wives; he might postpone or terminate the turns of any of his wives; if he sought a woman's hand, any other suitor must desist; and after his death, no other men might marry his widows. Moreover the Prophet's wives had no right to demand higher subsistence allowances.

In contrast with the privileges and freedoms given to the Prophet, exceptional restrictions were imposed on his wives. They were not like other women; they must not let themselves be seen by the people; they must speak to men from behind curtains; they must abstain from wearing ornaments customary in pagan times; they must be content with whatever subsistence allowances might be granted to them; they must not complain if their turns were not kept; and they must never remarry. The last sentence of verse 53, which is addressed to male believers, states categorically: "It would not be (right) for you to offend God's Apostle by marrying his wives after him at any future time. That would be an enormity in God's sight." In the Talmud there is a similar ban on remarriage of widows of Jewish kings.

'Abdollāh b. ol-'Abbās[72] is reported to have said that a man went to see one of the Prophet's wives, and the Prophet ordered him not to do so again. The man protested that she was the daughter of his paternal uncle and that he and she had no wrong intentions. The Prophet replied, "I am well aware of that, but there are none so jealous as the Lord and myself." The man took umbrage and walked out, muttering "He forbids me to speak to my cousin. Anyway I shall marry her after his death." It was then that the revelation of verse 53 of *sura* 33 took place.

A point which should be borne in mind is that at no time were all the prophet's twenty wives living together in his harem. The loss of his revered first wife, Khadija, has already been mentioned. At least one of his later wives, Zaynab b. Khozayma, died in his lifetime, and so too did his slave-concubine Rayhāna. He did not consummate two of his marriages. At the time of his death he did not have more than nine contractual wives.

Two rival factions arose among the Prophet's wives: on one side 'Ā'esha, Hafsa, Sawda, and Safiya, on the other side Zaynab b. Jahsh, Omm Salama, and three more.

Some of the wives were involved in incidents which have entered into Islamic history and literature. Best known is the story of the lie concerning 'Ā'esha and Safwān b. ol-Mo'attal.

After the Moslem raid on the tribe of the Banu'l-Mostaleq in 5 A.H./627, a quarrel between one of 'Omar's servants and a Khazrajite from Madina broke out. 'Abdollāh b. Obayy, the Khazrajite chief notorious in early Islamic history as leader of the hypocrites, took offense and said to his people, "We brought this misfortune (i.e. the presence of the Meccan Mohājerun) onto our own heads. The saying that if you feed a dog it will bite you is true of us. Let us return to Yathreb, where the majority of the people are our friends, and throw out this unwelcome minority!" The Prophet heard about this utterance and hurried back with his caravan to Madina to forestall any agitation or intrigue that 'Abdollāh b. Obayy might launch. He rode continually, with few halts on the way for rest. 'Ā'esha had been chosen by lot to accompany the Prophet on this raid. During a halt on the return journey, she walked into the desert to perform a natural function and then noticed that she had lost her beads. She searched and found them, but missed the caravan. The camel carrying her howdah had departed with the other camels. Thus 'Ā'esha was left alone in the desert, until Safwān b. ol-Mo'attal, who had been instructed to follow the caravan and collect any things that might be dropped, rode up and saw her. He mounted her behind himself on his camel and brought her to Madina. The adventure could not be hushed up. When Hamna, the sister of Zaynab b. Jahsh who was 'Ā'esha's rival, heard about it, she seized the opportunity to harm 'Ā'esha and accused her of adultery with Safwān. The famous poet Hassān b. Thābet and a Mohājer named Mestah b.

Othātha added their voices to Hamna's, and the disaffected 'Abdollāh b. Obayy was not slow to spread the rumor around the town. The circumstances were certainly not favorable for 'Ā'esha. After accompanying the Prophet on the raid, this very young and beautiful girl found herself up against two new and equally beautiful rivals, Zaynab b. Jahsh, whom the Prophet had recently been empowered by special Qor'ānic revelation to marry, and Jowayriya b. ol-Hāreth, the former wife of a Mostaleq tribesman named Mosāfe', who as already mentioned had been taken prisoner in the raid and was married to the Prophet not long afterward when he ransomed her from her captor for four hundred *derhams*.

It is of course possible that 'Ā'esha's womanly feelings had been so hurt and incensed by the appearance of a rival that she deliberately either sinned or staged the adventure as a warning to her husband. Certainly there is difficulty in believing that when her howdah was lifted onto the camel, nobody noticed that it was too light. Several more questions also spring to the mind. Why did not Mohammad, who was so fond of 'Ā'esha, ask whether she was all right before the caravan set off? How could 'Ā'esha have been so unaware of the departure preparations of several hundred Moslem warriors that she failed to get herself back to the caravan on time and was left stranded in the desert until Safwān found her? Although Safwān's task was to ride some way behind when the caravan was in motion, would not he have caught up with it when it next had to halt to rest the men and the animals? The story of Safwān's sudden appearance and rescue of 'Ā'esha quite a long time after the caravan's departure does not seem true to fact and logically coherent. Prima facie the evidence suggests that 'Ā'esha stayed behind in collusion with Safwān.

Malicious gossip began on the morning when Safwān rode into Madina with 'Ā'esha at his back, and became more and more scurrilous as it spread through the town. Since Madina was such a small place that even the most trivial matters quickly became common knowledge, the question arises whether credence can be given to the statement that no mention of this dangerous gossip reached 'Ā'esha's ear for twenty days, and that when it did, she fell ill. She may, of course, have feigned sickness. As a result of her indisposition, she was allowed to return to her father's house. The natural inference is that she had really known about the gossip from the start, and that she only feigned sickness and went back to her father when the Prophet had heard about the gossip and shown signs of aloofness and estrangement from her.

Yet despite all the outward appearances and unfavorable circumstances, 'Ā'esha's innocence is by no means improbable. The whole incident can arguably be taken for a childish and feminine charade. This seems all the more likely because Safwān b. ol-Mo'attal is said to have been a notorious misogynist.

In any case, reports of the rumors spreading among the people greatly distressed the Prophet and prompted him to consult two of his confidants, Osāma b. Zayd and 'Ali b. Abi Tāleb. Osāma held for certain that 'Ā'esha was innocent and, being Abu Bakr's daughter, would never have stooped to any impropriety. 'Ali, on the other hand, argued that there was no shortage of women for the Prophet to marry, and that the truth about the affair could probably be obtained from 'Ā'esha's maid. Afterwards 'Ali gave the unfortunate maid a beating to make her disclose the truth, but she knew nothing and swore that 'Ā'esha was innocent.

The Prophet, however, was still nagged by doubts. He therefore went himself to interrogate 'Ā'esha at Abu Bakr's house, where he encountered scenes of weeping and protestations of innocence. While he was there, an inspirational trance came over him. They wrapped him up and put a leather pillow under his head. He perspired so much that sweat poured from underneath his cloak. After a while he recovered, and sura 24 (on-Nur) was revealed. This sura begins with a lengthy section (almost the whole of verses 2–26) about penalties for adultery and false accusations of adultery and about the story of the lie. It exculpates 'Ā'esha.

Zamakhshari remarks that no other subject in the Qor'ān is pursued with such intensity. Verse 23 of the sura is the best example: "Those who cast aspersions on careless but believing married women will be accursed in this lower world and in the after-life. And they will get great torment."

The affair of the lie was concluded with the punishment of three of the scandal-mongers, namely Hamna, Hassān b. Thābet, and Mestah b. Othātha. They were punished with floggings (of eighty stripes) as enacted by verse 4 of sura 24. The penalty was applied retrospectively, because it had not been enacted at the time when they committed the offence.

Also recorded in the biographies and echoed in Qor'ānic verses are the Prophet's enamorment and marriage to Zaynab b. Jahsh, the wife of Zayd b. Hāretha who was his adopted son.

Zayd had been an enslaved captive, and Khadija had bought him and presented him to Mohammad. Later the Prophet freed him and, in accordance with a contemporary Arab practice, adopted him as a son. In pre-Islamic Arab custom, exactly the same rights and restrictions pertained to an adopted son as to a natural son, for instance with respect to inheritance and to kindred and affinity disqualifications in marriage. The Moslems maintained the old practices until they were prohibited by the revelation of verses 4 – 6 of *sura* 33 (*ol-Ahzāb*). On this subject, 'Abdollāh b. 'Omar[73] is reported to have said: "We who were close to the Prophet used to speak of Zayd as Zayd ben Mohammad. He was not only the Prophet's son, but also one of his most devoted and steadfast companions."

Zaynab's mother was Omayma, daughter of 'Abd ol-Mottaleb, and Zaynab was thus the daughter of Mohammad's paternal aunt. It was the Prophet himself who requested that she should be given in marriage to Zayd. At first she and her brother 'Abdollāh were reluctant to agree, because Zayd was a freed slave, but they withdrew their objection when verse 36 of *sura* 33 (*ol-Ahzāb*) was sent down: "When God and His Apostle have decided a matter, neither a believing man nor a believing woman has any choice in their matter. Anyone who disobeys God and His Apostle is in manifest error." After this revelation, Zaynab was given in marriage to Zayd.

The Prophet's love for Zaynab arose later, and the time and circumstances of its incidence are diversely reported. The account in the *Tafsir ol-Jalālayn* suggests that his attitude began to change soon after her marriage to Zayd: "After a time (probably meaning a short time) his eye fell on her, and love for Zaynab budded in his heart."

Zamakhshari, in his comment on verse 37 of *sura* 33, states that it was after Zaynab's marriage to Zayd that the Prophet's eye fell on her. She pleased him so much that he could not help saying, "Praise be to God who makes hearts beat!" The Prophet had seen Zaynab before, but she had not then pleased him; otherwise he would have asked for her hand. Zaynab heard the Prophet's exclamation and told Zayd about it. Zayd knew intuitively that God had cast an unease with Zaynab into his heart. He therefore went in haste to the Prophet and asked whether he might divorce his wife. The Prophet asked what had happened and whether he suspected her. Zayd replied that he had met with nothing but kindness from her, but was distressed because she considered herself more noble than himself and more suitable for the Prophet. It was then that the words "Keep your wife for yourself and fear God" in verse 37 came down.

This meaningful verse is an impressive example of the Prophet Mohammad's honesty and candor. A translation of the whole of it is given below:

"When you were saying to the person whom God had helped and you had helped, 'Keep your wife for yourself and fear God', you were concealing something in your heart that God always discloses and were fearing the people, whereas it is God whom you should rightly fear. Now that Zayd has fulfilled a wish concerning her, We make her your wife so that there shall be no impediment for believers with respect to wives of their adopted sons, provided that they (i.e. the adopted sons) shall have fulfilled a wish concerning them (i.e. shall have divorced them). And what God has commanded must be done."

The verse is sufficiently clear and does not need exegesis. The Prophet had taken a liking to Zaynab, but when Zayd had come to ask him for permission to divorce her, he had advised Zayd not to do so but to keep her. In giving this advice to Zayd, he had concealed his inner wish. But God told him that he had suppressed his inner wish for Zaynab's divorce because he feared that the people would speak ill of him, whereas he ought to fear God alone. When in spite of his advice, Zayd finalized the divorce, God authorized him to marry Zaynab so that the Moslems should no longer be debarred from marrying former wives of their adopted sons.

While the Prophet's change of attitude and amorous feeling toward Zaynab had probably started at the ceremony of her marriage to Zayd, the fact that Zayd went to ask for the Prophet's approval of her divorce on the ground of her estrangement suggests that Zayd and Zaynab had lived together in a normal conjugal relationship for some time, even if not for very long. In that case, the sequence of events given by Zamakhshari may be visualized as follows: the Prophet's exclamation "Praise be to God who makes hearts beat" occurred immediately after his glimpse of Zaynab at her marriage ceremony; the hearing of these words and perhaps the sight of a glint in Mohammad's eye made her aware of the true nature of his feelings; this awareness kindled in her mind an ambition to catch Mohammad and become the wife of the most eminent man of the Qoraysh tribe; with this motive, and on the pretext that she had never desired to be married to Zayd, she began to behave coldly toward Zayd, going so far as to boast of her more noble origin and even of the Prophet's feelings for her; Zayd, in his devotion to his patron and liberator, then decided to release her, and notwithstanding contrary advice proceeded with the divorce.

The unknown author of the Cambridge *Tafsir*[74] gives a different account: "One day when God's Apostle, blessings be upon him, went to Zaynab's house to look for Zayd, he saw Zaynab standing by a bowl in which she was pounding a fragrant perfume. She pleased him, and a wish that she might be his wife arose in his heart. When Zaynab saw the Prophet, she laid her hand on him. Then the Prophet said, 'Grace and beauty! O Zaynab, praise be to God who makes hearts beat!' He said this twice and went away. When Zayd arrived, she told him what had happened and said, 'You cannot have me any more. Go and ask for permission to divorce me!' Zayd then took such a dislike to Zaynab that he could not bear to see her face. After the finalization of the divorce, the Prophet requested Zayd to go and tell Zaynab that God on High had given her to him as a wife. Zayd went to Zaynab's door and knocked. She asked what he wanted of her now that he had divorced her. He answered that he had brought a message from God's Apostle. Zaynab said 'All hail to God's Apostle' and opened the door. Zayd walked in, and she wept. Zayd said, 'It is not a time for tears. God has given you a better husband than I was.' She answered, 'Never mind about you! Who is that husband?' He told her that it was God's Apostle, and she bowed to the ground in prayer."

This account accords with another report according to which Zayd said: "I went to Zaynab's abode and found her kneading dough. Since I knew that she was soon to become a wife of the Prophet, my reverence for him did not permit me to look her in the face. I kept my back turned to her while I gave her the news that the Prophet was seeking her hand."

According to the *Tafsir ol-Jalālayn*, the Prophet counted the days, and as soon as the waiting period before the divorced Zaynab could be remarried was over, went without any prior ceremony to her house where a sheep was killed and a wedding feast was prepared. The feast and the distribution of bread and meat to the people went on long into the night.

Both 'Omar and 'Ā'esha are reported to have said that verse 37 of the *Surat ol-Azhāb* gives proof of the Prophet's honesty and truthfulness. 'Ā'esha said that if the Prophet had been disposed to conceal things, his inner feelings for Zaynab would not have been mentioned in the Qor'ān (i.e. the words "you were concealing something in your heart that God always discloses" would not have been revealed).

Not only verse 37 of *sura* 33, but also many other Qor'ānic verses, give proof of the Prophet's honesty and truthfulness. Mohammad was not afraid to admit his human weakness. This fact, however, has never been appreciated by Moslem zealots wanting to be more royalist than the king and hungering for miracles with an avidity which has been described in an earlier chapter. Notwithstanding the clear evidence of the Hadith and the clear meaning of verse 37, the great early scholar Tabari[75] could not accept that the subject of the verb in the sentence "you were concealing something in your heart" is Mohammad; he therefore argues that the sentence is addressed to Zayd and that it was Zayd who was concealing something in his heart. To justify this baseless interpretation, Tabari alleges that "Zayd had a disease which he was concealing, and because of that disease he decided to divorce Zaynab, his motive being to keep the illness from public knowledge."[76]

The modern biographer, Mohammad Hosayn Haykal, is another writer more royalist than the king, or in the Persian phrase, "a nurse more caring than the absent mother". In his *Life of Mohammad*, he states: "Zaynab was the daughter of the Prophet's paternal aunt. He had seen her before and felt no desire to marry her. He therefore urged Zayd not to divorce his wife. But Zayd disregarded his patron's advice and did divorce his wife. The Prophet then married Zaynab in order to break pagan Arab custom in the matter of consequences of adoption by showing the believers that marriage to wives of their adopted sons was permissible. That was the only reason why he married Zaynab and probably why he went to her house for the wedding feast so soon after the end of her waiting period."

Mohammad Hosayn Haykal thinks that most of the Prophet's marriages were political or for the good of his religious cause. In support of this view he quotes a report about the Prophet's marriage to Hafsa, the daughter of 'Omar b. ol-Khattāb:

"One day 'Omar was discussing a matter with his wife. She was very argumentative and cantankerous. He grew angry and said,

135

'Women are not fit to discuss life's affairs with men and to have opinions of their own.' His wife replied, 'Your daughter sometimes argues with God's Apostle so much that the Apostle is left angry for the rest of the day.' After hearing his wife say this, 'Omar went straightaway to Hafsa's house to question her. He told her to beware of God's punishment and the Prophet's wrath, and added, 'Do not worry about this young girl (meaning 'Ā'esha) who is so proud of her beauty and of the Prophet's fondness for her! The Prophet married you because of me, not because he loves you.'"

Obviously some of the Prophet's marriages were contracted for the purpose of establishing bonds of kinship which would strengthen the cause of Islam. In Haykal's view, this purpose determined the Prophet's choice of 'Ali and 'Othmān to be his sons-in-law. It is well known that Khāled b. ol-Walid accepted Islam when the Prophet, on his visit to Mecca in 7 A.H./629 to perform the lesser pilgrimage, married his last wife Maymuna, who was Khāled's maternal aunt and a sister of the wives of the Prophet's uncles 'Abbās and Hamza b. 'Abd ol-Mottaleb.

Another conjugal matter which must be mentioned, because it caused a stir at the time and is the subject of Qor'ānic verses, is the Prophet's boycott of Māriya the Copt. One day Māriya went to see the Prophet at Hafsa's house. Hafsa was not at home. He took Māriya into the bedroom and lay down with her. Hafsa came back. In great indignation she shouted at him, "Why are you lying with your slave-girl on my bed?" In order to placate Hafsa, the Prophet swore that he would never touch Māriya again. When the storm abated, and perhaps because he was fond of Māriya or affected by her hurt feelings and complaints about the interdict, he changed his mind. His conduct was justified by the revelation of the first five verses of *sura* 66 (*ot-Tahrim*):

"O Prophet, why do you lay an interdict on something that God has made permissible for you, seeking to placate your wives? God is forgiving, merciful." (Verse 1)

"God has imposed on you people the duty of making amends to expiate your oaths. And God is your protector. He is knowing, wise." (Verse 2)

This is evidently a reference to verse 91 of *sura* 5 (*ol-Mā'eda*), which authorizes expiation of ill-considered oaths through compensatory good deeds such as feeding or clothing ten poor persons, freeing a slave, or fasting for three days. According to one account, which is attributed to Moqātel b. Solaymān,[77] the Prophet expiated his oath about Māriya by manumitting a slave, but Hasan b. 'Ali is reported to have said that the words "God is forgiving, merciful" in verse 1 mean that God forgave the Prophet.

"When the Prophet said something secret to one of his wives, and when she talked about it and God informed him thereof, he made part of it known and refrained from (making known) part of it. And when he spoke to her about it, she asked, 'Who told you this?' He answered, 'The One who knows all and is informed of everything told me.'" (Verse 3)

What had happened was evidently as follows. The Prophet had let Hafsa know in strict confidence that he undertook to have no more relations with Māriya, and had asked Hafsa not to tell anyone else; but Hafsa told 'Ā'esha, and God informed the Prophet that she had done so. He then spoke to Hafsa, mentioning part of what he had been informed but refraining from mention of part of it. Hafsa, thinking that 'Ā'esha had told the Prophet, asked him how he knew, and he answered that God had told him.

Every reader of the Qor'ān must be amazed to encounter these private matters in a scripture and moral code valid for all mankind and for all time.

Even more amazing are the explanations given by the Qor'ān-commentators. One example is the following statement in the Cambridge *Tafsir*: "When Hafsa told 'Ā'esha about the Prophet's secret and when God informed His Apostle that Hafsa had told his secret to 'Ā'esha, the Prophet reminded Hafsa of part of what she had said to 'Ā'esha."

Is such women's talk, which may occur at any time and in any corner of the world, a fit matter for inclusion in the text of the Qor'ān? Do not the commentators degrade God, the Creator of the Universe, to the level of a tale-bearer reporting on Hafsa's conversation with 'Ā'esha? In any case, the subject of the first three verses of the *Surat ot-Tahrim* is a commonplace dispute between a husband and a wife.

The next two verses give warnings to Hafsa and 'Ā'esha. If they persisted in grumbling and showing wifely jealousy, they would incur the Prophet's displeasure. God was the Prophet's protector, and the Prophet could in the last resort divorce them.

"If you two women repent to God, and your hearts have indeed become (so) inclined, (all will be well). If you support each other against him (i.e. against the Prophet), God is his protector. And

137

Gabriel, and the righteous among the believers, and the angels are his supporters as well." (Verse 4)

"Maybe if he divorces you, his Lord will give him better wives than you instead – women who are Moslem, believing, submissive, penitent, devout and ready to fast, widows or divorcees, and virgins." (Verse 5)

Although both the meaning and the occasion of the revelation of this verse are clear, commentators have tried to explain it in ways which can only make the reader smile at their naivety. According to the Cambridge *Tafsir*, the word *thayyebāt* (widows or divorcees) refers to Pharaoh's wife Āsiya, and the word virgins (*abkār*) refers to Jesus's mother Mary, both of whom are waiting to be married to the Prophet Mohammad in heaven.

A quite different account of the occasion of the revelation of the first five verses of *sura* 66 should perhaps also be mentioned. According to it, the Prophet had eaten some honey at Zaynab's house, and after he had left, 'Ā'esha and Hafsa, being jealous of Zaynab, said to him, "Your breath smells bad." On hearing this, the prophet swore that he would never eat honey again. Afterwards (presumably after he had regretted his oath), the verse of rebuke (i.e. verse 1) in the *Surat ot-Tahrim* was sent down, and then the principle of compensatory expiation for breach of an oath was instituted and the Prophet's wives were threatened with divorce in the event of persistence in their jealousy and rivalry. This report is unlikely, however, to be an authentic Hadith because it omits the matter of Hafsa's knowledge and disclosure of the Prophet's secret.

# CHAPTER IV

# *Metaphysics*

## GOD IN THE QOR'ĀN

> Beside these nine enamel domes,
> the earth is like a poppy-seed floating on the ocean.
> When you see what size you are beside this poppy-seed,
> you should laugh at your beard.
>   Shabestari[78]

This poppy-seed, as the poet Mahmud Shabestari described our
earth, weighs six thousand billion ($6 \times 10^{21}$) tons and has a
circumference of 40,076 km. and a surface of 510,100,000 square
km. It is one of the smaller planets of the solar system. The time
which it takes to revolve around the sun is a little over 365 days. Its
eight known fellow-planets move in similar predetermined orbits.
The most remote of them is Pluto, which has a smaller mass (about
the same as Mercury's) and an orbit varying between 4.5 and 7.5
billion km. from the sun. The distance is made easier to visualize
by the calculation that if a jet aeroplane flying at a steady 1000 km.
per hour could reach Pluto, the journey would take at least seventy
years. Scientific and mathematical evidence indicates that Pluto is
not the last heavenly body governed by the sun's pull, and that a
journey one hundred times longer, i.e. of 7000 years at 1000 km.
per hour, would be needed to reach the limit of the gravitational
field of another star.

Our sun, for all its glory and importance to us, is only a
medium-sized star in the galaxy known in Persian as the Kah-
kashān (Straw Ribbon) and in European languages as the Milky
Way, because on a summer night it looks like a straw-colored or
milk-colored stripe across the sky. Within this particular galaxy
alone, it has so far been possible to identify seven thousand stars,
each of which is a sun and may be supposed, on a priori if not on

empirical grounds, to have a planetary system of its own more or less similar to the solar system.

The poppy-seed floating on the ocean, with its surface of 510,100,000 sq. km., has a volume of 1,082,842,210,000 cubic km., which in relation to the sun's volume is tiny. If, for the sake of comparison, the sun could be supposed to be a hollow shell, one million globes of the size of our earth could be fitted into it. The sun contains 99.86 per cent of all the matter in the solar system, the share of its nine planets and their satellites being only 0.14 per cent of the total and that of the earth and its moon being less than 0.0014 per cent.

In space there are stars five hundred times bigger than the sun with its circumference of 1,392,000 km. and mass of approximately 1,200,000,000 billion tons. The sun, as already mentioned, is one of the stars in the Milky Way. It has been estimated that every galaxy contains at least one hundred billion stars, and on the basis of telescopic observations and mathematical calculations up to the present time, it has been conjectured that at least one hundred million galaxies (including our Milky Way) lie scattered through space.

The remoteness of the stars cannot conveniently be denoted by ordinary numerals and is therefore expressed in terms of light years. The speed of light being roughly 300,000 km. per second, one light year is equivalent to roughly 9.4608 billion km. The distances of certain stars from the earth are so great that the time needed for their light to reach us ranges from one hundred to one thousand years.

These figures bewilder our minds and convey only a vague idea of the universe's vastness; but they show clearly that the earth is a very small poppy-seed floating on a very large ocean. Every thoughtful man or woman who tries to visualize this immensity is bound to feel powerless and humble. If the apparently infinite universe has any limits at all, they lie beyond the grasp of the human intellect.

If the apparently infinite universe not only has a boundary in space but also had a beginning in time, this again is something which our minds cannot conceive. If we postulate the existence of a creator of so vast a universe, we necessarily presuppose that the creator is bigger than it and surrounds it. If we assume that this huge and awesome mechanism has a controller, we necessarily presuppose that the controller possesses infinite power. The nature of this creator-controller is therefore bound to be too remote, lofty, and abstract for comprehension by our limited and limiting intellects. In the words of Jalāl od-Din Rumi, "That which we cannot conceive is He."

In general, mankind has not been capable of far-reaching thought. Study of religious beliefs shows that human beings, with rare exceptions, can only visualize God's immense scheme as an enlarged replica of whatever system they have known in their own petty lives, and can only visualize God's unique nature as similar to their own natures, somewhat superior of course, but subject to essentially the same reactions, emotions, weaknesses, desires, and ambitions.

There is an Arabic saying, found in the Hadith and derived ultimately from the Old Testament, that God created man in His own image. It would be truer to say the exact opposite, namely that men have created God in their own image.

Some time ago, a satirical but intelligently written book entitled "And Moses created God" came by chance to my notice. Referring to the sentence "And God created Man" in the Old Testament, the book argued that the reverse is true and that God is a figment of Moses's imagination.

Throughout the Old Testament, the God who is presented to us is an imperious being, quick to anger, unwilling to relent, and avid for praise and worship. Out of the millions of His creatures, He preferred Abraham who was submissive, and therefore made Abraham's descendants His chosen people. Hence it would be right that these people should rule over the whole earth.

The choice fell on Abraham because, in the period after Noah, he was the most obedient and respectful slave whom God could find. For the same reason, God enabled Abraham's wife Sarah to become pregnant and give birth to Isaac in her old age. Since there was no virgin in all the land of Canaan suitable to be married to Isaac and to become the progenitrix of the chosen people, Abraham on God's command sent a messenger to Chaldaea who requested the betrothal of Abraham's niece Rebecca to Isaac and brought her to Palestine. Then God obtained from the Children of Israel a covenant whereby they were not to worship anyone else and in return would have the rulership of the world. The entire attention of the Controller of the Universe was directed, not just to the solar system and the earth, but to one small part of the earth's surface, namely Palestine.

141

On one occasion, God was so angry when He saw the people of Sodom and Gomorrha turning to vice and sin that He decided to destroy those two towns. Even the intercession of Abraham, who was more lenient than God, proved ineffective. God sent down a thunderbolt which killed all the inhabitants, guilty and innocent, men, women, and children alike, with one exception; God, in order to please Abraham, also sent down an angel who rescued his nephew Lot from the general massacre. Throughout the Old Testament, God is similarly portrayed as a capricious, exacting, and relentless tyrant.

The texts indicate that Moses had similar despotic inclinations, and that David and Solomon cherished the same ideal of kingship when they ruled over the Israelites. The story of Uriah's wife shows how little respect King David had for other men's rights.

In the Qor'ān, God is endowed with all the qualities of perfection. He is knowing, strong, hearing, seeing, wise, independent of all needs, and benevolent. These are not His only qualities, however, as He is also often imperious and wrathful, and sometimes even sly; in verses 47 of *sura* 3 and 30 of *sura* 8, He is "the best of the schemers."

These attributes are not mutually compatible. If God is self-subsistent and intrinsically perfect, how can He be susceptible to accidents such as anger and desire for revenge? Why should He ever become angry when His strength is absolute and anger is an involuntary mood induced by weakness? Why should He, in His absolute independence, be angry about the ignorance and stupidity of some humans incapable of discerning His existence and mastership of the universe? Why too, when God is "the most merciful of the merciful" (*sura* 12, verse 92), should He warn people that He will never forgive those who imagine that He has partners (*sura* 4, verse 116), but will punish them with eternal torment? Despite God's own words "I am not unjust to (My) slaves" (*sura* 50, verse 28), He throws sinners into Hell for ever, and lest they think that incineration in its fire may end their torment, He states that "every time their skins are consumed, We shall give them other skins instead so that they may (continue to) taste the punishment" (*sura* 4, verse 59). Only an insatiable anger could induce such cruelty, and anger is a sign of weakness. Can weakness be attributed to Almighty God?

In the Qor'ān there are, on the one hand, numerous verses which state that guidance and error depend entirely on God's decision, and on the other hand, numerous verses which impose specific obligations on men and women together with harsh penalties on those who decide not to observe them.

There are also times when the Omnipotent and Omniscient God needs the help of humans. "Jesus, the son of Mary, said to the disciples, 'Who will be my supporters in God's cause?' The disciples said, 'We will be God's supporters'" (*sura* 61, *os-Saff*, verse 14). "And We sent down iron, (because) in it lie great power and benefits for the people, and so that God in the unseen world may know who support Him and His Apostles" (*sura* 57, *ol-Hadīd*, verse 25).

These problems are fundamental, but will not be pursued further here. For many centuries Islamic theologians and Qor'ān-commentators have striven to explain away the seeming contradictions or at least discordances. In the context of this book, it will be sufficient to proceed to a brief examination of some of the Qor'ānic passages concerning events in the twenty three years under study.

God, the omnipotent controller of the infinite universe, took offense with Abu Lahab for saying to the Prophet, "Perish you, Mohammad! Did you invite us here for this?" Like a thunderbolt, *sura* 111 (*ol-Masad*) came down onto Abu Lahab's head, and his wife was not spared from its blast: "Perish Abu Lahab's hands, and may he (himself) perish! His wealth will not give him security, nor will the gains that he has made. He will roast in a flaming fire. And his wife, the carrier of the firewood sticks, will have a rope of palm fiber on her neck!"

Abu'l-Ashadd's conceit brought down the stinging rebuke which Almighty God gave to him in *sura* 90 (*ol-Balad*).

*Sura* 104 (*ol-Homaza*) is a similar slap in the face for ol-Walīd b. ol-Moghira and Omayya b. Khalaf, who in Mohammad's presence had boasted of their wealth and mocked him with innuendos and winks. *Sura* 108 (*ol-Kawthar*) reprimands ol-'Ās b. Wā'el, who after the death of the Prophet's son had insultingly called him heirless.

Ka'b b. ol-Ashraf's journey to Mecca after the battle of Badr particularly angered the Master of the Universe because Ka'b, being a Jew and therefore a possessor of scripture, was expressing sympathy with the defeated polytheists and rating them higher than Mohammad, who was a strict monotheist. Verses 54–57 of *sura* 4 (on-Nesā) attest the vehemence of God's wrath over this matter.

In *sura* 59 (*ol-Hashar*), however, God takes pride in the eradication of the Nadir tribe and describes it as a merited punishment for their persistent adherence to Judaism. 'Abdollāh b. ol-'Abbās is reported to have given the name *Surat Bani'n-Nadir* to this *sura*.

In the Qor'ān, God not only refutes and denounces persons and groups who obstructed the advance of Mohammad's cause; He also intervenes in His Prophet's problems with women. One problem was the Prophet's love for Zaynab, the daughter of Jahsh and wife of Zayd, and the resultant estrangement of Zayd from Zaynab. After the execution of her divorce and completion of her waiting period, God gave her in marriage to His Prophet through the revelation of verse 37 of *sura* 33 (*ol-Ahzāb*). In verses 28 and 29 of the same *sura*, the problem of the demands of the Prophet's wives for higher allowances out of the booty taken from the massacred Banu Qorayza is settled by God's decision that the wives must be content with their present allowances or face divorce. The later problem of his wife Hafsa's complaint about his relations with his concubine Māriya is the subject of the numerous verses in *sura* 66 (*ot-Tahrim*) which were discussed in the preceding chapter. Hafsa's and 'Ā'esha's jealousy greatly displeased God, who warned these two women that unless they ceased to vex the Prophet and repented, God and Gabriel and the righteous believers would go to the Prophet's support, and that if the Prophet divorced them, God would give him better wives instead – obedient Moslem women ready to fast and pray, who had migrated from Mecca, and who might be widowed, divorced, or virgin. It has already been mentioned that one Qor'ān-commentary takes "widowed" to mean Pharaoh's wife Āsiya and "virgin" to mean Jesus's mother Mary, and states that both will be married to the Prophet in heaven; since the Qor'ān says nothing to this effect, the only significance of the statement is that it illustrates the mentality of the commentator.

*Sura* 24 (*on-Nur*) deals mainly with the lie about 'Ā'esha and prescribes the penalty of eighty lashes for slandering chaste wives. Through the retrospective infliction of this penalty on Hassān b. Thābet and Hamna b. Jahsh, 'Ā'esha's innocence was proclaimed.

Throughout the years 1 A.H./622–11 A.H./632, not only the infinite universe but also the earth's other regions were forgotten or ignored because some Arabs in the Hejāz and Najd had begun to think about the one great God but had sometimes, from fear or laxity, neglected duties such as participation in raids. To punish them, the fire of hell was made hotter, while to reward those who, from faith or hope of booty, had given proof of valor and steadfastness, gardens with rivers flowing beneath were prepared.

When the feelings of God's beloved Apostle were hurt by taunts or sneers, he was consoled by the assurance that "We have given you sufficient (protection) against the mockers" (*sura* 15, *ol-Hejr*, verse 95).

The Creator's most conspicuous and effective intervention in Arab affairs took place in 2 A.H./624 at the battle of Badr and is the subject of the whole of *sura* 8 (*ol-Anfāl*). A caravan, bearing a large cargo and led by Abu Sofyān, was on its way back from Damascus to Mecca. When the Prophet heard about it, he set forth from Madina with a party of his companions to attack it and seize the valuable goods. Abu Sofyān, having obtained information, requested help from Mecca, and Abu Jahl led out a Qorayshite force which was to guard the caravan. As an additional precaution, Abu Sofyān changed the caravan's route. He succeeded in bringing it safely to Mecca. The Prophet Mohammad and his party did not catch the caravan but ran into Abu Jahl's troops at a place called Badr. Not unnaturally some of the Prophet's men, who had been expecting to get a lot of booty without much trouble, flinched from battle with the large Qorayshite force and advised return to Madina. In verse 7 of *sura* 8, God reprimanded these men and called on them to fight the unbelievers. Verse 9 states that God had promised to reinforce them with a thousand angels, and verse 17 that not they, but God, had slain the enemies who fell in the battle. One of these fallen enemies was Abu Jahl, on whom the curse was thus fulfilled. Verse 17 goes on to address the Prophet, saying "You (singular) did not throw when you threw, but God threw." This refers to the Prophet's symbolic gesture of flinging a handful of sand in the direction of the polytheists for the purpose of blinding them, and means that it was God, not the Prophet, who thereby caused the unseeingness and defeat of the large enemy force.

This victory over the polytheists gave rise to problems of division of the booty. God allotted one fifth of it to His Apostle and the public treasury of the Moslems, and made provisions for its distribution (*sura* 8, verse 42).

The next problem was how to deal with the captives. At first God endorsed 'Omar's advice to behead them all and thereby intimidate adversaries: "It is not for a Prophet to have prisoners

145

until he has spread fear of slaughter in the land" (*sura* 8, verse 68). A little later, however, God accepted Abu Bakr's calmer advice to ransom them: "O Prophet, say (this) to the prisoners in your hands! 'If God knows of any good in your hearts, He will give you something better than that which will have been taken from you. And He will pardon you'" (verse 71).

The whole of *sura* 8 is devoted to solutions of problems arising from the relations of the Moslems with the polytheists and the Jews.

God's intervention in the crisis which arose when the Ghatafān tribe entered into an alliance with the Qoraysh, and their combined forces laid siege to Madina, is described in verse 9 of *sura* 33 (*ol-Ahzāb*): "O believers, remember God's bounty to you when armies came against you, and We sent against them a wind and armies that you did not see!" Verses 10–13 give more information about this crisis in which God so greatly helped the Moslems.

The Cambridge *Tafsir* gives the following account of what happened: "God on High sent a wind to uproot their tent pegs, blow out their fires, and smash the stable where they kept their horses, with the result that they all fell on top of each other. And the angels cried out, 'God is great.'"

The pious commentator never thought of asking why Almighty God had not sent the wind three weeks earlier. If God had done that, He would have relieved the Moslems of the grueling task of digging the defensive trench around Madina and would have spared them many days and nights of acute anxiety.

Nor did it occur to this commentator or to any contemporary or later Moslems to wonder why, at the battle of Mount Ohod, God had not sent a reinforcement of angels, as at Badr, or a windstorm, as in the war of the trench, in order to avert the painful defeat and the martyrdom of seventy Moslem fighters, one of whom was the Prophet's intrepid and popular youngest uncle, Hamza b. 'Abd ol-Mottaleb. If some angels or a tempest had helped at Mount Ohod, the Prophet would have been spared the embarrassment of a military reverse and the experience of being hit in the face by a stone and only rescued from martyrdom himself thanks to the bravery of 'Ali who shielded him.

A broad picture of contemporary social conditions in the Hejāz can be pieced together from the study of various passages in the Qor'ān. In addition to commandments and moral precepts, there are mentions of contemporary events and conflicts. Hundreds of verses are devoted to controversy, rebuttal of traducers, arbitrament of private disputes, exhortation to fight, censure of draft-dodgers, promise of booty and possession of other people's wives and property, and threat of hell-fire for opponents and disobeyers. The thunderbolt of God's wrath is suspended over the heads of righteous and wicked persons alike, ready to destroy a whole town if a few of its inhabitants are disobedient or sinful.

God in the Qor'ān has the typical characteristics of a human being. At times He is happy, at other times irate. He has likes and dislikes, and can be pleased. In short, all the propensities of our weak and unstable human nature, such as love, anger, vengefulness, and even guile, are also experienced by the Supreme Being. Yet if we postulate the existence of a creator and controller of the infinite universe, we must rationally believe him to be exempt from such accidents. We are therefore bound to interpret the Qor'ānic attributions of incongruous qualities to the Creator as expressions of the Prophet Mohammad's own human feelings, and all the more so because the Prophet himself said that he too was human. We know that, like any other man, he took offense, felt grief and mourned the loss of his son, and was so upset by the sight of Hamza's mutilated body at Mount Ohod that he heatedly vowed to mutilate the bodies of thirty Qorayshites.

The foregoing observations prompt the question whether a confusion between God and Mohammad is discernible in the Qor'ān. This is the only hypothesis capable of resolving the difficulties presented by a large number of Qor'ānic passages. A study of some of them will perhaps make the problem rather more clear.

All Moslems believe that the Qor'ān is God's word. This premiss is based on information frequently given in the text of the Qor'ān, e.g. in verses 3 and 4 of *sura* 53 (*on-Najm*), "And he (the Prophet) does not speak at will. It is nothing but revelation being revealed"; and in verse 1 of *sura* 97 (*ol-Qadr*), "We sent it down on the night of power." Thus the Qor'ān became for Moslems the sole document of the faith, incontrovertible, majestic, and sacrosanct.

The reverence for the Qor'ān was so great that after a hundred years a fierce controversy arose among the religious scholars on the question whether it was created or is, like God himself, uncreated, i.e. not preceded by non-existence. This controversy went on for centuries. All that need be said here is that the doctrine of the Qor'ān's uncreatedness conflicts with the factual evidence, the criteria of reason, and the basic principles of Islamic theology. Nevertheless, in the reign of the 'Abbāsid caliph Mo'tasem (218/833–227/842), the leading Sonnite exponent, Ahmad b. Hanbal, believed so strongly in this doctrine that, rather than abjure it, he endured a flogging of so many lashes that he fell unconscious. Presumably he even believed the words "Perish Abu Lahab's hands" to be as eternal as God Himself.

When a community has succumbed to a fever, it cannot be calmed with words and proofs. Yet for all who read the Qor'ān and study its contents, the facts are plain.

An immediately striking example is the content of the opening *sura* (*ol-Fāteha*). It is made up of seven verses,[79] called the seven repetitions,[80] and is placed first in the Qor'ān because of its great importance in Islamic prayer. A translation is given below:

> "In the name of God, the Compassionate, the Merciful!
> Praise to God, the Lord of the Worlds,
> the Compassionate, the Merciful,
> the Master of the Judgement Day!
> You (alone) we worship and from You (alone) we seek help.
> Guide us to the straight path,
> the path of those on whom You have bestowed bounty, not
> of those with whom You are angry and who have gone astray!"

These words cannot be God's words. From their content it is clear that they are the Prophet Mohammad's words, because they consist of praise to God, homage to God, and supplication for God's help. God himself would not say "Praise to God, the Lord of the Worlds, the Compassionate, the Merciful, the Master of the Judgement Day." This difficulty would not have arisen if the *Surat ol-Fāteha* had been introduced with the word "say" (Arabic *qol*) in the same way as many *sura*s and verses, for example *sura* 112, verse 1, "Say 'He is God alone'"; *sura* 109, verse 1, "Say 'O unbelievers'"; *sura* 18, verse 110, "Say 'I am only a human like you'". It is logically untenable, however, that God should say "Guide us to the straight path, the path of those on whom You have bestowed bounty, not of those with whom You are angry and who have gone astray."

Since the *Surat ol-Fāteha* cannot consist of God's words when its whole content is praise and supplication to God, it must be deemed to consist of the Prophet Mohammad's words and to be a prayer which he composed. For this reason 'Abdollāh b. Mas'ud, who was one of the scribes who wrote down the revelations and knew the Qor'ān by heart and later became a respected transmitter of Hadiths, considered that the *Surat ol-Fāteha* and also *suras* 113 (*ol-Falaq*) and 114 (*on-Nās*), both of which contain the words "I take refuge with the Lord", are not part of the Qor'ān.

Another utterance which, by the nature of its subject, cannot be attributed to the Sustainer of the Universe is *sura* 111 (*ol-Masad*), the retort to Abu Lahab. The Prophet had invited some relatives and influential Qorayshites to hear him expound the principles of Islam. When he began to speak, Abu Lahab angrily interrupted him, shouting "Perish you, Mohammad! Did you invite us here for this?" The *sura*, with its repetition of Abu Lahab's word "Perish", voices the Prophet's indignation at the rudeness of Abu Lahab and the malice of his wife, Omm Jomayyel, who had strewn thorns along the Prophet's route. The retort as such is not out of proportion. On the other hand, it ill becomes the Sustainer of the Universe to curse an ignorant Arab and call his wife a firewood-carrier.

In some Qor'ānic verses the verb is in the first person, and in others it is in the third person. Evidently God speaks first, and the Prophet Mohammad then speaks on God's behalf. In *sura* 53 (*on-Najm*), the first speaker is God, who confirms Mohammad's prophethood with the words "Your comrade is not lost, not astray, and he does not speak at will. It is nothing but revelation being revealed." In verses 21–28, however, the speaker is evidently Mohammad, who refers to the pagan notion that the idols Lāt, 'Ozzā, and Manāt were God's daughters and reproachfully asks the Arabs, "Do you have male (children) and does He (God) have female (children)?" These words cannot be words of God, who would not ask Himself whether He has daughters. They clearly express the Prophet's censure of the customs and morals of the Hejāzi Arabs, whose pride in having sons and shame in having daughters is the subject of several other Qor'ānic verses, for example verse 42 of *sura* 17 (*ol-Esrā*): "Has your Lord favored you with sons and chosen for Himself female (children) from among the angels? Surely you are saying a monstrous thing." This question can only have been asked by the Prophet Mohammad, because if it had been asked by God, the wording would be "Have I favored you with sons and chosen for Myself daughters?" Obviously God, for whom the sex of children makes no difference, would not have asked such a question.

149

The short-sighted prejudice against daughters is still wide-spread, even among civilized nations. The ancient Arabs boasted of having sons, and some of them were so barbarous as to practice female infanticide; but at the same time they absurdly supposed angels to be of the female sex. The Prophet Mohammad himself was not exempt from the traditional Arab desire to have sons. Every time that he married a wife, he hoped that she would bear him a son. When his son Qāsem died, he was sorely distressed, and at the same time deeply hurt by ol-'As b. Wā'el's taunt about his heirlessness, because in the Arab view only sons were real heirs. He rejoiced when Māriya the Copt gave birth to his son Ebrāhim, and wept with grief when the child died. Such was the Mohammad who said to the polytheists, "Has God favored you with sons?"

The Qor'ān contains many instances of confusion between the two speakers, God and Mohammad, in the same verse. One is the first verse of *sura* 17 (*ol-Esrā*), which is the only Qor'ānic mention, and for Moslems the sole proof, of the Prophet's night journey:

"Exalted is He who carried His servant by night from the Mosque of the Sanctuary to the Furthest Mosque, whose precincts We have blessed, so that We might show him some of Our signs. He is (all-)hearing, (all-)seeing." The praise of Him who carried His servant from Mecca to Palestine cannot be God's utterance, because God does not praise Himself, and must be Mohammad's thanks-giving to God for this favor. The next part of the sentence, describ-ing the Furthest Mosque "whose precincts We have blessed", is spoken by God, and so too is the following clause "so that We might show him some of Our signs". The closing words "He is (all-)hearing, (all-)seeing" seem most likely to be Mohammad's.

Another striking example of change of subject from the first to the third person is the opening sentence of *sura* 48 (*ol-Fat-h*): "We have given you a clear victory so that God may forgive your earlier and later sin." The sequence of thought would require the wording to be "so that We may forgive your earlier and later sin."

Among these many passages are some, like the above, which can easily be explained, but also others which present great difficulty. One of these is in *sura* 33 (*ol-Ahzāb*), verses 21–24. Verse 21 states: "In God's Apostle you (people) have had a good example for those who hope for God and the Last Day and have remembered God often." Surely if God had been the speaker, the sentence ought to have been worded in a way which would give the meaning "Those who seek Me should take My Apostle as their model." In verses 22 and 23, the sincere believers are commended for their steadfastness in the war of the trench, and in verse 24 a qualifying clause is appended: "in order that God may reward the sincere for their sincerity and punish the hypocrites, if He so wishes, or else absolve them. He is forgiving, merciful." Here again the speaker is clearly not God but the Prophet, because God would have spoken in the first person ("in order that We may reward the sincere for their sincerity . . .").

It is related that the Prophet, when preparing the expedition against the Romans (i.e. Byzantine Greeks) in 8 A.H./630, asked why ol-Jadd b. Qays, the chief of a Madinan clan, was not going to join in the fighting that year. In reply, ol-Jadd b. Qays said to the Prophet, "Excuse me from going and save me from temptation! I am very fond of women, and I fear that if I saw the Roman women, I might be unable to resist the temptation." This was the occasion of the revelation of verse 49 of *sura* 9 (*ot-Tawba*): "There is one of them who says, 'Excuse me and do not let me fall into temptation!' Have not they (already) fallen into temptation? Hell encircles unbelievers." Plainly the verse is from Mohammad's tongue, not from God, because ol-Jadd b. Qays had asked Mohammad, not God, for exemption from military service. God supported His Apostle by making hell available for the punishment of persons presuming to make this improper demand, but He did not speak on that occasion.

The presence of confusions between God and the Prophet in the Qor'ān cannot objectively be disputed. Sometimes God speaks, giving to the Prophet the command "say" (i.e. to the people). Sometimes the sentence structure proves that it is the Prophet who speaks, expressing devotion to God. The impression conveyed by the Qor'ān is that a hidden voice in Mohammad's soul or subconscious mind was continually impelling him to guide people, restraining him from lapses, and providing him with solutions to problems.

No other hypothesis can explain certain Qor'ānic passages which attribute excellence in guile and scheming to God. Verses 44 and 45 of *sura* 68 (*ol-Qalam*) advise: "Leave to Me those who call these words lies! We shall lure them on, (and) they will not know whence. And I shall give them rein. My guile is sure." In verses 181 and 182 of *sura* 7 (*ol-A'rāf*), the passage is repeated with the omission of "Leave to me", beginning "And those who call these words lies, We shall lure them on".

Verse 30 of *sura* 8 (*ol-Anfāl*) refers to a conclave of Qoraysh chiefs in their assembly hall (*dār on-nadwa*) and states: "When the unbelievers scheme against you, to arrest you or kill you or expel you, while they are scheming, God (too) is scheming, and He is the best of the schemers."

Guile is a substitute for strength, an expedient to which a person facing a more powerful adversary has recourse. In these two passages Almighty God, who created the universe by uttering the word "Be" and decides everything that happens in it, seems to have acquired the nature of an Arab shaykh wilier than his rivals. A historical analogy which springs to mind is the success of 'Amr b. ol-'Ās in outwitting Abu Musā ol-Ash'ari in the arbitration of 'Ali's and Mo'āwiya's claims to the caliphate.[81]

Confusion between God's and Mohammad's words is again apparent in two verses of *sura* 10 (*Yunos*). "And if your Lord so wished, all the dwellers on the earth would believe together. Are you going to compel the people to be believers?" (verse 99). "It is only (possible) for a soul to believe with God's permission. And He inflicts vileness on those who are not intelligent" (verse 100). In verse 99 the words are from God and addressed to the Prophet, but in verse 100 the words appear to be Mohammad's, a sort of self-consolation followed by an explanation of the obduracy of the polytheists who would not heed his teaching.

It is self-evident that God, having not wished that certain people should believe, would feel no anger with those people for their unbelief, because anger only arises in a person when action contrary to that person's wish takes place.

As already noted, it is obvious from the content that the Prophet (not God) spoke the words of verse 24 of *sura* 33: "in order that God may reward the sincere for their sincerity and punish the hypocrites, if He so wishes, or else absolve them. He is forgiving, merciful."

The Arabs, being temperamentally unstable and fickle, veered in whatever direction the wind might blow, and thus some Moslems from Mecca had actually joined Abu Jahl's force and fought against Mohammad at Badr. The inconstancy and disloyalty of these men, who were very poor, displeased God so much that verses 99 and 100 of *sura* 4 (*on-Nesā*) were sent down. "(To) those whom the angels took away while they were wronging themselves, (the angels) said, 'How were you off?' They said, 'We were impoverished on the earth.' (The angels) said, 'Was not

God's earth spacious enough for you to emigrate in it?' (For) those men, their shelter will be hell, a nasty destination" (verse 99). "But not for those impoverished men, women, and children who are incapable of guile and receive no guidance to a (right) path. Those God will perhaps pardon, as God is pardoning, forgiving" (verse 100).

At Mecca before the *hejra*, God had sent down to Mohammad the command: "Summon (people) to your Lord's path with wisdom and good preaching, and argue with them by (using arguments) that are better! Your Lord knows well who have erred from His path, and He knows well who have been (rightly) guided" (*sura* 16, *on-Nahl*, verse 126).

A few years later, after Islam's rise to power and Mohammad's triumphal entry into Mecca at the head of an army, God's tone changed and acquired a harsh, peremptory note: "When the sacred months are over, kill the polytheists wherever you find them! Catch them, besiege them, and lie in ambush for them everywhere!" (*sura* 9, *ot-Tawba*, verse 5).

In view of the limitations of human nature, it is only natural that a person should react in one way to difficulty and in another way to success, and should speak and act accordingly; but in view of the divine omnipotence and omniscience, it is inconceivable that God should experience such reactions. Nevertheless the assurance that "there is no compulsion in religion" (*sura* 2, 257), which God sent down in the first year after the *hejra*, was followed, probably one year later, by the command to "fight in God's cause" (*sura* 2, 186 and 245) and by the warning that "believers who sit (at home), other than the disabled, are not the equals of those who commit their properties and their lives to the war for God's cause" (*sura* 4, 97). Thus the believers were required to fight people who had been told a year earlier that they would not be compelled to become Moslems if they did not so wish; and at the same time the believers were told that they were not all equal, those who contributed to the war by giving their money or wielding their swords being superior to those who only professed Islam and followed its rules.

At Mecca before the *hejra*, God had revealed to His Apostle the moral precept that "The kind action and the unkind action are not equal. Repay (the unkind action) with that which is kinder! Then the person who is at enmity with you will become like a close friend" (*sura* 41, *Fosselat*, verse 34). At Madina, God sent contrary instructions to His Apostle: "Do not be weak and call for peace when you are uppermost!" (*sura* 47, *Mohammad*, verse 37).

Such changes of tone and method are bound to attract attention. Also noteworthy in the Qor'ān are some of the questions which the Controller of the Universe, with its myriads of stars and planets, put to the Arabs of the Hejāz. One example is the question about water in verse 68 of *sura* 56 (*ol-Wāqe'a*): "Did you bring it down from the clouds, or do We send it down?"

In some passages, the Creator seems to have the same need as any poor mortal for human help. One such passage (already quoted earlier in this chapter) is verse 25 of *sura* 57 (*ol-Hadid*): "And We sent down iron, (because) in it lie great power and benefits for the people, and so that God in the unseen world may know who support Him and His Apostles." This appears to mean that only human use of the sword could tell God who were supporting Him and His Apostle.

There are more than fifty Qor'ānic verses in which God states that the guidance of humans depends wholly on His will and choice. Three are quoted below.

"Those against whom your Lord's word has taken effect will not believe, even if every sign has come to them. In the end they will see painful punishment." (*sura* 10, *Yunos*, verses 95 and 96).

"And if We had so wished, We would have given every soul its guidance. But the word from Me has taken effect. I shall fill hell with genies and humans together." (*sura* 32, *os-Sajda*, verse 13).

"So taste (the punishment) for forgetting your encounter on this day! (i.e. with God on the judgement day). We have forgotten you. Taste eternal punishment for what you have been doing!" (*sura* 32, verse 14).

Reading these verses makes the hair stand on end. According to what they say, God does not desire to guide many humans aright, and then inflicts eternal and painful punishment on those humans for not being guided aright.

God's lack of desire for the right guidance of all mankind is explicitly affirmed in verse 25 of *sura* 6 (*ol-An'ām*) and again, with identical wording, in verse 55 of *sura* 18 (*ol-Kahf*): "We have put covers on their hearts, in case they might understand it, and a heaviness in their ears . . . . . . "

Yes, as already said, more than fifty verses threaten eternal and painful punishment for those whom God chooses not to guide. The subject cannot be pursued here. A different, but no less astonishing, matter requires attention. This is the presence of abrogating and abrogated verses in the Qor'ān.

The Qor'ān-commentators and theologians collected and explained all the cases of abrogation.[82] A previously revealed verse was abrogated by a subsequently revealed verse with a different or contrary meaning.

Change of mind after the taking of a decision or making of a plan is a normal and frequent occurrence in the lives of human beings, who cannot at any time know all the relevant facts. The human mind is limited and prone to deception by outward appearances, but is capable of learning from experience and recognising mistakes. It is therefore fitting and desirable that men and women should revise their past decisions or plans. It is contrary to reason, however, that God, who is omniscient and omnipotent, should revise His commands. This point prompted Mohammad's opponents to scoff that he issued an order one day and cancelled it the next day. Their protests are answered in verse 100 of *sura* 2 (*ol-Baqara*): "Whenever We abrogate a verse or order that it be forgotten, We bring a better one or a similar one. Do not you know that God is capable of everything?"

It is precisely because God is capable of everything that He would not reveal a verse and then abrogate it. Since omniscience and omnipotence are essential attributes of the Creator, He must be able to issue commands which do not need revision. Every thoughtful person who believes in One Almighty God is bound to ask why He should proclaim a command and then revoke it.

There is a contradiction in the above-quoted verse. Since God is capable of everything, why did not He reveal the better verse first?

It seems that there were hecklers in those days too, and that they were persistent. A reply was given to them in verses 103 and 104 of *sura* 16 (*on-Nahl*): "When We have replaced a verse with (another) verse – and God knows well what He sends down – they say, 'You are a mere fabricator.' But most of them have no knowledge. Say (to them), 'The Holy Ghost brought it down from your Lord, truly (so), in order to confirm the believers.'"

On the assumption that the Qor'ān is God's word, there ought to be no trace of human intellectual imperfection in anything that God says. Yet in these two verses the incongruity is obvious. Of course God knows what He sends down. For that very reason the replacement of one verse by another made the protesters suspicious. Evidently even the simple, uneducated Hejāzi Arabs could understand that Almighty God, being aware of what is best for His servants, would prescribe the best in the first place and would not have changes of mind in the same way as His imperfect creatures.

Study and reflection lead to the conclusion that this incongruity can only be explained as the product of an inextricable confusion between God and Mohammad. God had manifested Himself in the depths of Mohammad's mind and made Mohammad His messenger to guide the people. Mohammad was fulfilling the mission while retaining his human characteristics. The verses of the Qor'ān are outpourings from both parts of his personality.

The observations made by Ignaz Goldziher at the start of chapter 3 of his valuable book *Le dogme et le loi de l'Islam* may seem startling, but perhaps come near to solving the problem; they certainly deserve consideration. "Prophets," he writes, "are not philosophers or theologians. The messages which their consciences prompt them to convey, and the religious beliefs which they call into being, do not form a corpus of doctrine built on a premeditated plan and are not as a rule capable of systematization."

In other words, teachings inspired by a prophet's conscience pour forth from his inner soul; people are drawn to his teachings, and the number of believers grows until a new religious community takes shape; scholars then appear and try to coordinate the popular beliefs into a system. If the scholars find a lacuna, they fill it, and if they find an inconsistency, they explain it away. For every simple statement by the prophet, they imagine or invent some hidden meaning, and for every inspired utterance some logical sequence. In short, they bring up meanings and concepts which never passed through the prophet's mind, and reply to questions and difficulties which never troubled him. They do all this with the aim of creating a theological and philosophical system which, they hope, will be an impregnable fortress against internal doubters and external opponents. They base the whole edifice on the Prophet's own words. These zealous scholars do not go unchallenged, however, because other theologians and commentators extract different meanings from the same words of the prophet and construct other systems at variance with the system of the first group.

Although Goldziher's perceptive observations are expressed in general terms and about all religions, his insight must have been

greatly sharpened by his study of the fierce controversies which
raged in the early centuries of Islam between the Khārejite,[83]
Shi'ite, Morje'ite,[84] Mo'tazelite,[85] and Ash'arite[86] sects. Being a
Jew and having acquired a thorough knowledge of the history of
the Christian churches, he was well aware of the similar controversies in the Jewish and Christian religions; but he clearly owed his
keen insight to his extensive studies of the developments in Islam.
A few more brief illustrations of the nature of the basic issue may
fittingly be included in this chapter.

The Qor'ān contains many figures of speech, whose meaning
ought to be obvious to every intelligent reader. For example, the
words "God's hand is above their hands" in verse 10 of *sura* 48
(*ol-Fat-h*) clearly means that God's power is superior to all other
powers. Likewise the meaning of "The Merciful occupied the
throne" in *sura* 25 (*ol-Forqān*), verse 60 (also in 7, 52; 10, 3; 32, 3;
57, 4) is not that God, who has no body, sat on a ceremonial chair,
but that God was and is the supreme master. In *sura* 75 (*ol-
Qiyāma*), the words of verses 22 and 23 "On that day (i.e. the
judgement day), faces will be radiant, looking toward their Lord"
appear from the context to mean that on that day righteous men
and women will turn their thoughts to God. The repeated statement that God is hearing and seeing (*suras* 22, 60 and 74; 31, 27;
42, 9; 58, 1) manifestly mean that nothing is unknown to God.

Many Moslems, however, have had rigid minds. Such men only
accepted interpretations which are confirmed by Hadiths, and
they considered any use of reason in religious matters to be
misleading and impermissible. They took the above-quoted
Qor'ānic phrases literally and believed that God possesses a head,
mouth, eyes, ears, hands, and feet just like those of a human being.
In the opinion of Abu Ma`mar al-Hodhali (d. 236/850), a
preacher at Baghdād, anyone who denied this belief was an infidel.
Adherents of the school of the famous traditionist and lawyer
Ahmad b. Hanbal (164/780–241/855) have stuck to the same
unthinking literalism ever since. The school's chief later
exponent, Ahmad b. Taymiya, was so fanatical that he called the
Mo'tazelites infidels and Ghazzali a heretic; on one celebrated
occasion, after quoting the Qor'ān in a sermon, he said to the
congregation as he stepped down from the pulpit of the Great
Mosque at Damascus, "God will step down from His throne in the
same way as I am stepping down from this pulpit."

These narrow-minded bigots considered not only the Mo'tazelite but even the Ash'arite theologians to be un-Islamic and condemned any sort of divergence from their own crudely simplistic views as pernicious innovation. Abu 'Āmer ol-Qorashi, a Moor from Majorca who died at Baghdād in 524/1130, declared that it was heretical to understand the sentence "There is nothing similar to Him" in verse 9 of *sura* 42 (*osh-Showrā*) as meaning what it says; it meant, in his opinion, that nothing resembles God in respect of His divinity, because "God possesses limbs and organs like yours and mine." As proof of God's possession of such limbs and organs, Abu 'Āmer ol-Qorashi cited the description of the last judgement in verse 42 of *sura* 68 (*ol-Qalam*) "On the day when the leg will be bared and they will be bidden to kneel but cannot," and then slapped his thigh and said, "God has legs just like mine."

The beliefs of these literalists or, as they are sometimes called, fundamentalists cannot fail to remind those who study them of the primitive notions and customs prevalent in pre-Islamic Arabia. The Arabs did not suddenly lose their materialistic outlook, their inability to think in abstract terms, their unconcern with spiritual matters, and their unruliness and obstinacy. On the whole, their minds were not much influenced by their intermingling with other nations such as the Iranians or by their contacts with intellectually inclined Islamic groups such as the Mo'tazelites, the Sufis, the Shi'ites, the Ekhwān os-Safā, and the Bātenites.[87]

It is on record that all of the chief exponents of fundamentalism were of Arab descent, and that most of the intellectuals of early Islam were not of Arab descent. The Mo'tazelite and later religious thinkers were either non-Arabs or Arabs who had dropped the primitive outlook under the influence of Greek and Iranian ideas. These facts confirm the opinion, expressed at the start of this chapter, that men create God in their own image.

## GENIES AND MAGIC

Genies resemble humans but are normally invisible. There are male genies (*jenni*) and female genies (*jenniya*), malevolent genies, and benevolent genies or fairies. On rare occasions a genie is seen by a human, and it is even possible for a fairy princess to fall in love with a man or for a male genie to love a woman. There are also evil spirits, which sometimes enter human bodies and make them epileptic. Notions like these have long been found in all peoples and communities.

Equally widespread and long-standing is belief in magic. It is a notion that incantations, amulets, and drugs or other substances can procure results unobtainable by ordinary means; for instance that these things can cause a person to die, fall in love, or go mad, or that making a wax doll and sticking pins into its eyes can immediately cause a person living hundreds of miles away to go blind. Such fatuities have been in vogue among all nations since the dawn of recorded history, and are still deplorably common even among the more advanced nations.

These two types of illusion are not difficult to explain. Man is a perceptive and inquisitive animal. The human mind searches for causes of the phenomena which it perceives, and has difficulty in finding them. When the weak human mind cannot penetrate the darkness of the unknown, it has recourse to guessing and fantasy. Failure of the rational faculty gives scope to the imaginative faculty. Man is weak against nature, and subject to fears and desires which cannot be appeased by normal means.

Factors like these push mankind into the abyss of superstition. Notions such as the predictability of the future by means of omen-reading, astrology, geomancy, or arithmomancy get a grip on benighted minds, and phantasms of every kind and shape proliferate. Not surprisingly the Arabs of the 7th century A.D. were sunk in superstition. What is surprising is that in the Qor'ān the two illusions which were discussed above are not only mentioned but also presented as facts.

The effects of magic and the evil eye are the subject of two *suras*, 113 (*ol-Falaq*) and 114 (*on-Nās*). The explanation of these *suras* given by most Qor'ān-commentators is that the Qorayshite polytheists induced Labid b. A'sam to make a charm which would prevent the Prophet from pursuing his work, and that the Prophet consequently fell ill until Gabriel came down and informed him. According to the Cambridge *Tafsir*, the Prophet, when asleep during his illness, dreamed that two angels hovered over his head and one asked the other, "Why is this man sick and groaning?" The other angel answered, "Because of the charm which Labid made for him and buried in the well of Dorwān." When the Prophet woke, he sent 'Ali b. Abi Tāleb and 'Ammār b. Yāser (an early convert) to take the charm out of the well. They removed the water from the well, lifted the stone from the bottom, and as the angels had foretold, found the charm, which was a string on which eleven knots had been tied. They brought it to the Prophet.

Thereupon the two *suras*, in which together there are eleven verses, began to come down, and every time that a verse was recited a knot became untied, with the result that the Prophet was cured. Tabari gives a more highly colored account, while the *Tafsir ol-Jalālayn* simply states that the recitation of each verse caused the untying of each knot. Zamakhshari, who did not accept that magic has effects, omits this story in his *Kashshāf*; like other rational thinkers, he interprets "the evil of what He (God) has created" in verse 2 of *sura* 113 as probably referring to poison or some such created thing which one human can use to injure another.

No commentator or theologian, however, has denied the existence of genies, because they are mentioned in more than ten Qor'ānic passages and are explicitly stated, in verse 14 of *sura* 55 (*or-Rahmān*), to have been created by God out of smokeless fire. Moreover *sura* 72, which is known as the *Surat ol-Jenn*, states in its first two verses that a company of genies listened (to the Qor'ān being recited) and said, "We have heard a wonderful Qor'ān. It guides to righteousness, so we have believed in it and will never ascribe any partner to our Lord."

The ancient Arabs, like other primitive peoples, believed in the existence of good and evil spirits, and all the more readily because of the harshness and solitude of their desert environment. There is a report that when an Arab dismounted to spend the night in an uninhabited waste, he would be so frightened that he would utter supplications to the king of the fairies to shelter him and to the king of the genies to prevent impudent genies from molesting him. Verse 6 of *sura* 72 warns that taking shelter with genies only makes them more impudent.

While it is easy to understand why illusions and irrational ideas are so common among primitive peoples and lower classes of advanced nations, it is surprising to find them in a book deemed to be God's word and in the preaching of a man who challenged his own people's superstitions and sought to reform their customs and morals.

It is conceivable that the contents of the *Surat ol-Jenn* describe a dream which Mohammad saw. His glimpse of the angel during the first revelation, when he was appointed to the prophethood, has been called the beatific vision, and his second glimpse of the angel during his night journey to the Furthest Mosque has likewise been interpreted as a dream.

Another possible hypothesis is that the ideas of Mohammad's

compatriots had such a strong influence on his imaginative mind that he actually came to visualize a race having the same perceptive and rational faculties and moral obligations as humans and requiring similar exhortation to belief in One God and the life to come. In that case, however, it may be asked why the genies were not aided by the appointment of an apostle of their own race to guide them, because in several Qor'ānic passages (e.g. *sura* 10, 48 and *sura* 16, 38) it is stated that every nation receives its own messenger from God, i.e. one who belongs to the nation and speaks its language. Moreover it is stated in verse 97 of *sura* 17 that if the angels had been walking safely on the earth, God would have sent down an angel from heaven as an apostle to them.

It is also possible to regard the *Surat ol-Jenn* as a piece of allegorical preaching. As the poet Jalāl od-Din Rumi said, "When you are dealing with children, you must use childish language." Perhaps the Prophet, making allowance for the mentality of his people, invented the story that the genies had heard the Qor'ān and been so impressed that they had become Moslems.

Whatever the explanation may be, no blame attaches to the Prophet Mohammad. The great philosophers of ancient Greece, with all their lofty ideas and achievements in mathematics and natural and social sciences, could not ignore the ideas of their people; indeed they were steeped in Greek religious mythology. Nevertheless there is a dilemma. Moslems believe that the Qor'ān consists of God's revelations to Mohammad and deny that any part of it was composed by Mohammad. Furthermore the *Surat ol-Jenn* begins with the command "Say". Does God concur with beliefs about genies and fairies once held by Hejāzi Arabs? Or were these beliefs spread and perpetuated by the Prophet Mohammad's utterances?

# COSMOGONY AND CHRONOLOGY

The Old Testament is a precious legacy of records from the history of human thought. It illustrates the naïvety of primitive people's ideas about the creation and the creator. According to its account, God created heaven and earth in six days and rested on the seventh day, which was the Sabbath day; but since the sun obviously did not exist before the creation of heaven and earth, the phenomena of sunrise and sunset, which enable humans to measure time in units of day and night, cannot then have been present. In any case, why did God need a human scale to measure the time taken in the creation? Why did He measure it in terrestrial days rather than the days of some other planet, for instance in Neptune-days? Sunrise and sunset are the ascent and descent of the sun as seen from the earth's surface. If God had not yet created the sun and the earth, how could there have been any days and nights? Did Moses place the effect before the cause?

However that may be, God's creation of the universe in six days is reaffirmed eight times in the Qor'ān, as follows:

(i) "Your Lord is God who created the heavens and the earth in six days, then occupied the throne" (*sura* 10, *Yunos*, verse 3).

(ii) Exactly the same words as in (i) in *sura* 7 (*ol-A'rāf*), verse 52.

(iii) "And it was He who created the heavens and the earth in six days, while His throne was on the water, in order that He might test you (to find) which of you are better in conduct" (*sura* 11, *Hud*, verse 9). In this verse the theme of creation in six days is supplemented with the statement that during the creation the throne was on the water, which implies that the throne and the water existed before the creation of the heavens and the earth. In *sura* 10, 3, and *sura* 7, 52, it is stated that God mounted the throne after the creation of the heavens and the earth, and this may perhaps be a partial echo of the biblical story of God's rest on the seventh day. It is noteworthy that the account of the creation in the three above-quoted verses is given in the third person, and that the speaker must therefore be the Prophet Mohammad. In the verse quoted below, the speaker is God.

(iv) "And We created the heavens and the earth and what is between the two in six days, and no weariness touched Us" (*sura* 50, *Qāf*, verse 37). This verse differs from the three previous ones in that it mentions not only the heavens and the earth but also the space between the two, and denies that the heavy task of creating these structures wearied God. Weariness, being an involuntary diminution of vital energy experienced by weak and mortal humans and animals, obviously cannot be attributed to an omnipotent and everlasting creator. The words "no weariness touched Us" are therefore surprising, but may perhaps be a refutation of the biblical statement that God rested on the seventh day, which implies that God was weary on that day.

(v) "Say, 'Do you disbelieve in Him who created the earth in two days?'" (*sura* 41, *Fosselat*, verse 8). Here again the speaker is not Mohammad, but God, who specifies the time taken in the creation of the earth as two days. The sentence implies that it was because all the Arabs of Mecca knew about the creation of the earth in two days that they ought not to deny the existence of the person who had accomplished that heavy task in two days. But the Arabs must have lacked this knowledge; otherwise they would not have been asked why they disbelieved in the Creator. Although God is the speaker, the wording is inappropriate for a divine utterance. God would not expect people to believe in Him because some Arabs acknowledged that there was a person who had created the earth in two days. The sentence must therefore be regarded as a product of the Prophet Mohammad's imagination.

(vi) "And He fixed towering mountains in it, on top of it, and blessed it, and predetermined its nutrients in it, in four days, equally for all who ask" (sura 41, verse 9).

(vii) "Then He occupied the heaven while it was smoke and said to it and to the earth, 'Come, both of you, willingly or unwillingly!' They both said, 'We come (and) are willing'" (sura 41, verse 10). God's throne is not mentioned in sura 41, but the heaven or sky takes its place in verse 10. Sky and earth in Arabic are feminine nouns, and the verb "said" in verse 10 is accordingly feminine and dual; but the adjective "willing" at the end of the verse is masculine and plural, and thus at variance with the rules of Arabic grammar.

(viii) "Then He disposed them, seven heavens, in two days, and inspired into each heaven its function" (sura 41, verse 11). In this verse two extra days for the stratification of the seven heavens are added, and the time taken in the creation is thereby increased from six to eight days. This further confusion makes it impossible to regard the words as God's words.

Another dilemma is posed by the calendar ordinance in verse 36 of sura 9 (ot-Tawba): "The number of the months in God's sight is twelve, (as written) in God's book on the day when He created the heavens and the earth. Four of them are sacred. That is the right religion."

The world's peoples understand a year to be the period of roughly 365¼ days in which the earth revolves around the sun. They perceive four seasons in the year and arrange their work according to the seasons. Early civilized peoples, such as the Babylonians, Egyptians, Chinese, Iranians, and Greeks, used the solar year in their time reckoning and divided it into four quarters of three months each, making twelve months in the year; they determined the quarters by observation of the sun's varying positions in the sky. For primitive peoples with little or no knowledge of mathematics, accurate observation of the sun was difficult; they therefore preferred the simpler method of time measurement by observation of the phases of the moon. The lunar months, however, are useless for timing agricultural operations, which are mankind's main means of subsistence.

The Arabs used the lunar months, and in order to obtain regular suspensions of fighting and feuding, treated four of those months as sacred. Some of the Arabs tried to bring their year of twelve lunar months into line with the solar calendar by periodically "postponing" the new year, i.e. increasing the length of the old year. In the Qor'ān, however, the old Arab use of the lunar year is seen as an inviolable law of nature, and intercalation is prohibited in verse 37 of *sura* 9: "Postponement is an increase in unbelief." The Lord who made observance of ancient Arab lunar time-reckoning compulsory everywhere and for ever must have been either a local Arabian god or the Prophet Mohammad.

In like manner the Arab national custom of pilgrimage to Mecca was made a religious duty for Moslems, and the running from Safā to Marwa became an Islamic rite.

In verse 185 of *sura* 2 (*ol-Baqara*), a human custom or rule is stated to be the cause of a natural phenomenon: "They ask you about crescent moons. Say, 'They are appointed times for the people and for the pilgrimage.'" The *Tafsir ol-Jalālayn* makes the absurd comment that the reason for the moon's waxing and waning is to inform people of the right times for sowing, reaping, pilgrimage, fasting, and fast-breaking. The moon's phases are of course no help in agricultural timing, and the lunar months were prescribed for the timing of pilgrimage and fasting because the solar months had not come into general use in Arabia. The real reason for the moon's waxing and waning is its orbital movement around the earth with consequent change of position of its earth-facing disc in relation to the sun, and the coincidence of this phenomenon with the terrestrial phenomenon of night and day. The crescent moon and the full moon had been visible for thousands of years before the Arabs lived in the Hejāz and Najd, and no doubt been potentially visible for many millions of years before the human race existed. The

Creator of the Universe is certainly aware of these facts; He would therefore not have uttered words which put an effect in the place of its cause.

Even more astonishing is the question in verse 31 of *sura* 21 (*ol-Anbiyā*): "Have not the unbelievers seen that the heavens and the earth were (one) stitched piece and We unstitched them?" The unbelievers were not the only people who could not see how the heavens had once been stitched to the earth and were then unstitched; people who are not unbelievers also find it hard to understand.

# CHAPTER 5

# *After Mohammad*

## THE SUCCESSION

Early in the year 11 A.H. (probably on 8 June 632 A.D.), the star which had beckoned to the Arab peoples for nearly twenty three years ceased to shine.

The event caused immediate tumult. Before the Prophet Mohammad's corpse was cold, a clamor for "an *amir* of ours and an *amir* of yours" rang out in the hall of the Banu Sā'eda, where the Ansār had hastily assembled. Rivalry for power between the Madinan Ansār and the Meccan Mohājerun was already at boiling point.

Study of the history of Islam shows it to be a sequence of struggles for power in which the contestants treated the religion as a means, not as an end.

In the thirteen years between Mohammad's appointment to the Prophethood and his move to Madina, his mission was purely spiritual. The Qor'ānic revelations from that period consist entirely of preaching, guidance, and exhortation to do good and shun evil. In the Madinan period, the spiritual tone is less marked and much of the content is made up of instructions and laws intended to strengthen the Moslems against their foes and to lay the foundation of a political and national entity. The intention was fulfilled. Favorable circumstances also helped to bring a new Islamic community and state into being.

While it is clear from the Qor'ān and the reports of the Prophet's actions that the Meccan and Madinan periods were very different, there can be no question that his goal was always to implant Islam. It was eventually achieved under the flag of a state.

All the Prophet's decisions were taken in pursuit of this goal. Use of force, political assassination, and bloodshed with no apparent legal or moral excuse were among the tactics chosen to promote Islam's advance.

After the Prophet's death, however, ambition for the leadership replaced zeal for the religion as the pivotal motive. At the same time there was unanimous agreement that Islam, having been the cause of the new state's rise, was necessary for its survival or, in simpler language, that the religion which had made the leadership possible must be resolutely maintained. In the event, Islamic principles and Prophetic custom were strictly observed in the twelve years of the caliphates of Abu Bakr (11/632–13/634) and 'Omar (13/634–23/644); but the further the Prophet's death receded into the past, the greater became the tendency to treat the religion as a means rather than as an end in itself – to use it as an instrument for seizure of the leadership and the rulership.

As soon as the Prophet's death became known, Sa'd b. 'Obāda (the chief of the Khazrajite Ansār) made a bid for the leadership of the whole Moslem community. An adroit move by 'Omar secured the leadership for Abu Bakr and consigned Sa'd b. 'Obāda to oblivion. Abu Bakr repaid his debt to 'Omar by defining the leadership as the "succession (khelāfat) to the Prophet", i.e. caliphate, and by recommending that 'Omar should be chosen as the next caliph. 'Omar, on his deathbed after being stabbed, appointed a six-man committee to choose his own successor, though he was actually in favor of 'Abd or-Rahmān b. 'Awf. The committee's choice, however, fell on 'Othmān, whose caliphate was ended by assassination in 35/656. Despite the allegiance then given to 'Ali, the five years of his caliphate were spent in fighting civil wars (at the battles of the camel, Seffin, and Nahrawān) and in contending with the hostile designs of Mo'āwiya and 'Amr b. ol-'Ās until he too was assassinated in 40/661. The Omayyad caliphate of Mo'āwiya and his successors, the killing of 'Ali's son Hosayn in 61/680, the desecration of the Ka'ba in the fighting against 'Abdollāh b. oz-Zobayr in 64/683, the Hāshemite propaganda and the fall of the Omayyads, the 'Abbāsid takeover of the caliphate, the rival Fātemid caliphate in the west and the revolutionary Esmā'ilite movements in the east, the events which culminated in the fall of Baghdād to Hulāgu Khān's Mongols in 656/1258 – all these were symptoms of the same mania for power in the guise of succession to the Prophet of Islam.

How was the government which Mohammad's spiritual energy and the Qor'ānic revelations had brought into being to be run after his decease? Ought the Prophet to have designated his successor and thus made clear to the new community of Moslems where their duty lay? Ought the Prophet's companions to have somehow reached agreement on the choice of his successor? Since the prophethood had been a God-given trust, ought the future spiritual leadership (emāmate) of the Moslems to partake of the same characteristics? If the Prophet had named a successor, whom would he have chosen? Would he have selected his nephew and son-in-law 'Ali, the finest man in his own clan of Hāshem, the first male convert to Islam, a warrior whose bravery had served the cause well and protected his own life from danger? Would his choice have fallen on Abu Bakr, a senior and much respected man whose conversion in the early days of the mission had brought credit to Islam, who had accompanied him and shared the shelter of a cave with him on his flight to Madina, who had given him a beautiful daughter in marriage? Or would he have preferred 'Omar, a man of firm will and keen political acumen and a staunch defender of the faith? But had the Prophet ever thought of naming his successor? Why had he shown no sign of such an intention during the ten years of his career at Madina? Yet is it conceivable that the Prophet, who had built up the Islamic community and government from nothing and always shown great statesmanship and foresight, should have neglected such an important matter? Would the Prophet, who in the last days of his life had identified Arab nationalism with Islam by saying that there must henceforth be only one religion in Arabia, have left the future of the new state to chance?

Many such questions spring to the mind. They can never be answered. All the suggestions that have been made are mere conjecture. The problem lay at the root of most of the conflicts which were to trouble the future course of Islam.

It certainly appears that the Prophet made no definite provision for the succession. Well authenticated reports state that the Prophet, during a stop at the Pool of Khomm (Ghadir Khomm) on his way back to Madina after his farewell pilgrimage in 10 A.H./632, took 'Ali by the hand and said, "Those whose friend I am, 'Ali is their friend." (The word *mawlā*, literally "made near", was used with two meanings: "protector and befriender", or "protégé and befriended"). In the Shi'ite belief, these words of the Prophet were his designation of 'Ali to be his successor. The Sonnites reject this belief; if they accept the truth of the statement

168

at all, they interpret the Prophet's words as commendation of 'Ali for his services to the Islamic cause, which all Moslems acknowledge. If it can be argued that the Prophet's utterance at Ghadir Khomm was his designation of 'Ali, it can be equally well argued that his order from his deathbed to Abu Bakr to go to the mosque and take his place as leader of the prayer indicated his desire to be succeeded by Abu Bakr.

The theory of the caliphate held by the Sonnite Moslems conflicts with the Shi'ite belief but at first sight may seem convincing. They maintain that the revelation of the words "Today I have perfected your religion for you and completed My bounty to you" (in verse 5 of *sura* 5, *ol-Mā'eda*) marked the end of Mohammad's prophetic mission and limited the obligations of Moslems to those laid on them by the Qor'ān. On this assumption, the Qor'ānic legislation is perfect and complete. Hence it is not necessary that there should be a divinely guided and infallible successor to the Prophet (as the Shi'ites believe); it is sufficient that the leadership of the Moslems should be held by a man who is earnest in enforcing the Qor'ānic commandments and in following the example of the Prophet's conduct. The Prophet's companions therefore had the right to appoint a successor who was well qualified to direct the Moslem community's affairs in accordance with the Qor'ān and the *sonna* (Prophetic custom and precedent).

This Sonnite theory, for all its plausibility, is an example of ex post facto reasoning, being based on a particular interpretation of the course of events under the first four caliphs. Careful study of the history of the caliphate proves the theory to be unsound.

The dispute in the hall of the Banu Sā'eda shows clearly that what was uppermost in the minds was ambition for the leadership, not concern to find a successor capable of directing affairs in accordance with the Qor'ān and the *sonna*. At that meeting both the Ansār and the Mohājerun claimed precedence, the former on the ground of their help, the latter on that of their kinship, to the Prophet.

Nobody from the Prophet's own clan, the Banu Hāshem, took part in this meeting of chiefs to decide the succession. His cousin 'Ali and his uncle 'Abbās, who were his closest relatives, did not attend. Also absent were two of "the ten to whom paradise was promised" (i.e. the first ten male converts to Islam), namely Talha b. 'Obaydollāh and Zobayr b. ol-'Awwām; they were at 'Ali's house, busy making arrangements for the washing and burial of the Prophet's corpse. When 'Ali was told that the meeting had been held and that the Mohājerun had prevailed over the Ansār on the strength of the argument that they were of the Prophet's "tree", he is reported to have said, "They have put up the argument of the tree, but they have lost (sight of) the fruit."

As for Zobayr, the news of the meeting reportedly made him shout in anger, "I shall not sheathe my sword until I get them to swear allegiance to 'Ali."

The reports of Abu Sofyān's remarks run as follows: "O descendants of 'Abd Manāf (the common ancestor of the Omayyad and Hāshemite clans), a sandstorm has blown up which cannot be calmed with smooth words. Why should Abu Bakr thwart you? Have they placed the succession in the poorest clan of the Qoraysh (i.e. Abu Bakr's clan) because they do not find 'Abbās and 'Ali lowly enough?" Then he turned to 'Ali and said, "Give me your hand so that I may swear allegiance to you! I will fill Madina with mounted men and foot-soldiers if you so wish." 'Ali refused his offer of allegiance.

It certainly appears that, with the single exception of 'Ali, whose sincere devotion to the Prophet and faith in Islam had raised him to a moral plane well above the old Arab standard, all the chief figures were actuated by ambition to rule. A report which confirms this view, and is quoted in Tabari's Annals as well as Ebn Heshām's Biography, deserves repetition here: "'Ali went out of the Prophet's house on the last day of his illness. People thronged around 'Ali, asking him about the Prophet's health, and 'Ali answered them, 'He is recovering, thank God.' 'Abbās took 'Ali aside and said, 'In my opinion he is dying. I have seen on his face the same signs that were on the faces of the sons of 'Abd ol-Mottaleb before their deaths. Go back to the Prophet and ask who is to take charge after him! If the authority is to be with us, we shall be informed; if it is to be with others, he will recommend us (to them).' 'Ali replied, 'I shall never ask such a question. If he withholds it from us, nobody in future will turn to us.'"

It is an undeniable fact that the reigns of the first two caliphs turned out well. While their accessions may have been contrived by questionable means and without unanimous agreement of the Prophet's companions, their methods of government did not deviate from the Qor'ān and the *sonna*. Abu Bakr and 'Omar were honest men. Although 'Ali, as the most eligible candidate for the succession, waited for six months before he swore allegiance to

Abu Bakr, he did not, according to the reports, show any similar hesitation to swear allegiance to 'Omar.

The same cannot be said of the third caliph. In 'Othmān's reign, deviation from Qor'ānic norms took place on such a scale that the whole Moslem community smoldered and a revolt flared up,

There had been a semblance of democracy in 'Othmān's succession, in that the choice was made by a committee and supported by public opinion. 'Omar had appointed the six members of the committee and instructed them to choose one of themselves as his successor. The six men were 'Ali, 'Othmān, Talha, Zobayr, Sa'd b. Abi'l-Waqqās, and 'Abd or-Rahman b. 'Awf. On the proposal of 'Abd or-Rahmān b. 'Awf, the caliphate was offered to either 'Ali or 'Othmān; when 'Ali expressed reluctance, 'Abd or-Rahmān b. 'Awf swore allegiance to 'Othmān, and the others followed his lead. In order to gauge public opinion, 'Abd or-Rahmān had conducted a sort of referendum in the preceding three days.

Nevertheless the reign of this caliph who had risen to power with the whole community's approval soon fell short of the standard set by the Prophet. No fewer than fifty wrongdoings by 'Othmān have been recorded. For most of these the ambition and greed of members of his clan were to blame. 'Othmān himself was a modest man, but he was too weak to resist the importunities of his relatives. His weakness stood in marked contrast to 'Omar's firmness. Not even the advice of wise companions of the Prophet could make him take heed.

The most popular of all the choices for the caliphate was that of 'Ali. His accession was welcomed by public opinion at Madina and by most companions of the Prophet. In his short reign, however, he had to fight three civil wars and to face conspiracy and perfidy from many different quarters. Even the Prophet's veteran companions Talha and Zobayr broke their oaths of allegiance to 'Ali, and took up arms against him because he refused to give them the governorships of Kufa and Basra respectively.

Dozens more cases of this kind could be cited. History shows that the Sonnite theory of the caliphate, even if it can be accepted in principle, was belied in practice and did not work to the good of the Islamic community. Greed for power and wealth prevailed over concern to enforce the commandments of the Qor'ān and rules of the *sonna*.

This again raises the question whether the Prophet Mohammad was more competent than any other person or group to appoint his successor. Surely, it will be thought, he was uniquely well qualified to do so, not only by his gift of inspiration and prophethood but also by his possession of intellectual and moral strengths and other qualities far exceeding those of his contemporaries, by his absolute devotion to the Islamic cause, and in particular by his knowledge of human nature and of the characters of his companions. Yet he refrained from this step, even at the zenith of his career when nobody would have dared to oppose him. Why did he refrain? Did he give no thought to such an important matter as the choice of his successor? Or did he think that the time was not ripe and that he would have many more years in which to make the choice?

The Prophet was not very old when he fell ill; by all accounts he was in his sixty third year. His illness was short. There are grounds for supposing that he did not regard it as mortal but expected until the last day that he would recover. This must have been the reason why on the first day he asked his wives to let him be nursed at 'Ā'esha's house. He is reported to have said jokingly to 'Ā'esha, who had a headache, "Are you going to die before me and give me the tasks of getting your corpse washed and saying the prayer at your funeral?" Her reply, also jocular, was "In that case you could enjoy the company of your wives at my house without having to worry." Clearly the Prophet did not then expect his illness to be fatal.

This supposition is supported by the following fact. Shortly before that time the Prophet had mustered a force to attack the Christian Arabs in Syria and had appointed Zayd b. Hāretha's son Osāma, who was only twenty years old, to be its commander. This choice caused annoyance among the Moslem troops, because many worthy veterans from the Mohājerun and the Ansār were to serve in the force. Reports of widespread grumbling angered the Prophet so much that, after the start of his fever, he wound a wrap around his head and walked to the mosque, where he declared from the pulpit that the people's discontent was a form of disobedience and that Osāma b. Zayd was in every way the best choice. This action silenced the grumblers; it also indicates that the Prophet expected a short illness and a quick recovery.

Weight is added to this supposition by the fact that the Prophet died before he had attended to another matter just as important for the future of Islam as the choice of a successor. He had not arranged for the Qor'ān to be collected and edited under his supervision.

The Qor'ān is the warrant of Mohammad's prophethood and the

authoritative scripture of the Moslems. At the time of Mohammad's death it had not been collected and stored in one place, but was scattered among his companions and the scribes of the revelation. Many problems which were to trouble future theologians and commentators would have been solved if he had ordered its collection and personally supervised its editing. Different textual readings would not have gained currency, abrogating and abrogated verses would have been identified, and above all, the *suras* and verses would have been placed in the chronological sequence of their revelation, as 'Ali is reported to have done.

According to certain accounts, Zayd b. Thābet, who had been one of the Prophet's two chief scribes, made the following statement: "Abu Bakr summoned me and said, "Omar has for some time been pressing me to have the Qor'ān collected and edited. I was unwilling, because if collecting and editing the Qor'ān had been necessary, the Prophet himself would have attended to the matter. But at the battle of Yamāma (fought in Central Arabia against the rival prophet Mosaylema), so many companions of God's Apostle have been killed, and so many pieces of the Qor'ān which they took with them have been lost, that I now concur with 'Omar's opinion.'"

The significant point is that it was 'Omar who saw the need for this step and persuaded the caliph Abu Bakr to take it. Many years passed, however, before the editorial work was completed. The text which was finally prepared under the supervision of a committee appointed by 'Othmān is regrettably not ordered in chronological sequence of the revelations. The texts in the possession of 'Ali b. Abi Tāleb and 'Abdollāh b. Mas'ud were not consulted. The *suras* are placed illogically in order of decreasing length, when at least the Meccan *suras* might have been placed first and the Madinan *suras* last. There are also misplacements of Meccan verses inside Madinan *suras* and of Madinan verses inside Meccan *suras*.

In any case the fact that the Prophet did not arrange for the Qor'ān to be edited suggests that death caught him off guard. There is evidence that not until the last day did he sense that the illness would be fatal. That day has been recorded as either 28 Safar 11 A.H., or (more probably) 13 Rabi' ol-Awwal 11 A.H. corresponding to 8 June 632. It was then that the fever became acute and made him unconscious. Later he awoke and, in evident awareness of death's approach, said to those around him, "Bring

173

me an inkwell and a sheet so that I may write something (or cause something to be written) for you! After that, you will not err in future." Regrettably this last request of the Prophet was not carried out. Those present were at first astonished and then began arguing among themselves. One of them said, "Is he raving? Ought we to chant an exorcism?" Zaynab b. Jahsh and some of the companions said, "You ought to bring the things that the Prophet has said he wants." 'Omar said, "His fever is too severe. You have the Qor'ān. God's book is enough for us." The argumentation, between those in favor of letting the Prophet write or dictate a letter which would avert future error and those against letting him do so on the ground that the Qor'ān gave sufficient guidance, went on for a long time and distressed the Prophet so much that he told them to stop quarreling in his presence. None of them knew what the Prophet wished to write or, since he probably could not write, to dictate. Did he intend to name his successor? To pronounce on a matter not already determined in the Qor'ān, or to abrogate a Qor'ānic ordinance? To spell out a policy for the advancement of the Arab nation? If it was a matter of importance for the future of Islam, why did not he make it known orally? The enigma can never be solved.

There is a further vexed question which has caused much controversy. Why did 'Omar, a strong and steadfast man wholly committed to Islam and its founder, argue against bringing the writing material and recording the Prophet's last testament on the pretext that the Qor'ān was sufficient? Did 'Omar really think that the Prophet's fever had made him speak deliriously? Or did 'Omar, with his keen eye and realistic prescience, sense that the Prophet was going to name a successor before death came and would probably name 'Ali, in which case 'Omar would never hold any real power because the Prophet's testament would be respected by the great majority of the Moslems? This is what the Shi'ites believe; they may well be not far off the mark, because no other convincing reason can be found to explain why 'Omar objected to fulfillment of the Prophet's last request.

'Omar was an outstanding figure in Islam, one of the Prophet's most respected and influential companions and a pillar of support in political matters. In addition to statesmanship, he had always shown ability to judge character and think ahead. It is therefore likely that he made a calculation. If the Prophet was about to name a successor, the choice would probably fall on either 'Ali or Abu

174

Bakr. 'Ali was the most distinguished member of the Hāshemite clan, being a son-in-law of the Prophet, a valiant fighter, and a scribe of the revelation, and he had a mind and will of his own; he would naturally not be susceptible to another man's influence. Abu Bakr was 'Omar's staunch friend; throughout the ten years at Madina, 'Omar had been in closer touch with Abu Bakr than with the Prophet's other companions, and on most matters the two saw eye to eye. If the choice of the successor lay between 'Ali and Abu Bakr, 'Omar was bound to prefer Abu Bakr. Since Abu Bakr's clan was not influential, and since his temperament was modest and placid, 'Omar could look forward to becoming his right-hand man. Under 'Ali, who would have the support of the whole Hāshemite clan and the respect of many companions of the Prophet, 'Omar could expect to be side-tracked. Another point unlikely to have escaped 'Omar's sharp mind was Abu Bakr's age; he was then over sixty. This seniority, which was one of the reasons why Abu Bakr enjoyed general respect, must have strengthened 'Omar's hope that the choice would fall on Abu Bakr rather than 'Ali, whose age was then only thirty two. In short, Abu Bakr's appointment would in several ways offer a better prospect for 'Omar's political ambition.

Such considerations may well explain 'Omar's unease over the Prophet's request for writing material and probable intention to make a will. Also present in his mind may have been another concern. It would not be easy to accept that after the prophethood, the rulership should remain in the Hāshemite family and that the door should be closed to other aspirants.

It is of course possible that the Prophet's intention was not to appoint a successor but to deal with a different matter; but it certainly looks as if 'Omar's intention was to avert the risk of being faced with a fait accompli. Not wishing to disclose his intuition that the Prophet was about to make a will, he pretended that the Prophet had spoken in the extremity of fever and was not in a state to add anything to the Qor'ān, which had been revealed to him when he was in good health and contained all the commandments that were needed.

In this context another question springs to the mind. If the Prophet intended to appoint his successor, why did not he announce the name orally? When the argumentation began and 'Omar prevented the bringing of the writing material, could not the Prophet have said enough to indicate his decision, which in the

Shi'ite belief was that 'Ali should succeed him? Since the number of those present in the room was quite large, the news of his last wish would soon have spread around the Moslem community. Was there a reason why he did not make his decision known orally? At first sight this is another unfathomable mystery.

It must not be forgotten, however, that Mohammad always acted with a purpose. During the twenty three years of his prophetic career, an idea had taken root and gathered such strength in his mind that it can be said to have become a part of his personality. This was the goal of creating a new society based on Islam and incorporating Arab nationalism.

The Prophet, with his innate sagacity and exceptional understanding of human nature, was well aware of the idiosyncrasies and merits of his companions. He certainly understood the character of 'Omar, having had many occasions to observe his objectivity and foresight, his tenacity of purpose, and his moral strength. The Prophet also knew of 'Omar's friendship with Abu Bakr. 'Omar ever since his conversion had been one of the Prophet's closest companions and on several occasions had pressed the Prophet to take decisions or initiatives which had contributed to the progress of Islam. In other words, 'Omar was not a dutiful follower like Abu Bakr, but a man with his own ideas and opinions, which he often propounded to the Prophet and which the Prophet often adopted. In Soyuti's *Etqān* there is a chapter entitled "Passages in the Qor'ān which were revealed at the suggestion of the companions"; among them are many which were revealed at the suggestion of 'Omar. According to Mojāhed b. Jabr (an early traditionist), "'Omar used to express an opinion, and then it was sent down in the Qor'ān." 'Omar himself is reported to have thought that three verses were revealed at his suggestion; the verse of veiling (*sura* 33, *ol-Ahzāb*, 53), the verse of the prisoners (i.e. those taken at Badr; *sura* 8, *ol-Anfāl*, 68), and the verse of Abraham's stopping-place (i.e. the Ka'ba; *sura* 2, *ol-Baqara*, 119). The traditionists, biographers, and Qor'ān-commentators have much to say on this subject. Their writings make it amply clear that 'Omar was intelligent and wise and that the Prophet trusted him. Certainly there were not more than five men of comparable worth among the Prophet's companions.

Such a man would not have obstructed the writing of the testament unless he had a motive. If the Prophet named 'Ali orally, there would be a risk that after his death the appointment might be challenged by 'Omar, Abu Bakr, and their associates and that the Islamic cause might thereby suffer great damage. In Mohammad's lifetime, the boundless prestige of the prophethood had enabled him to take whatever steps he deemed right. Not long ago he had given an army command to the young Osāma b. Zayd in the face of widespread criticism, which he had silenced with a terse rebuke. But after his death how would matters stand? When he was no longer there, who would have the ability to suppress tribal strife and curb ambitions for wealth and power? What would happen to the new Islamic community whose creation had been his great goal? Would the Arabs relapse into internecine feuding and fighting? Perhaps reflections such as these crossed the Prophet's mind and prompted him to stay silent, apart from his request to the people to leave the room. Other reasons why the Prophet did not, after all, appoint a successor can of course also be surmised.

As for 'Ali, he had a record of merits which both his friends and his foes acknowledged. He had never worshipped idols and had become a believer at the age of eleven. He had fought in the principal raids, shielded the Prophet from mortal danger at the battle of Mount Ohod, felled the Qorayshite champion 'Amr b. 'Abd Wodd in the war of the trench, and stormed the fortress of Nā'om at Khaybar. On the night before the *hejra* (which the Prophet, together with Abu Bakr, had spent in a cave), 'Ali had slept on the Prophet's bed and faced the risk of assassination. He had killed more enemies than any other companion of the Prophet had done. He had won esteem for his courage, frankness, eloquence, and exactness in following the Prophet's example. He was the most distinguished man of the Prophet's own clan, the Banu Hāshem.

All these virtues, however, may have been offset by 'Ali's youth, because he was the youngest of the Prophet's companions, and by his double kinship to the Prophet as cousin (son of the Prophet's paternal uncle) and son-in-law (husband of the Prophet's surviving daughter, Fātema). There was a risk that designation of 'Ali as the successor might be attributed to nepotism and thus kindle clan jealousies which could impair Moslem unity and well-being.

Other virtues for which 'Ali was well known may perhaps have been obstacles in the way of his advancement to the leadership. To govern men of unbridled ambition, the future leader would require composure, moderation, and regard for the legitimate needs and aspirations of his subordinates – qualities which the Prophet himself had amply evinced. After the conquest of Mecca, the Prophet had refrained from inflicting the death penalty on stubborn adversaries except in a very few cases, and he had distributed the booty taken from the Hawāzen tribe among the Qoraysh chiefs. 'Ali, however, was inflexible in his handling of such matters. He was never willing to consider demands which he deemed improper. In the campaign in the Yaman under 'Ali's command in 10 A.H./631–2, the troops had demanded that the abundant booty should be distributed among them on the spot, but 'Ali had ignored them and insisted on delivering all the booty to the Prophet; the outcome had been that the Prophet determined an equitable distribution and exonerated 'Ali from complaints made by the troops. At a later date, when 'Othmān, after becoming caliph, consulted 'Ali about the case of 'Obaydollāh b. 'Omar who had killed Hormozān (an Iranian general taken captive and employed as an adviser at Madina) because he suspected Hormozān of complicity with his father's assassin,[88] 'Ali unhesitatingly advised that 'Obaydollāh was liable under Islamic law to the penalty of retribution in kind. 'Othmān did not act on 'Ali's advice; he spared the life of the second caliph's son by letting him pay blood money instead and then sending him to Iraq.

The Prophet fully understood 'Ali's character. He was well aware of 'Ali's virtues and also knew that 'Ali was an uncompromising stickler for what he deemed to be right. This idealism, while intrinsically praiseworthy, might not be altogether appropriate in the practical handling of men whose religious faith would probably be coupled with ambition or cupidity. If 'Ali's leadership would alarm the men of that type, the community might be rent by dissension and the great goal might not be achieved.

In the short period of 'Ali's caliphate (18 Dhu'l-Hejja 35/17 June 656–17 Ramadān 40/24 January 661), the self-seekers were indeed alarmed. His unwillingness to let sinners continue, even temporarily, to rule over Moslems brought him into conflict with Mo'āwiya, the governor of Syria. His view of the matter also antagonized the two senior companions of the Prophet, Talha and Zobayr, who likewise took up arms against him.

Whatever the reasons may have been, the succession was undecided when the Prophet passed away. This fact may perhaps be an indication of the Prophet's wisdom and foresight. It is possible that the Prophet finally resolved not to set one faction over another but to let the struggle for power and leadership take its natural course, in expectation that the principle now called the survival of the fittest would ensure Islam's survival.

The matter brings to mind a somewhat similar event in modern history. Lenin from his sickbed sent a letter to the Soviet communist party's central committee. Being unable to attend the committee's meetings, he was obliged to write this letter, which came to be known as Lenin's testament. In it he praised the qualities of the committee's two leading members, Stalin and Trotsky, and described both men as vital components of the new régime, but could not conceal his anxiety about the risk of future conflict between them. He even mentioned the demerits as well as the merits of each. Yet he too chose silence on the succession problem, leaving its solution to the workings of the law of survival of the fittest (or strongest).

Before the advent of Islam, the Arabs used to boast about the superiority of their tribe, clan, or genealogy over those of others. Their claims to superiority were not based on virtues and graces but on prowess in killing, plundering, and abducting other men's women. The teachings of Islam negated this concept and made piety the measure of a person's merit. Unfortunately the new standard was not long maintained in practice – to be precise, not after 'Omar's death in 23/644. During 'Othmān's reign, nepotism prevailed over piety. Devout men such as Abu Dharr ol-Ghefāri[89] and 'Ammār b. Yāser[90] were thrust aside, and members of the caliph's clan such as Mo'āwiya b. Abi Sofyān and ol-Hakam b. Abi'l-'Ās were appointed to governorships.

Under the Omayyad caliphate (41/661–132/750), the great Islamic principle of nobility through piety was simply ignored. Tribal and national pride again held sway, but in a broader setting. The demands of Arab nationalism could now be satisfied at the expense of the conquered peoples.

Men from the barren deserts of Arabia had overrun large parts of the civilized world. The conquest of peoples formerly renowned for imperial power and material wealth intoxicated the Arabs with pride. Supposing their own nation to be superior and the conquered nations to be inferior, they despised those nations and never recognised them as equal. They did not even concede to those who became Moslem the equality of rights enshrined in Islamic law.

It is related that when a converted Iranian protégé of an Arab tribe, the Banu Solaym, married one of their women, a tribesman named Mohammad b. Bashir went to Madina and complained about the matter to the governor, Ebrāhim b. Heshām b. ol-Moghira. The governor then sent agents who gave the Iranian a flogging of two hundred lashes, shaved his head, face, and eyebrows, and forced him to divorce his wife. Mohammad b. Bashir composed an ode on the subject which is preserved in the *Ketāb ol-Aghāni*.[91] Some lines from it are translated below:

> You respected custom and judged justly.
> You had not inherited the governorship from an alien.
> The (non-Arab) protégé received an exemplary punishment
>   in the two hundred (lashes),
> in the shaving of the eyebrows and cheeks.
> When the daughters of Kesrā[92] are suitable mates for them,
> are the protégés to get still more?
> What do protégés rightly deserve?
> Marriage of slaves to slaves.

Another informative story comes in the *'Oyun ol-akhbār* of Ebn Qotayba:[93]

"An Arab went to a *qādi* (judge) and said, 'My father has died leaving a will that his property be divided between my brother, myself, and a *hajin* (an Arabic word meaning ignoble which was applied to a son by a non-Arab woman). What is the share of each?' The *qādi* answered, 'There is no problem. Each brother is entitled to one third of the property.' The Arab said, 'You have not understood our problem. We are two brothers and one *hajin*.' The *qādi* answered, 'Each has the right to an equal share.' The Arab asked angrily, 'How can a *hajin* be equal to us?' The *qādi* answered, 'That is God's commandment.'"

Hundreds of similar reports from the early Islamic centuries have been handed down. They give proof that Islam was used as a means to power and as an instrument of domination over other peoples. The humane commandments and teachings of the Qor'ān were neither enforced nor observed. Pagan Arab notions of superiority were reasserted in the Islamic context. Non-Arab Moslems, however, remained mindful of Islam's great precept, "The noblest among you in God's sight are the most pious among you" (*sura* 49, *ol-Hojorāt*, verse 13). The Sho'ubiya movement (of Iranian cultural revival) began in reaction to these Arab pretensions and might never have arisen if the Islam of Mohammad b. 'Abdollāh and the course of Abu Bakr, 'Omar, and 'Ali had been maintained.

# THE QUEST FOR BOOTY

Certain Western scholars who have studied Islam regard it as a regional phenomenon and criticize many of its commandments as unsuitable for advanced societies. Among the examples which they cite are the obligations to perform ritual prayer and ablution five times in every twenty four hours and preferably in a mosque; to measure time in years of twelve lunar months; and to fast and refrain from vital activity from sunrise to sunset during one of those months, regardless of the geographical fact that in high latitudes there are seasons when the sun does not set and the daylight is continuous. In the view of these Western scholars, the legislator of the Ramadān fast only had knowledge of conditions in the Hejāz in the 7th century, and standardized them because he was ignorant of conditions elsewhere. The ban on lending at interest is criticized as harmful to capital investment and economic development. The permissibility of slavery is seen as legalizing treatment of human beings as animals. The inequality of women's inheritance rights with those of men, when women have the greater need because they do not normally perform wealth-producing functions, is considered irrational, and the presumption that women's testimony has half the value of men's is judged to be a denial of human rights. The penalties of hand-amputation for theft and foot-amputation for repeated theft are deemed antisocial because they make the convicts disabled and unemployable. Polygamy up to the limit of four contractual wives, unlimited concubinage with slave women including married women whose husbands have been taken prisoner, and the adoption of stoning for adultery from Jewish law are condemned as inhumane. The restriction of freedom of testamentary disposition is regarded as inconsistent with the Islamic legal principle that "people have control of their properties and their persons." The upshot of all the criticisms is that such a religion cannot be universally and permanently valid.

It is of course a fact that many of these commandments, such as stoning, amputation, and "eye for eye, tooth for tooth" retaliation, are no longer observed in most Moslem countries, and that banks which pay and charge interest have been started in all Moslem countries. When this fact is mentioned, the critics make caustic comments on the *hajj*. They say that calling an idol-temple God's house, treating the ancient pagan rite of kissing a black stone as an Islamic ceremony, and all the other pilgrimage rites are inconsistent with Islam's claim to have saved people from idolatry and superstition and must be interpreted as expressions of racial feeling. No religion, they argue, can be universal and permanent unless it guides the whole of mankind to goodness and transcends all racialism and fanaticism.

These critics too often forget that the best laws are those which fill gaps and combat evils existing in the society concerned. In a land where killing, plundering, and violation of other people's rights and honor were commonplace, sternness alone could be effective. Amputation, stoning, and retaliation might be the only remedies in such circumstances. Slavery was and had been practiced by contemporary and earlier civilized peoples such as the Romans and the Assyrians and Chaldaeans; and in Islam manumission of a slave atones for many a sin. As already noted in the section on Women in Islam in chapter 3, pagan Arab women had no rights; a deceased man's wife could even be transferred to his heir as a part of his estate. The Qor'ānic legislation concerning women marked a revolutionary advance. It is absurd to assess the deeds and commands of a leader who lived in the 7th century by standards current in the 19th and 20th centuries; to argue, for instance, that the Prophet Mohammad ought to have acted like Abraham Lincoln in regard to slavery.

Many of the criticisms can be met with counterclaims. Even on the important point of freedom of thought and belief, it can be argued that the Moslems were justified in giving inhabitants of conquered territories the choice between profession of Islam and payment of tribute.

By the standards of advanced 20th century thinking, however, the use of the sword to compel profession of Islam was obviously improper and unjust. Nor can modern thought accept that Almighty God chose the Arabs of 7th century Arabia to guide the whole of mankind. If God had been so concerned that the peoples of Syria, Egypt, and Iran should become Moslem, gentler means were available, because in the words of the Qor'ān (e.g. *sura* 16, verse 95) "He leads astray whomsoever He wills and guides aright whomsoever He wills." The fact that people cannot be guided by the sword is made clear in verse 44 of *sura* 8 (*ol-Anfāl*): "Those who perish shall perish by clear proof and those who survive shall survive by clear proof." Verse 6 of *sura* 109 (*ol-Kāferun*), which states "You have your religion and I have my religion," and dozens of other Qor'ānic verses with the same import can be cited in confirmation of this thesis.

Study of the matter leads to the surprising conclusion that the grant of choice to profess Islam or pay tribute was a policy for dealing with the inhabitants of Arabia, and that it was only adopted after the capture of Khaybar and, above all, the conquest of Mecca and submission of the Qorayshites. The Prophet Mohammad intended to turn Arabia into a single political unit, and according to a well-authenticated *Hadith*, he therefore announced that "there must not be more than one religion in the Arabian peninsula." The conquest of Mecca was followed by the revelation of a verse (*sura* 9, *ot-Tawba*, 28) which declares that polytheists are unclean and may no longer approach the Mosque of the Sanctuary. Several passages in the same *sura* give evidence of the Prophet's resolve to form an Arab national entity under the banner of Islam. Stern measures and use of force are threatened against the Beduin, whom verse 98 describes as "the stubbornest in unbelief and hypocrisy and the most likely to ignore the limits of what God has revealed to His Apostle." The words "If We had sent it down to a non-Arab" in *sura* 26 (*osh-Sho'arā*), verse 198, suggests that foreigners were quicker than Arabs to understand and accept the Qor'ān and its teachings.

Among all the observations made by European scholars are two which remain virtually unanswerable. One concerns the irrationality of the idea that God commissioned the Hejāzi Arabs to teach morality and monotheism to the world's peoples at sword-point. Since this is hard to believe, the subject will not be pursued here. The other observation concerns the economic impulse to the Arab conquests.

In the previous section of this chapter, it was noted that ambition for leadership and rulership has shaped the political history of Islam ever since the death of the Prophet. There is also plenty of evidence that the Arab conquests were motivated by desire to seize the wealth of other peoples.

The rough men who eked meagre livings from their arid soil knew well that beyond their borders lay fertile lands and prosperous cities where necessities and luxuries were in ample supply.

Unfortunately these populous areas belonged to the mighty empires of Iran and Rome, and could not conceivably be seized by any band of poor, ill-equipped nomads. Islam, however, ended the internecine strife of the Arab tribes, broadened their horizons, and forged their dispersed strength into a powerful whole. The impossible then became possible.

These poor people had been wont to indulge their greed by rustling two or three hundred camels in a raid on a weaker tribe. Combined in a single force, they became able to seize far more booty, to conquer rich and fertile lands, to gain possession of beautiful, white-skinned women and priceless treasures. They had never feared to risk their lives in pursuit of loot or lust. Under the banner of Islam, they marched not only in hope of booty but also in confidence that if they killed they would go to heaven and if they were killed they would go to heaven. This belief satisfied a pressing spiritual need, as they also craved for glory and mastery. Attacks by the Tamim tribe on the Taghleb tribe, by the Aws on the Khazraj, by the Thaqif on the Ghatafān, were no longer possible; instead, the sights of all could be set on Syria and Iraq.

As already noted in the third section of chapter III, booty had been an important factor in the implantation of Islam and consolidation of the Moslem community. The capture of the Qorayshite caravan at Nakhla in the second year after the *hejra* had strengthened the position of the Moslems, and the subsequent seizure of part of the property of the Banu Qaynoqā' and all of the property of the Banu Qorayza had put their finances on a sound footing.

The insatiable Arab thirst for booty is vividly depicted in the Qor'ān (*sura* 48, *ol-Fat-h*, verse 15): "Those who lagged behind will say, when you set out to take booty, 'Let us accompany you!'" The verse refers to certain Beduin who had shrunk from fighting the Qoraysh and taking part in the Pledge under the Tree, but later wanted to join the expedition against the Jews of Khaybar in order to share in the abundant booty which God promised to the Moslems.

During the Khaybar campaign, the Prophet offered a share of the booty to the Ghatafān tribe and thereby dissuaded them from helping the local Jews, with whom they were allied.

The Accounts of the first decade after the *hejra* give many other instances of the Arab greed for booty. One which has already been mentioned in the fifth section of chapter III deserves particular note, namely the discontent of the Ansār when booty taken from

184

the defeated Hawāzen tribe was distributed among leading Qorayshites.

The reports give proof of the predatory instinct of the Arabs and at the same time of the Prophet's understanding of his people's mentality.

In discussion of this matter, it is important to bear in mind that the Prophet's recourse to measures such as attack on caravans and elimination or subjugation of Jewish communities was prompted by a higher aim than the Arab desire to amass wealth. Mohammad was also a statesman, and in the minds of statesmen the end justifies the means. He aimed to implant Islam, to eradicate the corrupt polytheists and the hypocrites, and to found a united Arab state under the banner of Islam. Any steps which conduced to that lofty goal were permissible.

The proceeds of the attacks and raids were used for the good of the still small Moslem community, not for the Prophet's personal benefit. He himself was content with a very modest life-style. After the confiscation of the houses and belongings of the Banu Qorayza, his wives demanded higher allowances out of the rich booty, but he gave them the choice of bearing with their present allowances or divorce.

The Prophet's chief companions, in keeping with his example, also lived modestly. As long as he was present, none of them fell into the grip of cupidity. After his death, however, and particularly after the great influx of booty from conquered lands far beyond the borders of Arabia, many of them succumbed.

The second caliph 'Omar took care to maintain a firm hand. In the apportionment of booty and pensions to leaders of the Mohājerun, the Ansār, and other worthies at Madina, he always acted moderately and equitably. Being anxious to keep the people on the Prophet's path, he himself led an austere life. The freedman Sālem (an early transmitter of Hadith) is reported to have said that the value of all 'Omar's clothes, including turban and shoes, during his caliphate did not exceed fourteen *derhams*, whereas it had previously amounted to forty *dinars*. 'Omar's frugality was so strict that, according to Tabari, widespread grumbling arose in the last years of his reign; having heard about it, he ascended the pulpit one day and declared bluntly, "I have striven to rear Islam. Now it is mature. The Qorayshites want to take God's bounty from the mouths of His worshippers. This will not be done while the son of ol-Khattāb remains alive. I stand alert. I shall prevent the

Qorayshites from leaving the straight path and going to hell."
Tabari also states that none of the leading companions were
permitted to move out of Madina without 'Omar's permission, and
that if he ever gave such permission, it was only for a short absence
or a journey within the Hejāz, because he feared that their arrival
in the conquered territories might cause division in the Moslem
ranks. If a prominent Qorayshite asked to join in one of the wars
against foreigners, 'Omar would answer, "The raid in which you
accompanied the Prophet is sufficient. It is better for you not to see
the foreign countries and for the foreign countries not to see you."

Commenting on 'Omar's strictness, the perceptive modern
Egyptian scholar Tāhā Hosayn[94] has written in his book *ol-
Fetnat ol-Kobrā* (2 vols., Cairo 1947 and 1953): "'Omar was suspicious of Qorayshites, being well aware of their tribal mentality
and greed for power and profit. The only ground for their claim to
be the noblest Arab tribe was their custodianship of the Ka'ba,
which had been the main pilgrimage center and idol-temple of the
Arabs. In reality they had made themselves the richest tribe by
exploiting the religious beliefs and customs of the Arabs. Thanks
to the assured safety of Mecca and its environs, they had been able
to concentrate on trade and gain a dominant position in that field.
'Omar knew that his Qorayshite fellow-tribesmen owed their
prestige and wealth to the Ka'ba and that they would not otherwise
have revered its idols. He also knew that their acceptance of Islam
had not been voluntary but had been forced on them by Mohammad's victory and by their fear of the Moslems. Moreover they still
viewed their move into the Moslem camp as a risky gamble.
Obviously it would be dangerous to give a free hand to such
grasping opportunists."

The soundness of 'Omar's judgement is attested by the course
of events after his death. Although 'Othmān left all 'Omar's ap-
pointees at their posts for one year in compliance with a request
in 'Omar's will and only made changes later, from the start of his
reign he made lavish payments from the public treasury to the
Mohājerun and Ansār, and on one occasion he increased their
pensions by one hundred per cent. While the third caliph maintained the modest life-style of his predecessors and never mis-
appropriated public funds for his private use, his undue largess
kindled envy and greed and discredited austerity and self-denial.

Reference has already been made to the modest attire and
life-style of 'Omar, one of the strongest caliphs in Islam's history

and the first to bear the title "Prince of the Believers." Equally well known is the austerity of 'Ali, to which his friends and foes alike bore witness. 'Ali's clothes were so full of patches that he was ashamed of having given so much work to the seamstress. He sternly rebuked his brother 'Aqil when the latter asked for help from the public treasury to pay his debts. 'Aqil's subsequent recourse to 'Ali's adversary Mo'āwiya b. Abi Sofyān is another token of the importance of the pecuniary factor in the determination of Arab attitudes.

In this context, the career of one of the greatest of the Prophet's companions, Sa'd b. Abi Waqqās, deserves notice. Converted in the early phase at Mecca, he became one of the ten to whom paradise was promised. In 'Omar's reign he commanded the army which defeated the Iranians at the battle of Qādesiya and took their capital, Ctesiphon, in 16/637. For this he was honored as the "knight of Islam" and made the first governor of Kufa. In 23/644 he was appointed by the dying 'Omar to be one of the committee of six companions who would choose the next caliph, and naturally was himself a candidate. When he died in 55/674-5 at his mansion in the valley of ol-'Aqiq near Madina, he left a fortune including cash to the value of between 200,000 and 300,000 *derhams*.

Nor should the conduct of this eminent companion's son be forgotten. In 61/681 'Omar b. Sa'd b. Abi Waqqās received from 'Obaydollāh b. Ziyād, the viceroy of Iraq, an offer of the governorship of Rayy in Iran if he would first take command of an expedition to intercept Hosayn b. 'Ali and compel the latter to acknowledge the caliphate of Yazid b. Mo'āwiya or face the consequences. 'Omar b. Sa'd was initially reluctant to accept this commission. His relatives, with whom he discussed the matter one night, unanimously disapproved on the ground that it would be wrong for the son of a respected companion of the Prophet to risk having to fight the Prophet's grandson. Nevertheless 'Omar b. Sa'd's ambition and 'Obaydollāh b. Ziyād's insistence prevailed, and 'Omar b. Sa'd agreed to march against Hosayn. When he encountered Hosayn's party, however, he preferred to negotiate and spent three days trying to persuade Hosayn to surrender and give allegiance to Yazid. The protracted parleys caused 'Obaydollāh b. Ziyād to fear that feelings of honor or Islamic zeal might induce 'Omar b. Sa'd to go over to Hosayn. 'Obaydollāh therefore sent a message to one of the officers, Shemr b. Dhi'l-Jowshan, ordering him to take command of the force if 'Omar b. Sa'd continued to procrastinate. As soon as 'Omar b. Sa'd learned of this, he forgot his father's record of service to Islam and his own concern to show respect for the Prophet's family. It was he who shot the first arrow at the Prophet's grandson. The governorship of Rayy meant more to him than religion, honor, and morality.

Talha b. 'Obaydollāh, another eminent companion and one of the ten to whom paradise was promised, was likewise one of 'Omar's nominees for the committee of six and also a candidate for the succession; but absence from Madina prevented him from taking part in the committee, which made its choice without hearing his opinion. After his return to Madina, he adopted a dissentient attitude and refused allegiance to 'Othmān. Finally 'Othmān went in person to his house and offered to abdicate in his favor. Talha was embarrassed and then gave allegiance to 'Othmān, who rewarded him with a loan of 50,000 derhams from the public treasury and, in recognition of his helpfulness, did not demand repayment of this substantial sum. Thereafter Talha became one of 'Othmān's closest friends and arranged many transactions with his help; for example, if Talha wished to exchange some lands or money in Iraq for some in the Hejāz or Egypt, 'Othmān was ready to help by sending orders to officials anywhere in the Islamic empire. When murmurs of opposition to the third caliph arose, Talha at first spoke in his favor; when they grew louder, he prudently held his tongue, and when the dissidents laid siege to 'Othmān's house, he glibly declared himself to be on their side. Talha was killed at the battle of the camel in 36/656. There is a report that 'Othmān's cousin, Marwān b. ol-Hakam, shot the arrow which killed Talha and that he said, "To avenge 'Othmān's murder, I need no more than Talha's blood." (Marwān, who was also an opponent of 'Ali, became the fourth Omayyad caliph in 64/684–65/685.) Although Talha had been far from rich at the time of his conversion and no more than moderately well-off at the end of 'Omar's reign, the fortune which he left was estimated at 30,000,000 derhams comprising 200,000 dinārs in cash and the rest in buildings, farmlands, and chattels. A different account (in Ebn Sa'd's Tabaqāt) gives Talha's cash holdings as 100 leather sacks each containing 3 qentārs (quintals or hundredweights) of pure gold.

Another of the six appointed by 'Omar to decide the succession was (oz-)Zobayr b. ol-'Awwām. He was a kinsman of the Prophet, being the son of Mohammad's paternal aunt and related in other ways also. Moreover he was an early convert and one of the ten to whom paradise was promised. Later he fought in many of the raids and wars. The Prophet had called him "my disciple". He was thus one of the most highly respected companions. There is a report that the third caliph gave 600,000 *derhams* from the public treasury to Zobayr, and that Zobayr himself did not know what to do with such a large sum but acted on the advice of some of his friends. He used it to buy houses and farmlands in and around various cities, and by the time of his death had numerous properties in Fostāt (the later Cairo), Alexandria, Basra, and Kufa, as well as Madina where he owned eleven tenanted houses. Estimates of the total value of his estate ranged from 35,200,000 to 52,000,000 *derhams*. Ebn Sa'd states in his *Tabaqāt* that Zobayr was too pious to accept deposits, for fear that the deposited goods or money might be lost or damaged in some calamity, but was willing, if people insisted, to accept loans from them, because he could invest their funds as profitably as his own funds and because his heirs would be obliged to pay his debts after his death. He in fact left debts amounting to about 2,000,000 *derhams*, which his son repaid.

'Abd or-Rahmān b. 'Awf, a close companion of the Prophet and one of the ten to whom paradise was promised, is remembered as a shrewd and experienced merchant. He was a trusted counsellor of Abu Bakr and 'Omar, and a member of the committee of six. Never ill-off, he took the lead in charitable activities. The wealth which he left, however, far exceeded any that could be gained from business in the Madina bazaar. When he died, he had four wives, each of whom inherited 50,000 gold *dinārs* together with 1000 camels and 3000 sheep; in his will he advised them to spend their riches in God's cause.

In the third caliph's reign, there were few men of the caliber of Hakim b. Hezām, who would not accept a penny from the treasury and refused a pension when public funds were distributed to the Mohājerun and the Ansār.

Better known are the piety and austerity of Abu Dharr ol-Ghefāri,[95] an early convert and companion of the Prophet and an important transmitter of Hadith. He held that verse 34 of *sura* 9 (*ot-Tawba*), "Those who hoard gold or silver and do not spend it in God's cause, give them notice of painful punishment!", is a commandment to all Moslems not to accumulate wealth but to spend it on charity. While living in Syria, Abu Dharr reproached the governor, Mo'āwiya, for breaking this commandment. He was then banished as an undesirable and sent back to the Hejāz. At Madina he repeated the same truths, and his words reached the ears of the third caliph. He was then flogged and expelled. For the rest of his life this devout companion dwelt in a cave.

All but a few, however, succumbed to cupidity and joined in the scramble for wealth. Even the unskilled and the unconnected could make money. A man named Jannāb, who had been a porter and errand-boy at Mecca, reportedly left 40,000 *derham*s in cash when he died at Kufa.

The shares of captured booty given to the warriors when they were on campaign and the pensions paid to them from the treasury at other times enabled them to become rich. Each of the cavalry-men who fought in Efriqiya (now Tunisia) under the command of ʿAbdollāh b. Saʿd b. Abi Sarh received 3000 *methqāl*s of pure gold, and each of the infantrymen received 1000 *methqāl*s. (One *methqāl* is equivalent to about 4.7 grams.)

From the hundreds of instances which are reported in the reliable sources of early Islamic history, it is obvious that the hope of taking booty, of appropriating other people's farmlands, and of capturing and enslaving other people's women was a major incentive to the Arab fighters. In their quest for these gains they neither lacked courage nor shrank from cruelty. Under the cover of Islam, they sought power, property, and ascendancy. In so doing they ignored Islam's great precept that "the noblest among you in God's sight are the most pious among you" (*sura* 49, verse 13).

Sooner or later this conduct was bound to provoke reactions. Other peoples, in particular the Iranians, would not submit to such tyranny. They accepted Islam's spiritual and humane teachings, but rejected the Arab pretension to racial superiority and refused to be bled by Arab exploiters. Arab spokesmen retorted by accusing them of nationalism (*shoʿubiya*) and even heresy (*zandaqa*).

The present writer remembers reading a book entitled *oz-Zandaqa waʾsh-Shoʿubiya* which had been published in Egypt with a preface by a Cairo university professor. The book was an attempt to portray the national self-assertion of the Iranians as a form of heresy or deviation from Islamic principles; it contained no mention of Arab breaches of the commandment "God enjoins justice and charity" (*sura* 16, verse 92).

Among the caliphs styled "Princes of the Believers" were men so debauched that they reportedly bathed in pools of wine. In flagrant disregard of the Prophet's highminded teaching that honesty and virtue are the measure of human worth, the Omayyad caliphs were bent on Arab ascendancy over other Moslems and Omayyad ascendancy over other Arabs.

There were so-called "Princes of the Believers" who mounted the pulpit to utter insults about 'Ali b. Abi Tāleb, the most devout and learned of the Prophet's companions. The caliph Motawakkel (232/847–247/861), himself a descendant of the Prophet's other learned cousin 'Abdollāh b. ol-'Abbās, went so far as to have a clown masquerade as 'Ali and dance before his assembled courtiers. He also caused the site of the grave of Hosayn b. 'Ali to be ploughed and irrigated in the hope that memories of this brave grandson of the Prophet would thereby be effaced.

The Iranians correctly judged that men who were so profligate and so heedless of the Prophet Mohammad's teachings did not deserve the title "Prince of the Believers".

# CHAPTER VI

# *Summary*

The rise and spread of Islam constitute a unique historical phenomenon. Study of former times is always a hard task, requiring thorough and comprehensive research to uncover and clarify all aspects of the events and to ascertain their cause or causes. Study of the history of Islam is made relatively easy by the abundance of authentic records and does not present insuperable obstacles to careful scholars, provided that they can think objectively and keep themselves free from prejudice. It is essential that the researcher should wipe inherited or inculcated notions off the slate of his mind.

This short book is not a product of profound research but at most an attempt to provide a concise, even if over-generalized, outline of the salient points of the twenty three years of Mohammad's prophetic career. These points are recapitulated below.

1    An orphan, left on his own from the age of six with no father and mother to care for him, lived at a relative's house in much less comfortable circumstances than other children of the same age and rank. He spent his time taking camels out to graze in the barren country around Mecca. His percipient and intelligent mind had an imaginative bent. Long hours of solitude in the desert over a span of five or six years developed his power to dream and see visions. Awareness of his own deprivation and of other people's relative affluence gave him a complex which gradually evolved, being directed first at his playmates and relatives, next at the rich families, and finally at the source of the wealth of those families. This was their custodianship of the Ka'ba, the famous idol-temple at the center of Arab religious life. Perhaps it was after addressing fruitless prayers to the idols that he conceived his intense hatred of idolatry.

In this way of thinking he was not alone. Among the inhabitants

192

of Mecca were possessors of scriptures and other thoughtful persons who saw the absurdity of the worship of lifeless images. Contact with such persons reinforced the process at work in his inner mind. Journeys to Syria in certain years gave him glimpses of the contrast between the outside world and the superstitious backwardness of his own people. Visits to places of worship of possessors of scriptures, conversations with their pastors, and hearing about their prophets and doctrines added to the strength of his conviction.

2 At the time when belief in one God and ideas heard from Jews and Christians were becoming the central concern of his mental life, marriage to a wealthy widow relieved him of the anxieties of his material life. Frequent meetings with her mono-theistic cousin Waraqa b. Nawfal turned his conviction into an obsession. The concept of an omnipotent and jealous God totally filled his mind. He was sure that the one God resents a people's worship of other deities. The people of 'Ād and Thamud had been wiped out for this offense, and his own people must soon be due for similar punishment. It was therefore his urgent duty to guide them.

As time passed, this grim foreboding merged with his visions and took the form of revelations. Khadija and Waraqa b. Nawfal believed his revelations to be true and divinely inspired. Surely he now ought to warn his people, just as Hud and Sāleh had warned the people of 'Ād and Thamud. Surely prophets did not have to come solely from the Jews but could also arise among their Arab cousins.

This spiritual process, or rather spiritual crisis and obsession, led him to start preaching to his people in his fortieth year.

3 Since everyone of any intelligence acknowledged the futility of the worship of man-made images, he could feel confident of his ability to rouse the people from their indifference. A few already shared and endorsed his belief. There were no grounds for des-pondency. He must start straightaway to fulfill God's command "Warn your tribe, your nearest kin" (sura 26, osh-Sho'arā, verse 214).

From the first day, however, he encountered derision and scorn. It had not occurred to his simple, devout mind that the people whom he hoped to convince through his salutary messages and sound arguments were strongly attached to their old ways, and above all that his preaching called for overthrow of the system which had given wealth and prestige to the leading men of the Qoraysh tribe. These men were bound to fight hard in defence of their position. The first to declare war on him was his own uncle Abu Lahab, who at his meeting with the Qoraysh chiefs shouted, "Perish you, Mohammad! Did you invite us here for this?"

4 The mentality of Mohammad's opponents is illustrated by Abu Jahl's remark to (ol-)Akhnas b. Shariq about the old rivalry between the Makhzum clan and the descendants of 'Abd Manāf and his allegation that it was because the former had caught up that the latter had produced a prophet in the hope of getting ahead again. The same notion appears in the verse of poetry said to have been composed fifty years later by Yazid b. Mo'āwiya with reference to Hosayn b. 'Ali: "The Hāshemites gambled for power, but no message came, no revelation was sent down."

The motives for opposition are made clear by Abu Jahl's words to Akhnas b. Shariq. Mohammad, a poor orphan dependent on his wife's wealth, was not comparable in social and personal standing with the rich and influential chiefs of the Qoraysh tribe. If his preaching met with success, their position would be weakened or perhaps wholly lost, and the Banu 'Abd ol-Mottaleb (or Hāshemites) would become the tribe's dominant clan. In actual fact, the Banu 'Abd ol-Mottaleb did not adhere to Mohammad; even Abu Tāleb and his other uncles wished to avoid a breach with the other Qoraysh clans.

Perhaps if Mohammad had foreseen the opposition of the chiefs and the heedlessness of the people which he in fact encountered during the thirteen years of his mission at Mecca, he might either not have embarked on it so unwarily or, like other monotheists such as Waraqa b. Nawfal, Omayya b. Abi's-Salt, and Qass b. Sā'eda, he might have been content to voice his faith and go his own way.

Mohammad, however, as the record of his prophetic career shows, was a man of too deep conviction to be daunted from pursuit of his goal by any obstacle. Wholly absorbed in one belief, which had taken hold in almost thirty years of reflection, he saw himself as duty-bound to guide his people to the right path.

In addition to the force of faith, he possessed another great gift, that of a unique eloquence which was indeed remarkable in an illiterate and uneducated man. In fervent tones be besought the people to be virtuous, honest, and humane. As proof that decency, righteousness, and piety are the only road to salvation, he quoted impressive reports about earlier peoples and past prophets.

5    Research has established that the preaching of Islam was a response to social conditions in Mecca. The number of persons in the town who disapproved of idolatry had been gradually increasing. Side by side with the rich and powerful magnates there was a class of indigent and destitute people. Islam spoke up for these people and was therefore likely to gain ground. History shows that the discontent of a deprived or oppressed class has been a factor in all revolutions. The Meccan magnates, however, did not stay idle. They constantly persecuted and even tortured poor, defenceless Moslems, though they did not molest Mohammad himself and the few Moslems such as Abu Bakr, 'Omar, and Hamza who had influential kinsfolk. Every sort of deterrent was brought to bear on members of the needy class, who ought to have formed the base of the pyramid of the new religious community. Thus in the course of thirteen years of continual preaching, Mohammad could not win more than a small number of converts, perhaps not much more than a hundred. From this only one conclusion could be drawn, surprising though it may seem. Neither the soundness of Mohammad's preaching, nor his austerity, nor his eloquence, nor his warnings of punishment after death, nor his moral and humane precepts had sufficed to give Islam the diffusion which it deserved.

6    The eventual solution was recourse to the sword, which became a major and essential factor in the diffusion and implantation of Islam. Killing and coercion were unsparingly used as means to this end. It must of course be added that use of force was not an innovation by the Prophet Mohammad but a long-established Arab practice. In the harsh environment of the Hejāz and Najd, the Arabs had little or no agriculture and industry and lived without man-made or God-given laws. They were normally engaged in raiding and fighting each other. Needing time for rest and recuperation, they treated four months in every year as sacred and refrained from warfare in those months. At other times a tribe's only security against plunder of its property and women was its own alertness and capacity for self-defence.

The decision to make similar use of force was taken after Mohammad's acceptance of the protection of the Aws and Khazraj tribes and his migration to Madina. Almost all the Moslem raids were undertaken in compliance with that decision. The main targets were the Jewish tribes of Madina and the adjacent districts.

195

In this way resources were obtained for the foundation of an Islamic state with the Prophet as its legislator, executive head, and commander-in-chief. Development of the new state was then put in hand.

7  Before the advent of Islam, the Arabs had generally been shallow-minded, materialistic, and impulsive. A verse of poetry could enrapture them and a nasty phrase could move them to kill. Their thoughts were fixed on tangible things and everyday experiences. Spiritual and mystical ideas, indeed any sort of interest in the supernatural, were alien to them. They were accustomed to violence and unconcerned with justice. There were no lengths to which they would not go in their greed for booty. A European scholar has cited evidence that, when defeated, they sometimes abandoned their own camp and went over to the other side; but such behavior was certainly exceptional.

In any society lacking organized government, order and security necessarily depend on balance of power and mutual fear.

The Arabs were fond of boasting and self-praise. They not only exaggerated their personal and tribal merits, but even took pride in their faults. They were incapable of self-criticism. On the morning after the rape of a captured woman, they would compose verses vaunting their prowess and reviling their victim. The primitive simplicity with which the Beduin poets spoke of their instincts sometimes seems quite animal-like.

In so far as the Beduin thought about spiritual and supernatural matters at all, they formed mental pictures from the concrete world around them. The same way of thinking persisted in the Islamic period, above all among the Hanbalites who denounced any use of logical categories as heresy or unbelief.

8  Study of the events of the first decade after the *hejra* shows that Mohammad took advantage of these Arab characteristics to win success and strength for Islam. There were occasions when a weak tribe was attacked in order to counterbalance a defeat and keep people in awe of the Moslems. Every victory over a small tribe caused it to gravitate toward Islam or at least to conclude a non-aggression pact.

The capture of booty was a potent factor in Islam's advance. Hope for a share certainly quickened eagerness to obey the commandment to wage holy war. The promise of abundant booty for the Moslems, given after the truce of Hodaybiya in *sura* 48 (*ol-Fat-h*), verse 20, was a stronger incentive than the promise of future bliss in gardens under which rivers flow (*sura* 85, *ol-Boruj*, verse 11).

Although no reliable statistics of devotees and opportunists among the Prophet's followers have yet been compiled, it can be inferred that about ninety per cent of those who had professed Islam by the time of his death had done so from either fear or expediency. The subsequent apostasy (*redda*) of many Arab tribes and the wars against the secessionists lend weight to this supposition.

Even at Madina, the capital and fountainhead of Islam, devotees such as 'Ali b. Abi Tāleb, 'Ammār b. Yāser, and Abu Bakr os-Seddiq were far less numerous than men whose loyalty to the faith and the Prophet was coupled with worldly aims. This became immediately apparent in the leadership contest between the Mohājerun and the Ansār which delayed the burial of the Prophet's remains for three days. 'Ali, Talha, and Zobayr were at Fātema's house and did not hear about the wrangling between the rival factions. Abu Bakr, 'Omar, Abu 'Obayda,[96] and some others were at 'Ā'esha's house, where a man came and warned them to act quickly if they did not want power to fall into the hands of the Ansār, who were rallying around Sa'd b. 'Obāda. 'Omar then asked Abu Bakr to go with him to see what the Ansār were doing. When they reached the hall of the Banu Sā'eda where the Ansār had gathered, Sa'd b. 'Obāda turned to them and said, "We Ansār are the army of Islam. We were the Prophet's supporters. Our doughty forearms made Islam strong. You Mohājerun also helped, and we shall let you join us." 'Omar impetuously started to walk out, but Abu Bakr grabbed his hand and stopped him. Then Abu Bakr, with his usual dignity and calm, said to Sa'd b. 'Obāda, "I acknowledge what you said about the Ansār. But this authority rightly belongs to the Qoraysh because they are superior to the other Arab tribes." He then shook hands with 'Omar and Abu 'Obayda and said, "Give allegiance to one of these two men!"

'Omar, being gifted with realism and foresight, did not let himself be flustered by this offer. He knew that in the excited state of public feeling, the only solution acceptable to all would be to choose Abu Bakr, the most senior and respected of the Mohājerun, the man who had shared danger with the Prophet in the cave and had been appointed by the Prophet to lead the prayers during his illness. For this reason, 'Omar promptly rose and shook hands with Abu Bakr, thereby pledging allegiance to him and presenting all the others with a fait accompli. The Mohājerun naturally followed 'Omar's example. Stirred by 'Omar's bold move, the Ansār soon also swore allegiance to Abu Bakr. According to one account, 'Omar was so anxious to get the matter conclusively settled that he dragged Sa'd b. 'Obāda out of the hall and with the help of some other men gave the elderly and ailing Ansār leader such a beating that he died on the spot.[97]

'Omar likewise brought pressure to bear on 'Ali, who was at first unwilling to recognise the caliphate of Abu Bakr. Knowing that 'Ali's example would be followed by other Hāshemites and that Abu Bakr's authority would not be secure without the Hāshemite clan's full support, 'Omar repeatedly met and argued with 'Ali until, at the end of six months, 'Ali gave in and swore allegiance to Abu Bakr.

9   Apart from the thirteen years of the Prophet's mission at Mecca, the history of Islam is indisputably a record of violence and power-seizure. As long as the Prophet lived, force was used primarily for the purpose of spreading Islam and imposing it on polytheists. After his death, rivalry for power and leadership was the motive for the recurrent violence.

Abu Bakr owed his accession to the adroitness of 'Omar, as described above. On his deathbed he indicated his desire that 'Omar should succeed him, and thanks to this, 'Omar took over the caliphate without opposition. Ten years later 'Omar in his last hours appointed a committee to choose his successor, consisting of 'Ali, 'Othmān, 'Abd or-Rahmān b. 'Awf, Talha, Zobayr, and Sa'd b. Abi Waqqās. When the committee met, none of them proposed a candidate because each aspired to the caliphate for himself. 'Abd or-Rahmān b. 'Awf then withdrew, but nobody else expressed an opinion. At 'Abd or-Rahmān's suggestion, the committee adjourned for three days to sound the feelings of the Mohājerun and the Ansār. During these three days 'Abd or-Rahmān questioned the other committee members about their views. Reportedly he asked 'Othmān which of the other four he would recommend if the choice did not fall on him, and 'Othmān answered that 'Ali had the best claim and qualifications to become the caliph. 'Abd or-Rahmān then put the same question to 'Ali, who answered that 'Othmān was the worthiest. When the committee reassembled in the Prophet's mosque at the end of the three days, it was clear to almost everyone that the next caliph would be either 'Ali or 'Othmān.

The characters of the two men differed. 'Othmān was known to be easy-going, unpretentious, and generous. 'Ali had a reputation for courage, devotion, and rigidity in religious matters. The worldly-minded circles, already sick of the strictness of 'Omar's ten year reign, were apprehensive of the possible accession of 'Ali because they knew that he would keep to 'Omar's line. According to Tabari, these people used 'Amr b. ol-'Ās as their go-between. One evening 'Amr went to see 'Ali and said that 'Abd or-Rahmān would first turn to him and propose him for the caliphate. But hasty acceptance would be unbecoming in a man like 'Ali. The dignity and stability of the caliphate would be better assured if 'Abd or-Rahmān had to repeat the proposal. On the day of the resumed committee meeting, 'Abd or-Rahmān ascended the pulpit and first turned to 'Ali, saying that he was the Prophet's cousin and son-in-law, the first Moslem, and the foremost fighter for the faith. If 'Ali would promise to act in accordance with the book of God, the custom of the Prophet, and the examples of the two *shaykh*s (i.e. Abu Bakr and 'Omar), 'Abd or-Rahmān would swear allegiance to him as caliph. 'Ali replied that he would adhere to God's book and the Prophet's custom, and otherwise act as he deemed right. 'Abd or-Rahmān then addressed 'Othmān, saying that after 'Ali, he was the worthiest candidate. If 'Othmān would conform to the book of God, the custom of the Prophet, and the examples of the two *shaykh*s, 'Abd or-Rahmān would swear allegiance to him. 'Othmān gave the promise unconditionally and became the caliph.

This is the gist of Tabari's account. At the risk of repetition, the full report, as it appears in Bal'ami's[98] Persian translation of Tabari's Annals, is appended below because it gives a revealing glimpse of the social scene at that time when ambition for power and weariness with 'Omar's strictness were uppermost in the minds of some of the Prophet's old companions.

"All the leading men of the desert-dwellers came to Madina after 'Omar's death to join in the mourning. 'Abd or-Rahmān consulted them, and each one of them said that 'Othmān would be best. One evening Abu Sofyān went to see 'Amr b. ol-'Ās and said that 'Abd or-Rahmān had called on him earlier in the same evening to tell him that the choice now lay between 'Othmān and 'Ali. 'As for myself,' Abu Sofyān added, 'I would prefer 'Othmān.' 'Amr answered that 'Abd or-Rahmān had come to see him too, and added, 'I likewise would prefer 'Othmān.' Then Abu Sofyān asked, 'What shall we do? 'Othmān is easy-going and may let the matter slip from his hands. 'Ali may win by default.' Abu Sofyān stayed with 'Amr that night and kept on asking how they could make sure that 'Othmān would be chosen. During the same night, 'Amr went to 'Ali's house and said to him, 'You know that I am your friend and have been fond of you since the old days. Everyone else is out of the running, and the choice lies between you and 'Othmān. This evening 'Abd or-Rahmān consulted all the leading men and asked whom they would prefer. Some want you and some want 'Othmān. Then he called on me, and I let him know that I want you. Now I have come to tell you that the post will be yours tomorrow if you will listen to my advice.' 'Ali answered, 'I will listen to whatever you say.' 'Amr replied, 'You must first promise never to tell anyone about our conversation.' 'Ali gave the promise. 'Amr then said, 'This 'Abd or-Rahmān is a wise and prudent man. He will want you if he finds you diffident and slow to accept. He might turn against you if he found you eager and in a hurry to accept.' 'Ali answered, 'I will act accordingly.' Later in the same night, 'Amr went to 'Othmān's house and at once said to him, 'The post will be yours tomorrow if you will heed my words. If you do not, 'Ali will snatch it from you.' 'Othmān answered, 'I will pay heed. Speak!' 'Amr then said, 'This 'Abd or-Rahmān is an honest and straightforward man. He does not mind whether things are said discreetly or bluntly. So do not show reluctance when he offers it to you tomorrow! If he lays down any conditions, do not refuse them! Assent immediately to whatever he says!' 'Othmān answered, 'I will do as you advise.' 'Amr then rose and went home.

"On the following day 'Amr went to the mosque. 'Abd or-Rahmān led the morning prayer and then ascended the pulpit. Standing on its platform, he said, 'You should all know that 'Omar, God bless him, did not name his successor. He was unwilling to incur the reward or punishment for so doing. He laid the task on the shoulders of five of us. Sa'd and Zobayr have transferred their rights to me, and I have withdrawn. The choice now lies between 'Ali and 'Othmān. Whom do you choose? To whom shall I swear allegiance? Before anyone in this congregation goes home, all must know who is to be the Prince of the Believers.' Some replied that they wanted 'Ali, others that they wanted 'Othmān, and all argued heatedly. Sa'd b. Zayd said to 'Abd or-Rahmān. 'It is you whom we like best. If you will swear allegiance to yourself, nobody will oppose you.' 'Abd or-Rahmān replied, 'It is too late for that now. Think carefully which of these two will be best, and stop arguing!' 'Ammār b. Yāser said, 'If you want to avoid dissension, swear allegiance to 'Ali!' Meqdād[99] said, "Ammār is right. If you swear allegiance to 'Ali, there will be no opposition.' 'Abdollāh b. Sa'd b. Abi Sarh (who was 'Othmān's foster-brother and had reverted to Islam after his earlier apostasy[100]) stood up in the crowd and said to 'Abd or-Rahmān, 'There certainly are people who will resist if you do not swear allegiance to 'Othmān.' 'Ammār then cursed 'Abdollāh, saying 'What business is this of yours, you apostate? What sort of Moslem are you to tell us who should be the Prince of the Believers?' A man of the Makhzum clan said to 'Ammār, 'You slave and son of a slave, what have you to do with the affairs of the Qoraysh?'

"Thus the people split into two groups and bitter strife arose. Sa'd b. Abi Waqqās stood up and said to 'Abd or-Rahmān, 'Hurry up, man! Unless you settle the matter soon, there will be a riot.' 'Abd or-Rahmān then rose again and said to the people, 'Be silent so that I may settle the matter as I deem right!' The people stopped talking. 'Abd or-Rahmān called out, "Ali, stand up!' 'Ali rose and walked up to 'Abd or-Rahmān. After gripping 'Ali's right arm with his left hand and raising his own right arm in readiness to shake 'Ali's right hand, 'Abd or-Rahmān asked 'Ali, 'Do you swear to God that you will conduct the affairs of the Moslems in accordance with the Qor'ān and the Prophet's custom and the examples of the two caliphs who succeeded him?' Mindful of the advice given by 'Amr that night, 'Ali answered, 'The task might be difficult on these conditions. Does anyone know all the commandments in God's book and all the precedents in the Prophet's custom? But I would undertake the task to the best of my knowledge, ability, and strength, and pray to God to grant me success.' 'Abd or-Rahmān dropped his left hand from 'Ali's arm, and with his right hand still stretched out, said to 'Ali, 'Your conditions would allow slackness and weakness.'

"Then 'Abd or-Rahmān called out, "Othmān, come here!' 'Othmān rose and walked up. After gripping 'Othmān's right arm with his left hand, 'Abd or-Rahmān asked, 'Do you swear to God that you will conduct the affairs of this community in accordance with the Qor'ān and the Prophet's custom and the examples of the two caliphs?' 'Othmān answered, 'I do.' 'Abd or-Rahmān moved his right hand from over 'Ali's hand, which he had not touched, and laid it on 'Othmān's hand. At the same time he swore

201

allegiance to 'Othmān, saying 'May God bless you in what He has ordained for you!' All the people then walked up and swore allegiance to 'Othmān, while 'Ali was left standing in amazement. 'Ali said to 'Abd or-Rahmān, 'You have played a trick on me.' He thought that 'Amr b. ol-'Ās had given him the advice in collusion with 'Abd or-Rahmān, 'Othmān, Zobayr, and Sa'd.

"Having thus been disappointed, 'Ali turned around to leave. When he turned, 'Abd or-Rahmān asked him, "Ali, where are you going? Are you unwilling to swear allegiance? God said that those who break their promise break it to their own hurt (*sura* 48, *ol-Fat-h*, verse 10). Did not I withdraw from this contest on the understanding that you would accept whatever I might decide? Did not 'Omar say that whoever opposed 'Abd or-Rahmān's decision ought to be put to death?' After hearing these words, 'Ali walked back and swore allegiance. The taking of the oaths was completed before the afternoon prayer on the same day. Thereafter 'Othmān was the Emām."

Such is Tabari's full account. It indicates that Abu Sofyān schemed with 'Amr b. ol-'Ās to secure 'Othmān's succession for fear of what might happen if 'Ali became the caliph. Twelve years earlier, Abu Sofyān had been so angry about the choice of Abu Bakr that he had urged 'Ali not to swear allegiance and had threatened to fill Madina with Qorayshite troops; but when the choice lay between 'Ali and 'Othmān, he preferred 'Othmān, whose protection would make life easy for him, and feared 'Ali, whose zealous piety might be dangerous.

It can be taken for certain that if 'Ali had succeeded 'Omar, the golden age of Islam would have lasted longer and the subsequent conflicts and deviations from Islamic norms would not have arisen. 'Othmān's self-seeking kinsmen would not have appropriated the chief posts in the government, and many of the events which led to the rule of Mo'āwiya and the Omayyad dynasty would have been averted.

10   After the Prophet's death, his companions can be said to have fallen into two groups: those who thought of him primarily as God's Prophet, and those who thought of him as also the founder of a state. Members of the second group had personally contributed to the state's rise. They saw themselves as having virtually inherited it and as being duty-bound to preserve and defend it. The two groups were at one in their great veneration of the Prophet.

In the second group, the outstanding man was unquestionably 'Omar. Concern for the state's survival was the reason why he stood, threateningly brandishing his sword, by the door of the Prophet's mosque and said to the people, "Mohammad is not dead but absent for forty days like Moses." Abu Bakr, however, reminded 'Omar of the words "You are mortal and they are mortal" (*sura* 39, *oz-Zomar*, verse 31). He then ascended the pulpit and said to the people, "If it is Mohammad whom you worship, Mohammad is dead. But if it is God whom you worship, God will never die." After saying this, Abu Bakr recited the verse "Mohammad is only an apostle. The apostles before him passed away. If he dies or is killed, will you turn about on your heels?" (*sura* 3, *Āl 'Emrān*, verse 138).

Thanks to 'Omar's wisdom and adroitness, the leadership was extricated from the rivalry of the Mohājerun and the Ansār, and the succession of Abu Bakr was secured. Prompted by 'Omar, Abu Bakr pursued the wars of the *redda* (apostasy) and ruthlessly subdued the dissident tribes.

Naturally the question arises whether to 'Omar's mind the Islamic religion or the Islamic state meant most. In any case a state apparatus had been set up and needed to be preserved. The new régime founded by Mohammad had put an end to the ignorance and barbarism of the Arab tribes and must therefore be consolidated. The Beduin must be made to stop their petty feuding and join in a new community under the banner of Islam.

This was why 'Omar, with his realism and understanding of the Arab character, launched the troops which became available after the crushing of the *redda* on the unprecedented venture of war with Iran and Rome. He knew that the tribes would not settle down to agriculture and industry, of which they were ignorant, and that they needed an outlet for their latent energy. What could be better than to train this restless force on lucrative targets beyond the frontiers? History was to show that 'Omar judged soundly when he adopted this policy.

11  The long series of wars between the Iranians and the Romans had greatly weakened the political and social fabrics of both empires. An even more important factor was the presence of numerous Arabs within their territories. For two or three centuries Arabs from North Arabia had gradually infiltrated into Transjordan and Syria and Iraq, where they had set up states under Roman and Iranian suzerainty. These Arab communities,

or at least their lower classes, fraternized with the armies of Islam. It was above all their collaboration that made 'Omar's conquests possible. They may perhaps have urged him to move, because Islam had become an organization for the advancement of Arab nationalism. The epic of conquest not only satisfied the Arab desire for booty and ascendancy; it also removed the stigma of vassalage and subservience to foreigners.

12   While there were undoubtedly people who embraced Islam from sincere conviction and joined in the invasions of Syria and Iraq out of respect for the Islamic commandment of holy war, the evidence in the recorded history of the conquests shows clearly that the basic motive was desire to seize other people's property. Asceticism and unconcern for worldly wealth were confined to a small circle. The rest of the Moslems, including some of the Prophet's chief companions, made great gains from the conquests. Talha and Zobayr, two of the ten to whom paradise was promised and members of the succession committee appointed by 'Omar, each left fortunes of thirty or forty million *derhams* in cash and real estate in Mecca, Madina, Iraq, and Egypt. After the murder of 'Othmān, both swore allegiance to 'Ali but rebelled against him when they saw that he would not continue 'Othmān's extravagance and would allow no further tampering with the public funds.

The Prophet's widow 'Ā'esha became one of Islam's most respected women, not only because he had dearly loved her but also because she was one of the few who knew the Qor'ān by heart and could give reliable reports of his sayings and actions. When 'Ali was chosen to be caliph, she took 'Othmān's murder as her pretext to defy the consensus and instigated the challenge to 'Ali at the battle of the camel. This was because 'Ali discontinued the allowance which 'Othmān had paid to her from the public funds, and probably also because she remembered 'Ali's unfavorable opinion of her in the affair of the lie.

The civil wars marked by the battles of the camel, Seffin, and Nahrawān arose basically from 'Ali's switch away from 'Othmān's laxity. All the men who after enduring 'Omar's strictness had lived in clover under 'Othmān were upset by 'Ali's policy of austerity. These men, and in particular the astute Mo'āwiya, used all available means to strengthen their personal positions.

13   The Prophet, during his lifetime, imposed Islam on the predatory and spiritually apathetic tribes by dint of the Qor'ānic revelations and by means of diplomacy or, in the last resort, force.

After his death, caliphs claiming to act in his name set up an Arab national kingdom.

It was then that myths attributing superhuman abilities and miracles to Mohammad were first put into circulation. The Mohammad who throughout his prophetic career had described himself as just one of God's servants was subjected to posthumous dehumanization and apotheosis. Fabrication of myths about great men after their deaths is a widespread and long-standing phenomenon. It does not alter the fact that great men, for all their greatness, are human and prone to human weaknesses. They experience hunger and thirst, feel cold and heat, and have sexual instincts which may possibly carry them beyond the bounds of discretion. There are times when they falter before obstacles and when they resent opposition. It is even possible that they may succumb to envy. Once they are dead, however, all their frictions with other men are forgotten and only their good achievements and thoughts are remembered. The books which Abu 'Ali ebn Sinā (370/980–428/1037) wrote on medicine (ol-Qānun in Arabic) and on philosophy and science (osh-Shefā in Arabic and Dāneshnāma-ye 'Alā'i in Persian) are remembered, and so is his courage in an adventurous career, but his human failings are either kept hidden or glossed over.

In the cases of founders of religions professed by millions of people, the process is naturally carried to extremes.

During the war of the trench, the Qoraysh chiefs sent an envoy, 'Oyayna b. Hesn of the Ghatafān tribe, to Mohammad with an offer to withdraw the besieging forces if he would let them take the whole of that year's Madinan date crop. The Prophet refused. The envoy then said that they would raise the siege in return for one third of the crop. The Prophet, who had caused the trench to be dug for the town's defence, knew that the tribal alliance still posed a dangerous threat. He therefore saw fit to accept the second offer. When he called for the peace terms to be written down, Sa'd b. Mo'ādh (one of the chiefs of the Aws tribe) asked whether his acceptance was a divine revelation. The Prophet replied that it was not, but it would get rid of the allied besiegers and avert the risk of collaboration between them and the Jews, who could be dealt with later. Sa'd retorted that in the old days, when his people were pagans, nobody had been able to extort a single date from them, and now that they were Moslems, they were not going to submit to such humiliation and pay such blackmail; the only right answer was the sword. The Prophet changed his mind. He accepted Sa'd's argument and decided not to pay the blackmail.

Frequent incidents of this kind are mentioned in the histories of the twenty three years of the prophetic mission. A companion would consult the Prophet, or the Prophet would take the advice of his companions. They would ask him how God judged a matter, and he would leave it to their own decision.

After his death, however, his human characteristics were forgotten. Everything that he ever did or said became a model of perfection and a manifestation of God's will. Governmental and judicial authorities took his actions as precedents for the solution of every sort of problem. The simple-minded believers of that time imagined him to have been even greater than he really was. Anybody who could claim to have heard some words from the Prophet's mouth was assured of prestige.

The Qor'ānic commandments and laws are not wholly clear and precise. Believers therefore had to find precedents in the Prophet's own conduct. For example, prayer is prescribed in the Qor'ān, but the ritual and number of the daily prayers had to be determined from the Prophet's usual practice. It was this need which prompted the collection of reports or traditions about his custom (sonna) and his sayings and doings (Hadith). The subsequent proliferation was such that by the 3rd/9th–4th/10th century thousands of reports were in circulation and hundreds of inquirers were rushing around the Islamic countries to collect more reports. A class of professional traditionists arose and acquired great respect in the Islamic world. They knew thousands of traditions by heart. One of them, Ebn 'Oqda (d. 332/943), is credited with having known 250,000 together with each one's chain of transmitters.

In the words of a Persian proverb, "when somebody picks up a big stone, you can be sure that he will not throw it." The vast bulk of the Hadith compilations is in itself proof that not all of their contents can be authentic. A more important aspect of the matter is the motive of these people who devoted their lives and energies to collecting Hadiths so assiduously. Basically their purpose was to leave no room for the use of human reason. Ebn Taymiya (661/1263–728/1328) said, "Nothing is true except what came to us through Mohammad." A learned scholar, Hasan b. Mohammad ol-Erbili (d. 660/1261) is reported to have said on his deathbed, "God told us the truth. Ebn Sinā told us lies."

14   It is an undeniable fact that the greater the lapse of time after the Prophet's death and the further the distance from the Hejāz, the more the number of miracles ascribed to him grew. Imaginations got to work and turned a man whose mental and moral strengths had changed the world's history into a being capable of existence only in the realm of fable.

15   The Iranians were routed. Their successive defeats at Qādesiya in 15/636 or 16/637 and Nehāvand in 21/642 were so shameful and painful that their failures against Alexander and the Mongols pale in comparison. The long record of disasters in Iranian history shows how vulnerable the country can be whenever it lacks a competent king or leader and good statesmen and generals. In this case Iran fell to quite small forces of ill-armed and untrained Arabs. City after city and province after province surrendered, accepting the Arab terms of conversion to Islam or inferior status as tribute-payers. Some became Moslems to avoid the poll-tax, others to escape from the oppressive grip of the Zoroastrian *mōbed*s (priests). All that was needed to become a Moslem was acknowledgement of God's unity and Mohammad's prophethood. Gradually, and often at the point of the sword, the simple faith of Islam gained general acceptance.

It was in keeping with the national character of the Iranians that after the conquest they sought to ingratiate themselves with their conquerors. They obeyed, served, and placed their brains and knowledge at the disposal of the new masters. They learned the language and adopted the manners of the Arabs. It was they who systematized Arabic grammar and syntax. There were no limits to their obsequiousness in their efforts to get the conquerors to employ them. They outstripped the Arabs in Islamic zeal and poured scorn on their own former beliefs and customs. They not only extolled the Arab nation and Arab heroes but even tried to prove that chivalry, generosity, and leadership inhere in the Arabs alone. They described Beduin poems and trite aphorisms from pre-Islamic Arabia as pearls of wisdom and models of behavior. They were content to be protégés of Arab tribes and lackeys of Arab *amir*s, and glad to give their daughters in marriage to Arabs and to take Arab names for themselves.

Iranian brains were soon at work in the fields of Islamic theology and law, Hadith-compilation, and Arabic literature. Approximately seventy per cent of the principal Arabic works on Islamic subjects were written by Iranians. Although the first conversions had been induced by fear, after two or three generations the Iranians were more Moslem than the Arabs.

The Iranians were so adept at infiltrating the new ruling class by means of flattery and cajolery that a famous *vazir* reportedly never looked at a mirror for fear of seeing an Iranian in it. At first they obeyed and served the Arab rulers because they hoped to become the rulers themselves in the long run and wanted to share in the spoils in the meantime. As the years passed, however, they became confused about their own identity. In the 3rd/9th and 4th/10th centuries there were Iranians who placed no value on their nationhood and imagined the Hejāz to be the sole source of God's blessings to mankind.

This may perhaps explain how the great growth of superstition and miracle-mongering became possible. The Iranians would not have been so credulous if they could have visualized the real circumstances at Mecca and Madina in the first thirteen and last ten years of the Prophet Mohammad's mission.

As an example of Iranian credulity, the following passage from the *Behār ol-Anwār* of Mohammad Bāqer Majlesi (1037/1627–1110/1699),[101] the leading *mojtahed* (authority on Shi'ite Islamic law and theology) in the later Safavid period, deserves repetition here. It is related, Majlesi states, that the Emāms Hasan and Hosayn asked their illustrious grandfather (the Prophet) for a present of new clothes on the day of the breaking of the fast. Gabriel came down and offered a white garment to each as a festival gift. The Prophet said that the two boys customarily wore colored clothes but Gabriel had brought white clothes. Gabriel obtained a tub and a jug from heaven and told the boys that if they would say what colors they wanted, he would fill the tub with a liquid in which each should dip his garment, and then the garment would be dyed the color he wanted. The Emām Hasan chose green and the Emām Hosayn chose red. While the clothes were being dyed, Gabriel wept. The Prophet asked why he wept when the children had been made happy that day. Gabriel answered that Hasan's choice of green meant that he would be martyred by poisoning with a poison which would turn his body green, and Hosayn's choice of red meant that he would be martyred when his blood would turn the ground red.

It is worthy of note that this absurd story is also quoted by the Bābi writer Mirzā Jāni in his book *Noqtat ol-Kāf*.[102] Inherited

Shi'ite superstitions evidently remained alive in the minds of the Bābis, who claimed to be reformers and founded a new religion. Mohammad and his companions are known to have lived in extreme poverty during the first year after the *hejra* up to the time of the Nakhla raid. Few of the companions had the commercial flair of 'Abd or-Rahmān b. 'Awf, who as soon as he arrived at Madina set up a business in the bazaar and made profits. Others found work as laborers in Jewish-owned palm-groves and were put onto hoeing and well-digging because they knew nothing about date-cultivation. The Prophet himself did not take an employment but lived on charity. He often went to bed without having eaten more than a few dates to appease his hunger, and sometimes without any supper at all. This fact is not mentioned in order to disparage Mohammad. On the contrary, it attests the greatness of his achievement. He did not let poverty and lack of resources hold him back from his resolve to establish mastery over Arabia. History records few self-made men of such caliber.

The events of the time prove that Mohammad was human like the rest of mankind and did not receive help from any superhuman or supernatural power. The battle of Badr ended in victory because of the courage and steadfastness of the Moslems and the negligence and slackness of the Qorayshites. The battle of Mount Ohod ended in defeat because the Moslems did not adhere to Mohammad's strategy. If it had been predestined that God should always help the Moslems, there would have been no need for the Moslem raids, for the digging of the trench around Madina, or for the massacre of the men of the Banu Qorayza. In view of verse 13 of *sura* 32 (*os-Sajda*), "if We had so wished, We would have given every soul its guidance," it would have been more logical for God to infuse the light of Islam into the hearts of all the unbelievers and hypocrites.

When the Jewish Qaynoqā' tribe surrendered after the fortnight-long blockade of their food and water supplies, Mohammad intended to put them all to death. Their old ally, 'Abdollāh b. Obayy, protested and blustered so much that Mohammad went black in the face with anger; but after full consideration of 'Abdollāh b. Obayy's vow to continue protecting the Banu Qaynoqā' and threat to come out in open opposition, Mohammad changed his mind. He decided not to put them to death, and was content to evict them from Madina within three days.

These and the dozens of similar incidents reported in the

biographies of the Prophet and histories of the rise of Islam are conclusive evidence that no supernatural power was at work. The events in Mohammad's life, like those in every other time and place, were determined by natural causes. Far from demeaning him, this fact makes the greatness of his mind and character all the more outstanding.

Unfortunately human beings are not accustomed and, it seems, often not able to investigate and ascertain causes of events. Their imaginative faculty is always ready to explain things by inventing gods. Primitive peoples in their ignorance can only explain thunder and lightning as the voice and flash of a potentate angered by their disobedience of his commands. Highly intelligent and learned men have ignored relations of cause and effect, preferring to postulate divine intervention even in petty incidents. They have supposed the omnipotent governor of the infinite universe to be a being like themselves. Men who thought in this way could believe that the governor of the universe sent gifts of clothes from heaven for Hasan and Hosayn and that his messenger-angel dyed the clothes red and green and wept.

Majlesi's *Behār ol-Anwār* is not exceptional. It is not the only book which states that a fish named Karkara son of Sarsara son of Gharghara told 'Ali b. Abi Tāleb where to ford the Euphrates before the battle of Seffin. Hundreds of books of this type are in circulation in Iran, for example *Helyat ol-Mottaqin*,[103] *Jannāt ol-Qolub, Anvār-e No'māni, Mersād ol-'Ebād*,[104] and many collections of stories of prophets and 'olamā. A single one of them is enough to poison a nation's mind and impair its capacity to think. Miracle-mongering is trafficking in a drug which deprives men and women of their reason.

People know what Mohammad accomplished in his prophetic career. They know too that he felt hunger, ate food, and had the same natural functions and instincts as they have. Mystification of his personality does him no honor and does mankind no good.

# Notes

1 Mohammad b. Jarir ot-Tabari (224/839–310/923), an Iranian by birth, author of two great works in Arabic: the Annals of the Prophets and Kings, and the oldest surviving Qor'ān-commentary (*Tafsir*).

2 Mohammad ol-Wāqedi (d. 207/823), author of the Book of the Prophet's Wars.

3 This history of the rise of Bābism was reprinted at Leiden in 1910 (ed. by E. G. Browne, E. J. W. Gibb Memorial Series, XV). The author, Mirzā Jāni, was one of twenty eight early Bābis who would not recant and were put to death at Tehrān in 1268/1852.

4 Abu Jahl (Promoter of Ignorance) was the name given by the Moslems to 'Amr b. Heshām b. ol-Moghira, who succeeded his uncle Walid b. Moghira as head of the Makhzum clan. A firm opponent of Mohammad, he persecuted the first Moslems and in 2/624 led the Meccan force at the battle of Badr, in which he was killed.

5 A lote tree (Arabic *sedra*, Persian *konār*) is a variety of the jujube tree (zizyphus).

6 B. 1888; author of *Zaynab*, the first Egyptian Arabic novel (1914), and of biographies of Mohammad (1935), Abu Bakr (1943), and 'Omar (1944); Minister of Education and President of the Senate; d. 1956.

7 Author of *La vie de Mahomet* (Paris 1929) and *Mahomet et la tradition islamique* (Paris 1955).

8 Author of Persian works on mathematics, astronomy, chronology, and mineralogy, and reputed inventor of trigonometry (597/1201–672/1274). He also wrote a treatise on ethics (tr. by G. M. Wickens, *The Nasirean Ethics*, London 1964), which includes a chapter on politics and a thoughtful chapter on economics.

9 Grandson of Chengiz Khān and brother of Qobelāy Khān, the founder of the Yuan dynasty of China. As the first of the Ilkhānid dynasty, he reigned from 654/1256 to 663/1265 over Iran, Iraq, and most of Asia Minor.

10 The royal audience hall built for the Sāsānid Iranian king Khosraw I Anūsharvān (531–579). Part of its 26 metre (85 ft.) vault still stands in the ruin on the Tigris 22 km. (13 miles) downstream from Baghdād.

11 Khosraw II Parviz (591–628) was the Sāsānid king of Iran whose armies conquered Syria, Palestine, Asia Minor, and Egypt between 611 and 616. After their defeat and expulsion he was put to death and replaced by his son Shiruya, who retroceded the conquests and made peace with the East Romans. The early biographies and histories state that the Prophet Mohammad sent letters to Khosraw Parviz, the East Roman emperor Heraclius, the governor of Egypt, and the Negus of Abyssinia calling on them to embrace Islam.

12 See below, pp. 29, 149.

13 See below, p. 96.

14 See note 94.

15 Ebn Heshām ('Abd ol-Malek b. Heshām), who lived in Egypt and died in 213/828, wrote a revised version of the lost biography of the Prophet by Ebn Es-hāq (Mohammad b. Es-hāq), a native of Madina who died at Baghdād ca. 150/767. Ebn Heshām's work is the oldest surviving and fullest of its kind (tr. by A. Guillaume, *The Life of Muhammad*, Oxford 1955).

16 Mohammad b. Esmā'il ol-Bokhāri (194/810–258/270), of Bokhāra, compiler of the Hadith collection entitled the *Sahih* (Correct). He took great pains to verify the

211

reports (7397 in all) and especially the chains of transmitters. It is the Hadith collection most widely respected and used by Sonnite Moslems.

17  Zohayr b. Abi Solmā, one of the most admired pre-Islamic poets, said to have lived into the early years of Mohammad's prophethood but not to have become a Moslem.

18  Labid b. Rabi'a, a poet of the Hawāzen tribe, noted for his descriptions of nature and religious feeling; became a Moslem after leading his tribe's delegation to the Prophet Mohammad at Madina, and thereafter gave up poetry; died at a great age in 41/661.

19  Celebrated physician (250/864–313/925) of Rayy (near Tehrān), author of Arabic works including two medical encyclopaedias which were translated into Latin and used in medieval Europe, of a treatise on alchemy which he tried to transform into scientific chemistry, and of psychological and philosophical treatises now mostly lost. He rejected prophethood on the ground that God has endowed all humans with reason.

20  Arabic poet (369/979–450/1058) of Ma'arra near Aleppo, blinded in childhood by smallpox; noteworthy for his agnostic and anticlerical poems and his prose account of a journey to the next world (Resālat ol-Ghofrān).

21  In other accounts the Arabic words of the Prophet's answer are slightly different and could mean either "I cannot recite" or "What shall I recite?"

22  See Theodor Nöldeke, Geschichte des Qorāns, 2nd ed., 2 vols ed. by F. Schwally, Leipzig 1909–19; Richard Bell, The Qur'ān, translated with a critical rearrangement of the surahs, 2 vols, Edinburgh 1937–39.

23  Ed. by Ahmad Zaki, Cairo 1912; ed. with French tr. by W. Atallah, Paris 1969; Persian tr. by Sayyed Mohammad Rezā Jalāli Nā'ini, Tehrān (early 1970s); English tr. by Nabih Amin Faris, The Book of Idols, Princeton 1952.

24  According to some of the sources, the avenger of his father and the composer of the verses were the same person, namely Emro' ol-Qays, the semi-legendary prince-poet to whom some fine pre-Islamic Arabic poems are ascribed. See R. A. Nicholson, A Literary History of the Arabs, London, 1907, repr. Cambridge 1953, pp. 103–105; Encyclopaedia of Islam, 2nd ed., articles Dhu'l-Khalasa and Imru' al-Kays.

25  Also quoted in Ebn Es-hāq's Life of Mohammad, tr. A. Guillaume, Oxford 1955, p. 37.

26  An emāmzāda is a son, daughter, or descendant of an Emām and thus a scion of 'Ali and Fātema. Tombs of emāmzādas are found in many Iranian villages and towns and are visited by devotees who address appeals for help or intercession to the emāmzāda, either orally or in writing on a piece of paper or cloth called a dakhil. Many of these shrines are domed, and some are very old. Some may have been tombs of local saints or Sufi votaries. In most cases, no information about the careers, let alone the genealogies, of the revered persons have come down; nevertheless they are all popularly supposed to be descendants of Emāms.

27  This is the translation chosen by 'Ali Dashti. Another translation is "and a guide to every nation." Both are grammatically possible.

28  An introduction to study of the Qor'ān by the Egyptian Jalāl od-Din os-Soyuti (848/1445–910/1505), co-author of the Tafsir ol-Jalālayn.

29  A leading theologian of the Mo'tazelite school, which held that the Qor'ān was created, that human beings have free will, and that sinners are not necessarily unbelievers. He died between 220/835 and 230/845. Some passages from his lost writings are quoted in works of ol-Jāhez and other early authors.

30  An author of the 3rd/9th century whose writings were condemned by many theologians as heretical.

31  Abu Mohammad 'Ali b. Ahmad b. Hazm (384/994–456/1064), a celebrated Moorish theologian, jurist, historian, and poet. Among his surviving works is a book on religions and sects (ol-melal wa'n-nehal).

32  'Abu'l-Hosayn 'Abd or-Rahim b. Mohammad ol-Khayyāt (ca. 220/835–ca. 300/913), a Mo'tazelite theologian of Baghdād, author of many works of which a few survive.

33  In 'Ali Dashti's rendering, "by an angel"; generally taken to mean the angel Gabriel.

34  Shams od-Din Mohammad Hāfez of Shirāz, the most admired Persian lyric poet (726/1326?–792/1390).

35  Jalāl od-Din Rumi (604/1207–672/1273), known to the Iranians as Mawlavi, is the most widely admired of the Persian mystic poets. He lived at Konya in Asia Minor, which was then called Rum. In those days alchemists searched for a substance, the elixir, which would transform base metals into gold.

36  Ignaz Goldziher (1850–1921), professor of Arabic at Budapest and an outstanding scholar. Author (inter alia) of *Muhammadanische Studien*, 2 vols, Halle 1889–90, tr. by C. R. Barber and S. M. Stern, *Muslim Studies*, 2 vols, London 1967–71; *Vorlesungen über den Islam*, Heidelberg 1910, 2nd ed. 1923, tr. by Félix Arin, *Le dogme et la loi de l'Islam*, Paris 1920, 2nd ed. 1958, and by A. and R. Hamori, *Introduction to Islamic theology and law*, Princeton 1981; and *Die Richtungen der Islamischen Koranauslegung*, Leiden 1920.

37  Abu'l-'Abbās Ahmad b. Mohammad al-Qastallāni of Cairo, author of a biography of the Prophet and commentaries on the Hadith.

38  See note 15. The report appears on pp. 677–678 of A. Guillaume's translation.

39  His employmeny by Mohammad was arranged by his mother, shortly after the hejra when he was ten years old, and lasted until the Prophet's death. Later he fought in wars of conquest and opposed the Omayyads. He died at Basra in 91/709(?) or 93/711(?).

40  'Abd ol-Wahhāb osh-Sha'rāni of Cairo, a prolific author of mystic and theological works.

41  A Yamani who arrived at Madina and embraced Islam only four years before the Prophet Mohammad's death, but became a very prolific transmitter of Hadiths. He died ca. 58/678.

42  A blind man of Beduin origin who lived at Basra and was a prolific transmitter of Hadiths (60/680?–117/735?).

43  The Library of the University of Cambridge possesses the unique manuscript of the third part of a Persian *Tafsir* (Qor'ān commentary and translation) written by an unknown author probably ca. 1000 A.D. and copied in 628/1231. It covers *suras* 19–114 and is the only surviving part. It is thought to be the oldest work of its kind in the Persian language. The text was printed by the Bonyād-e Farhang-e Irān, Tehrān, 1349/1970 (2 vols, ed. and introd. by Jalāl Matini).

44  The event is the subject of the short *sura* 105 (*ol-Fil*). The Abyssinians brought an elephant, which for the Hejāzi Arabs was an unknown prodigy. Verses 3 and 4 state that the Abyssinians were smitten by stones of baked clay which swarms of birds dropped on them. In the opinion of 'Ekrema, an early traditionist, and Tabari, the historian and Qor'ān-commentator, the verses are an allegorical expression of the fact that the Abyssinians were smitten by smallpox.

45  Verses 14 and 15 of *sura* 34 are thought to refer to this disaster. Archaeological and epigraphic evidence indicates it occurred some time in the middle of the 6th century.

46  ot-Tā'ef, a relatively large town about 50 miles (80 km.) south-east of Mecca in a mountain oasis where cereals can be grown. It had some importance in the caravan trade and was the center of the worship of the goddess ol-Lāt.

47  In the Qor'ān the town is once named Yathreb (*sura* 33, verse 13) and four times named ol-Madina (*sura* 9, verses 101 and 120, *sura* 33, verse 60, and *sura* 63, verse 8).

48  *Le dogme et la loi de l'Islam*, tr. by Félix Arin, 2nd ed., Paris 1958, p. 3.

49  The word *ommiyin* is often taken to mean illiterate, but in this context evidently means those who have not been given scriptures, i.e. gentiles. See p. 53 above.

50  Cf. *sura* 2, 187 (p. 82 above); in both verses, the word *fetna* appears to signify "persecution" rather than "anarchy", which is the normal meaning.

51  Abu Hāmed Mohammad ol-Ghazzāli (450/1058–505/1111), of Tus in Khorāsān, was an outstanding theologian and mystic. Among his many works, the most widely read are *Ehyā 'olum ed-din*, an Arabic treatise on faith and morals, and *Kimiyā-ye sa'ādat*, a shortened and somewhat different Persian version; *Tahāfot ol-Falāsefa*, on the inconsistencies of philosophers (i.e. metaphysicians); and *ol-Monqedh men od-dalāl*, a spiritual autobiography (tr. by W. Montgomery Watt, *The faith and practice of al-Ghazālī*, London 1953). Although Ghazzāli was a Sonnite, his works are read and respected by many Shi'ites.

52  See note 20.

53  See note 6.

54  The Prophet's action probably set the precedent for the conferment of the robe of honor (*khel'a*) by Moslem rulers of the 'Abbāsid and later dynasties, though this practice had existed in the Near East since long before Islam. Another famous poem is also called the Ode of the Cloak. This is a religious peom by an Egyptian, Sharaf od-Din ol-Busiri (608/1212–695/1296), who wrote it after being cured of paralysis by a dream in which the Prophet threw his cloak over him.

55  'Ali Dashti explains this sentence as "Do not show yourselves to be waiting for the cooking of the meal," having probably read *enā* (pot). A. J. Arberry's rendering is "without watching for its hour" (*anā*, length of time).

56  The Arabic word *hejāb* means basically "covering" and in the context probably "curtain"; in later times it came to mean "veil".

57  According to Moslem traditions, 'Ād is the name of an ancient nation, and Eram is the name of its town, or in a less common opinion, of its chief tribe. The people of 'Ād spurned the Prophet Hud whom God sent to them, and were punished with a flood and then a drought which destroyed them.

58  Thamud is the name of an ancient nation whose existence is attested in Roman sources. They were akin to the Nabataeans of Petra and have left a few inscriptions in a similar Semitic language and script. After the Roman conquest of Petra, their town ol-Hejr (now Madā'en Sāleh) in the north of the Hejāz was a center of commerce for some time. Among the Thamudite remains at Madā'en Sāleh and ol-'Olā are rock-hewn monuments similar to those at Petra but smaller. According to Moslem traditions, Thamud was punished with destruction by an earthquake or thunderbolt for defying the Prophet Sāleh.

59  The normal meaning of the Arabic *watad* (pl. *awtād*) is "peg", particularly "tent-peg". No satisfactory explanation of "owner of the pegs" has been found by either traditional commentators or modern scholars.

60  See A. Guillaume's translation of Ebn Es-haq's *Life of Muhammad*, Oxford 1955, p. 651. "Prisoners" is 'Ali Dashti's and A. Guillaume's rendering of the Arabic word '*awān*, which means literally "intermediate" and in this context probably "intermediate between free and unfree"; in *sura* 2, 63, it means "intermediate between young and old". Another suggestion is that the word may be the plural of '*āniya*, meaning "afflicted with disabilities".

61  Mahmud b. 'Omar oz-Zamakhshari (467/1075–538/1144), of Khwārezm, has left important works including an Arabic Qor'ān-commentary entitled *ol-Kashshāf*, a treatise on Arabic grammar, and an Arabic-Persian lexicon. He adhered to the Mo'tazelite school of Islamic thought, believing in human free will and the createdness of the Qor'ān.

62  'Abdollāh b. 'Omar ol-Baydāwi, of Fārs, wrote an Arabic Qor'ān-commentary, which is still much used by Sonnite Moslems, and other Arabic and Persian works. His Qor'ān-commentary, entitled *Anwār ot-Tanzil*, is based on Zamakhshari's *Kashshāf* but amplified and expurgated of Mo'tazelite interpretations.

NOTES

63 Ahmad b. Hanbal (164/780–241/855) of Baghdād was the author of *ol-Mosnad*, a Hadith compilation completed by his son 'Abdollāh, and the founder of the literalistic and anthromorphic school of Sonnite Islamic theology and law known as the Hanbalite school. He suffered beatings and long imprisonment for his rejection of the Mo'tazelite theology then favored by the 'Abbāsid caliphate. Ahmad b. Taymiya (661/1222–728/1328) of Damascus revived the Hanbalite school and wrote books which in later times influenced the Wahhābite movement in Arabia.

64 Mohammad b. Sa'd (ca. 168/784–230/845) of Basra compiled the *Ketāb ot-Tabaqat*, which gives biographies of Mohammad, his companions, and 4250 Hadith transmitters.

65 The Arabic term for temporary marriage is *mot'a*, which means literally "enjoyment" or "usufruct"; it is from the same root as the word "you enjoy" or "you have the usufruct of" in *sura* 4, verse 28.

66 The waiting period (*'edda*) is the period in which a widow or divorced woman is not allowed to remarry because she may be found to be pregnant by her former husband. In Islamic law the waiting period is 4 months and 10 days for a widow, 3 months for a divorced wife, 2 months for a widowed slave-concubine, and 1½ months for a divorced slave-concubine.

67 Mohammad ot-Termedhi (d. 279/892), of Termedh, a town on the Oxus, compiled *ol-Jāme'*, one of the six Hadith collections held in high esteem by Sonnite Moslems.

68 See p. 14f.

69 Zaynab was married to Abu'l-'Ās, a son of Khadija's sister: Roqayya to 'Otba, a son of Abu Lahab; Omm Kolthum to 'Otayba, another son of Abu Lahab; and Fātema to 'Ali b. Abi Tāleb. After the start of the preaching of Islam, Abu Lahab forced his sons to divorce Mohammad's daughters. Later Roqayya was married to 'Othmān b. 'Affān, and after her death Omm Kolthum was married to the same 'Othmān b. 'Affān.

70 H. Reckendorf gives her name as Qayla (*Encyclopaedia of Islam*, 2nd ed., Leiden 1960, vol. 1, p. 697, article *al-Ash'ath*); W. M. Watt gives it as Qotayla (*Muhammad at Madina*, Oxford 1956, p. 397). Both state that she was betrothed to Mohammad, who died before she reached Madina.

71 Egypt was invaded by troops of the Iranian king Khosraw II Parviz in 616 and remained under Iranian occupation until 628. Māriya probably arrived at Madina before 628.

72 A son of the Prophet's uncle (ol-)'Abbās and an ancestor of the 'Abbāsid caliphal dynasty. Generally known as Ebn 'Abbās, he is the reputed source of very numerous Hadiths. He died ca. 68/687.

73 A son of the second caliph 'Omar b. ol-Khattāb. He fought in many campaigns, but refused high office. He is remembered as a careful and accurate transmitter of Hadiths. He died in 73/693.

74 See note 43.

75 See note 1.

76 Zayd had a son, Osāma, by a previous marriage. After divorcing Zaynab in 4 A.H./626, he contracted further marriages and had more children. He led several Moslem raids and was appointed by the Prophet to command the first campaign into Syria; on that campaign he was killed in the battle of Mo'ta (near Ma'ān in what is now Transjordan) in 8 A.H./629. Osāma, despite his youth, was put in command of another expedition into Syria in 11 A.H./632.

77 'Ali Dashti's text has Maqātel/Moqātel. Zamakhshari, in his commentary ol-Kashshāf (see note 61 above) on which 'Ali Dashti relied, attributes the statement to a man named Moqātel b. Solaymān. (Information kindly given by Dr. Paul Sprachman of the University of Chicago).

78 Mahmud Shabestari of Tavriz, d. ca. 720/1320, author of *Golshan-e Rāz*, a short

215

exposition of Sufism in verse; tr. by E. Whinfield, *The Rose Garden of Mystery*, London 1880.

79  In *sura* 1, the invocation (In the name of God, the Compassionate, the Merciful) is numbered as a separate verse, but in other *suras* it is not. The rest of *sura* 1 consists of six short verses.

80  The meaning of the word *mathāni*, translated above as "repetitions", is obscure. It comes in two verses of the Qor'ān, *sura* 15, 87 and *sura* 39, 24. One theory is that it means verses or passages which were sent down twice; another is that it means verses which ought to be repeated in prayer; another is that it means praises.

81  'Amr b. ol-'Ās, a Qorayshite, was the conqueror and first governor of Egypt. Abu Musā ol-Ash'ari, a native of the Yaman, was the governor of Basra and conqueror of Khuzestān. During the battle of Seffin between 'Ali's and Mo'āwiya's forces in 37/657, 'Amr proposed arbitration. Mo'āwiya chose 'Amr, and 'Ali chose Abu Musā, to be the two arbiters. When they met at Adhruh (near Petra) in the following year, 'Amr persuaded Abu Musā to declare that both 'Ali and Mo'āwiya were ineligible, and then himself declared that only 'Ali was ineligible.

82  Some examples are *sura* 4, 14, abrogating *sura* 2, 241, on inheritance rights of widows; *sura* 24, 2, abrogating *sura* 4, 19, on punishment of adultery by women; *sura* 5, 92, abrogating *sura* 2, 216, on consumption of intoxicants.

83  The Khārejites disapproved of 'Ali's agreement to arbitration of the claims to the caliphate and seceded from his camp in 37/657. They believed that the most pious Moslem man, even if a black slave, ought to be the Emām (i.e. head of the Moslem community), and that a Moslem who commits a major sin ceases to be a Moslem and ought to be punished in this world. Small Khārejite communities still exist in 'Omān and Algeria.

84  The Morje'ites believed that the sincerity of a Moslem's faith can only be judged by God and that punishment of Moslem sinners ought to be postponed until the judgement day, i.e. left to God's judgement. They recommended obedience to the Omayyad caliphate because, even though sinful, it was the established régime.

85  The Mo'tazelites believed that God is necessarily just, that humans have free will, and that the Qor'ān was created (i.e. by God in the lifetime of Mohammad). The 'Abbāsid caliphs Ma'mūn (198/813–218/833), Mo'tasem (218/833–227/842), and Wātheq (227/842–232/847) maintained an inquisition for the purpose of eliminating anti-Mo'tazelite judges and officials. The greatest and last Mo'tazelite writer was Zamakhshari (d. 538/1143).

86  The Ash'arites were followers of the Sonnite theologian Abu'l-Hasan 'Ali ol-Ash'ari (d. 324/935), who broke away from the Mo'tazelites. They rejected human free will and scientific causality, and believed in predestination and continuous creation.

87  Bātenite was a term used disparagingly by orthodox writers to denote those who sought inner (*bāten*) meanings in Qor'ānic texts and Islamic laws and rites. Though applicable to Sufis (mystics), the term was generally reserved for the various Esmā'ili Shī'ite groups, such as the Qarmatis of eastern Arabia in the 4th/10th century; the Fātemid dynasty of Egypt (358/969–567/1171); the Ekhwān os-Safā (Brethren of Purity), a Moslem Neo-Platonist group said to have been based at Basra in the 4th/10th century who have left a collection of 52 epistles; and the Nezāri Esmā'ilis of Alamut (483/1090–654/1256).

88  The second caliph 'Omar was stabbed on 26 Dhu'Hejja 23/3 November 644 by Abu Lo'lo'a Firuz, an Iranian slave said in some sources to have been a Christian. In the hours before his death he appointed the committee which chose 'Othmān to succeed him.

89  An early convert, noted as an ascetic and critic of the rich and as a transmitter of Hadiths. He was expelled from Syria by Mo'āwiya in 'Othmān's reign and died in 32/652. Abu Dharr ol-Ghefāri, ol-Meqdād b. 'Amr, and Salmān ol-Fārsi are described as the first Shi'ites.

90 An early convert who fought in the Prophet's wars. He was appointed governor of Kufa by 'Omar and played a part in the conquest of Khuzestān. He was dismissed by 'Othmān. He fought for 'Ali in the battle of the camel and at Seffin where he was killed in 37/657.

91 An anthology of Arabic songs and poems from pre-Islamic days to the time of Ebrāhim ol-Mowseli, the court musician of the 'Abbāsid caliph Hārun or-Rashid (170/786-193/809). Its compiler Abul'lFaraj `Ali ol-Esfahāni(284/897-356/967) was an Arab of Omayyad descent who lived at Esfahān.

92 Arabic for Khosraw, the name of a mythical Iranian King and of two Sāsānid kings, Khosraw I Anusharvān (531–579) and Khosraw II Parviz (591–628).

93 'Abdollāh b. Qotayba (213/828–276/889), of Iranian origin, held official posts mainly at Baghdād where he died. He was the author of 'Oyun ol-akhbār, a collection of edifying anecdotes, and of a poetic anthology, a treatise on the secretarial art, and many other Arabic works.

94 Tāhā Hosayn (1889–1973) went blind in early childhood. After education at a Qor'ān-school and the, Azhar theological college in Cairo, he studied in France and earned the doctorate of the University of Paris in 1919 for his thesis on La philosophie sociale d'Ibn Khaldoun. His scholarly studies of the pre-Islamic Arabic poetry (Fi'sh-she'r el-jāheli, Cairo 1926) and the life of Mohammad ('Alā hāmesh es-sira, 2 vols, Cairo 1933 and 1938) aroused controversy but have lasting value. He represented the liberal tendency in Egyptian nationalism. In his book on the Future of Culture in Egypt (Mostaqbal oth-theqāfa fi Mesr, Cairo 1938) he called for cooperation with other Mediterranean countries. He was Minister of Education from January 1950 to January 1952. Above all he is remembered for his account of his life at the Qor'ān-school and the Azhar, ol-Ayyām (2 vols, Cairo 1929 and 1939. Vol. I, tr. by E. H. Paxton, An Egyptian childhood, London 1932; vol. II, tr. by H. Wayment, The Stream of Days, London 1948).

95 See note 89 on p. 216 above.

96 Abu 'Obayda b. 'Abdollāh b. ol-Jarrāh was one of the early converts who temporarily emigrated to Abyssinia and one of the ten companions to whom paradise was promised. As governor of Syria from 15/36 until his death in a plague in 18/639, he conquered Homs, Aleppo, and Antioch.

97 According to other accounts, Sa'd b. 'Obāda died four or five years later.

98 Abu 'Ali Mohammad b. Mohammad Bal'ami (d. 363/974), the vazir of two Sāmānid amirs of Bokhārā, 'Abd ol-Malek I and Mansur I, translated Tabari's Annals into Persian at the latter's request. The work is the oldest important monument of New Persian prose. It is abbreviated from Tabari's Arabic original and supplemented with some additional material, mainly on Iranian subjects. There is a French translation by H. Zotenberg, Chronique de . . . Tabari traduite sur la version persane de . . . Bel'ami, 4 vols, Paris 1867–1874, reprinted 1948.

99 'Ammār b. Yāser and ol-Meqdād b. 'Amr were early converts and companions of the Prophet and prominent supporters of 'Ali. 'Ammār, whose mother was a slave owned by a member of the Makhzum clan of the Qoraysh, became governor of Kufa in 'Omar's reign and took part in the conquest of Khuzestān; he was killed while fighting for 'Ali at the battle of Seffin in 37/657. 'Ammār, Meqdād, Abu Dharr ol-Ghefāri, and Salmān ol-Fārsi are regarded as the first Shi'ites.

100 See p. 98f.

101 The Behar ol-Anwar is an immense Hadith compilation in Arabic, running to 102 volumes. Mohammad Bāqer Majlesi also wrote more popular books in Persian, including biographies of the Prophet and the twelve Emāms. His persecution of Iranian Sonnites, Sufis, Jews, and Zoroastrians was one of the causes of the weakening of the Safavid monarchy, which was overthrown by Sonnite Afghan rebels in 1135/1722.

102 See note 3.

103  A Persian book by Mohammad Bāqer Majlesi.
104  By Shaykh Najm od-Din Dāya (d. 654/1256), an exponent of Sufism. The *Mersād ol 'Ebād* contains one of the few early mentions of 'Omar Khayyām, who is denounced in it as a philosopher and an atheist.

# Index of Persons

219

# Index of Tribes, Clans, Dynasties, Nations, Religious and Other Groups

223

Sabaeans 84
Safavid dynasty 208
Semites 20, 75
Shi'ites 68, 117, 158, 168f., 174, 208f.
Sho'ubiya 180, 190
Solaym 180
Sonnites 59, 68, 177, 148, 168f.
South Arabians 75, 77, 125
Sufi(s) 61, 158
Syrians 48

Taghleb 184
Tamin 4, 113, 184
Thamud 15, 21, 45, 53, 112, 193,
    n. 58
Thaqif 14, 15, 76f., 79, 90, 107,
    184

Yamani(s) 77; see also South Arabians

Zoroastrians 207

# Index of Places

225

# General Index